The Catholic Family:
Image and Likeness of God

VOLUME 2

Family Values

The Catholic Family:
Image and Likeness of God

VOLUME 2
Family Values

Deacon Dr. Bob McDonald

Queenship

PUBLISHING COMPANY
P.O. Box 220 • Goleta, CA 93116
(800) 647-9882 • (805) 692-0043 • Fax: (805) 967-5843

Library of Congress Number #, Pending

Published by:
Queenship Publishing
P.O. Box 220
Goleta, CA 93116
(800) 647-9882 • (805) 692-0043
Fax: (805) 957-5843

Printed in the United States of America

ISBN: 1-57918-119-8

Dedication

"Now a great sign appeared in the sky, a woman clothed with the sun, standing on the moon and on her head a crown of twelve stars."

(Rev. 12:1)

This book is dedicated to the Queen of Heaven, on whose feast day I was ordained a Permanent Deacon.

For my ordination gift I asked her that I would always preach and teach the truth with love. *"Veritatem facientes in caritate"* (Eph. 4:15). May this work give her the honour she is due as the Mother of Jesus and may it give glory to God in the hearts of Catholic couples everywhere.

Acknowledgements

A book such as this can never be the work of one person alone. I am so grateful for the love, the work, the countless hours, the support and the dedication of my wife, Rita, without whose wisdom and patience this book could never have been completed. She typed and retyped, read and reread the manuscript, always suggesting modifications with wisdom and tact. She never lost faith in the importance of the task and she never lost faith in me. Above all, she never lost faith in God and continued to believe in his holy will for this work.

My very special gratitude to Mark Sebanc, author of the wonderful novel *Flight to Hollow Mountain,* for his fearless editing and the expertise which he generously shared with regard to grammar and my poor literary style. It is not easy to make a silk purse out of a sow's ear.

My heartfelt thanks to my equally talented friend and mentor Michael O'Brien, artist and author of *Father Elijah* and numerous other works of literature, for his reading of the manuscript, pointing out errors and the need for clarification of many points which might otherwise have been misunderstood.

I am deeply grateful for the expert editing by Chris Zakrzewski, former editor of *Nazareth Magazine.* His input was given with such gentleness, yet at the same time he was firm in his conviction that the book should be brought to completion.

A special mention must be made to my fellow Secular Franciscan, Eric MacDonald, who was the expert "glitch-remover" for my computer. He made himself constantly available at all hours to assist, to advise, and to correct. I am sure that St. Francis is delighted with his spiritual son.

Above all, I humbly give *all* the glory to the Holy Spirit, Spouse of Mary, to whom I have prayed throughout the entire task of writing, and I also pray that this work reflects his guidance and inspiration.

Feast of Pentecost and the Visitation
May 1998.

CONTENTS

CHAPTER 1

The Catholic Family: The Little Church

*"Every living soul belongs
to me, parent and child
alike are mine."*

(Ezek. 18:4)

Volume one of *The Catholic Family: Image and Likeness of God* has tried to describe the reality of the world in which the Catholic family lives and breathes and to provide an outline of what Catholic family life is meant to be. However, by the very fact that we are Catholic, we are called by our good master Jesus to live out his divine mandate and that means following his instructions for the life of holiness. By this obedience, our families can become formed more and more into an image and likeness of God. As a consequence, this volume is devoted to those issues which bear upon true Catholic family values, values which ought to be predominant in the minds of Catholic disciples and which, if adhered to, will lead to the sanctification promised by Jesus. He is indeed the "Way, the Truth and the Life" and his greatest desire is to lead us to his heavenly Father. The Sacrament of Matrimony was instituted for this very purpose. It is devoutly hoped that this book will help Catholic husbands and wives to more clearly understand the awesome teaching of the Church on a variety of issues vital to family life.

The early Church Fathers referred to the Christian family as "The Little Church." Later the term "Domestic Church was used (*Ecclesia Domestica*), and Pope John Paul II has also called it the "Church in miniature." This concept is vital to an understanding of who we are as persons, for all of us were born into a family. Even where that family was fractured and broken, as in the case of single motherhood, it is still a little church and we cannot find meaning in our lives if we do not come to an understanding of what God intended for his human families. It is only with this understanding that we can ever hope to call our existing family to a harmony in the Lord, or that our children can learn how to create a little church for themselves when they decide to marry.

The Catholic Church is made up of families which are like individual living cells in a living body. Therefore each cell or family unit is a little church which, living in cooperation with all the millions of other cells, makes up the entire living, breathing organism that we call the Catholic Church. Every individual human body is made up of countless single cells, each with a specific and specialized function. There are skin cells which protect the integrity of the body from a hostile environment. There are gastric cells which are responsible for breaking down and preparing our food for assimilation. There are heart cells which must work in unison if blood is to be pumped efficiently to the rest of the body. There are kidney cells which extract waste chemicals and eliminate these through the urinary system. There are brain cells which wondrously store new information by which we both learn and grow in experience.

Each cell is expected to carry out its own designated duty for the good of the whole, indeed for its very survival. It is like that with the Church. She is made up of families and each family cell must perform its God-given function if the Church is to be healthy. Likewise, just as each cell in the body is also made up of individual components such as DNA and enzymes, and each of these must function as intended if that cell is to remain healthy and do its job effectively, so also each family unit is made up of individual persons who must also do their job well if the family is to survive.

Imagine the chaos in the body if a liver cell were to decide that it did not like being a liver cell anymore and wanted to become freed from its duties. This actually does happen in our bodies whenever a healthy cell becomes, as it were, disobedient, abandons its proper function and becomes a totally undisciplined cancer cell. It is now called malignant because it maliciously attacks the integrity of the body, concerned only with its own needs and growth and ends up being the cause of death to the whole body. A person who decides to become self-serving, undisciplined and malignant towards others is like a dangerous cancer to the integrity of the family. A family which defies the laws of God also endangers the whole Church. Jesus did say, "And the gates of Hell will not prevail against it" (Matt. 16:18), but he did not say that Satan would not put the Church under siege. Disordered and disobedient Catholic families take part in this diabolical attack upon the Barque of Peter.

St. Paul understood this concept of the Mystical Body of Christ which is the Church when he wrote, "For as with the human body, which is a unity although it has many parts, all the parts of the body though many, still making up one single body, so it is with Christ. We were baptised into one body in a single Spirit, Jews as well as Greeks, slaves as well as free men, and we were all given the same Spirit to drink. And indeed the body consists not of one member but of many. If the foot were to say, 'I am not a hand and so I do not belong to the body,' it does not belong to the body any the less for that. Or if the ear were to say, 'I am not an eye, and so I do not belong to the body,' that would not stop its belonging to the body. If the whole body were just an eye, how would there be any hearing? If the whole body were hearing, how would there by any smelling? As it is, God has put all the separate parts into the body as he chose. If they were all the same part, how could it be a body? As it is, the parts are many but the body is one. The eye cannot say to the hand, 'I have no need of you,' nor can the head say to the feet, 'I have no need of you.' What is more, it is precisely the parts of the body that seem to be the weakest which are the indispensable ones. It is the parts of the body which we consider least dignified that we surround with the greatest dignity; and our less presentable parts are given greater presentability which our presentable parts do not need. God has comprised the body so that greater dignity is given to the parts which were without it, and so that there may not be disagreements inside the body but each part may be equally concerned for all the others. If one part is hurt, all the parts share its pain. And if one part is honoured, all the parts share its joy" (1 Cor. 12:12-26).

The family then, is a vital part of the whole and it must function in integrity for the good of the whole. The little church must be a holy little church if the entire Catholic Church is to be the "light of the world" (Matt. 5:14).

Fr. Federico Suarez, in his book *Mary of Nazareth,* writes, "Matrimony is the origin of the Christian family and every Christian family is like a cell of that living organism which we call the Church. In their families young Christians learn to know God, to pray to him, to look on him as their Father, to pray to the Blessed Virgin. From Christian families come the priests, other Christs, that spread good doctrine and administer the sacraments. The family is necessary for the perpetuation of the Church, to fill the ranks of the faithful."

The very first little church was the Holy Family of Nazareth. Jesus, Mary and Joseph were the perfect church cell, the very germ cell, from which the Catholic Church was to be born. As human families, we are called to be a trinitarian image and likeness of God. As such we form the human trinity of husband, wife and child, and it is intended by God the Father that we be a reflection of his holy face to the world. The unbeliever should see in the Catholic family "the way, the truth and the life" (John 14:6), that is to say, he should see Jesus himself in our lives. By living out the life of the Lord in our ordinary day-to-day duties, the love of God will shine in our eyes and that shining is the light of God. "In the same way, your light must shine in people's sight, so that, seeing your good works, they may give praise to your Father in Heaven" (Matt. 5:16).

For a Catholic family to be a true little church, it must be like its mother, which is the Catholic Church. We belong to the One, Holy, Catholic and Apostolic church. Therefore the family also must be one, holy, catholic and apostolic. Like the Church, which is true, the Catholic family must be true. It is these marks which distinguish the Catholic family from all others and they need to be understood more fully. The vocation of the family is so sublime and yet so demanding that if it is to become an authentic church, it will need a constant supply of sanctifying grace to fulfil its mission. The Catholic Church, founded upon Peter the Rock, constantly inspired by the Holy Spirit in truth and in love, is the very sacrament by which families are immersed in this essential grace. The Big Church mothers the little church so that it can become like itself and therefore like Jesus, its divine spouse.

First of all, the family, like the Church, must be *one.* Jesus prayed to his Father "that they may all be one as we are one" (John 17:22). This oneness is the deepest cry ever uttered from the Sacred Heart of Jesus to his heavenly Father. Being one is a sign of the presence of God in our hearts. It is the hallmark of the action of the Holy Spirit in our families. God intends that individual family members be of one mind and one heart in spiritual matters. Since we are human, we are prone to being divided on secular issues such as how to spend the family income or where to take a vacation, and we do have a sinful tendency to defend our own opinions on everything. But that is the challenge of love. In love we are called to defer to one another, to die to self and to give of ourselves unceasingly. Thus mere differences of opinion are really opportunities for us to show our love to the other by submitting our ego to the other. But in matters of faith and truth, there must be no compromise. We are called to be one in faith. "There is one Lord, one faith and one baptism" (Eph. 4:5). There is only one Lord and he is Jesus the Christ. There is only one faith and it is the faith given to the world by Jesus to the Church founded upon Peter, and there is only one baptism, which is that "in the name of the Father and of the Son and of the Holy Spirit" (Matt. 28:19).

Another word for oneness is communion. Pope John Paul II in *Familiaris Consortsio* wrote, "The conjugal communion sinks its roots in the natural complementarity that exists between man and woman, and is nurtured through the personal willingness of the spouses to share their entire life-project, what they have and what they are: for this reason such communion is the fruit and the sign of a profoundly human need. But in the Lord Christ, God takes up this human need, confirms it, purifies it and elevates it, leading it to perfection through the sacrament of Matrimony: the Holy Spirit who is poured out in the sacramental celebration offers Christian couples the gift of a new communion of love that is the living and real image of that unique unity which makes of the church the indivisible mystical body of the Lord Jesus."

The family then, is a communion of persons in Jesus and as such it is indissoluble. Our unity is intended to be for life. "What God has joined together, let no man put asunder" (Mark 10:9). This is not the forum for a discussion of the process of annulment in the Catholic Church. Suffice it to say that the Church has the mandate from God to discern whether a civilly recognised marriage was a true joining by God or not. That is to say, the Church and only the Church can decide that a marriage was a Sacramental union. If it indeed was a valid sacrament, then that marriage was joined by God and cannot be dissolved even by the Church. Our oneness therefore, is a lifelong commitment and only death can end it. *Familiaris Consortsio* states, "Being rooted in the personal and total self-giving of the couple, and being required by the good of the children, the indissolubility of marriage finds its ultimate truth in the plan that God has manifested in his revelation: he wills and he communicates the indissolubility of marriage as a fruit, a sign and a requirement of the absolutely faithful love that God has for man and that the Lord Jesus has for the Church."

The family then must foster unity within itself, not by placing the good of the family above the good of God, but by obedience to the good of God. This is done by means of care and love for the little ones, the sick and the aged. It is done by means of mutual service every day and it is done by a generous sharing of material things, of joys and of sorrows. Children foster this oneness by their obedience, their allegiance and above all their love, which they generously give to their parents. By obeying the commandment to honour their father and mother, they do honour to themselves in the eyes of God and help to foster this first of all the charisms of the Catholic Church, which is oneness.

Secondly, the family is called to be *holy* in imitation of Holy Mother Church. Holiness is the call of God. It is his Will that we "be perfect as your Father in heaven is perfect" (Matt. 5:48). Since this is the plan of our Creator God, it cannot ever be something which harms us. Holiness, in fact, is the *only* way by which we will find peace and joy within our hearts. The world does not offer us peace. It seduces us with the sadness of sin and trivial pleasure in trivial things. God, on the other hand, blesses the family which seeks holy things. Pope John Paul II writes, "On the contrary, by responding to the deepest demands of the human being created by God, it places itself at the service of that person's full humanity with the delicate and binding love whereby God himself inspires, sustains and guides every creature towards its happiness" *(Familiaris Consortsio).*

The pursuit of holiness therefore, is the very reason for our existence and it is the duty of every Catholic family to promote it within itself. This demands an awareness of sin, a sincere commitment to observe the moral law in all things and a willingness on the part of family members to forgive one another and to try again and again. The first charism of oneness is essential if the family is to grow in holiness. This is a lifelong struggle in the war against egoism, and for the little church to thrive, it must constantly listen to the loving exhortations of its Mother the Church. The big Church must not be seen as some kind of tyrannical policewoman trying to spoil our enjoyment of life. She must be seen for what she is, the nurturer of holiness and the guardian of our immortal souls. Just like the whole Church, the family should have a hunger for souls. It should give examples of holiness, teach holiness and be a living embodiment of the holiness of Jesus. No loving parents would expose their children to a polluted atmosphere since it would damage their lungs. This should be even more true for the spiritual atmosphere. Holiness should be the very air that the children breathe every day and all day so that they too will grow in "wisdom and stature and grace before God and men" (Luke 2:52).

The little church, just like the big Church, must be *Catholic.* This means being Catholic with a big "C" and a little "c." A big "C" Catholic is one who belongs to the one, holy and apostolic Church. Such a person is proud to be a Catholic. He does not hide his light under a bushel basket. He never pretends to his friends that he is anything else but Catholic. Not only is he faithful to the infallible teachings of the Church *in all things*, but he is also eager and fearless in proclaiming the truth to others. As my grandmother used to say, "He is never backward at coming forward!" Such a man or woman loves the Church as a mother, rejoices in the purity of her instruction and is willing even to lay down his or her life for her. This is oneness, this is truth, this is holiness and this is Catholic.

I meet so many Catholics who are not on fire with the love of the Church. They seem to think of only doing the minimum to get to heaven and so they go to Mass on Sunday and then go into hiding for the remainder of the week, trying very hard not to be noticed by others, as though being Catholic was some kind of affliction or something to be ashamed of. The true little church is thrilled to be Catholic. It is filled with jubilation at belonging to the true Church and marvels at the privilege of belonging to Jesus in truth and holiness. When we are overjoyed at some good fortune in our lives, are we not propelled into voicing it at the top of our lungs and sharing it with all whom we meet? We are the unworthy recipients of the grace of being baptised into the Catholic church and so we should be on fire with the urge to share it with others. We should be better evangelisers than the Evangelicals, better singers of God's music than the Baptists, better Bible scholars than the Pentecostals, better participants in the liturgy than the Orthodox and better praisers of God's glory than all denominations put together. Big "C" Catholics are lovers of the Pope, who is the successor to Peter, the first pope, and to whom has been handed on "the keys to the Kingdom of Heaven" (Matt. 16:19).

To be Catholic with a small "c" is to recognize that the word catholic means *universal*. It means to believe that Jesus came and died for all men and women of the earth, regardless of race, sex or creed. Therefore the Catholic family must, like Jesus, love all men and women. This love discriminates against no one and is the most fundamental commandment of the Lord. Jesus did not disdain to eat with prostitutes and tax collectors, nor did he balk at staying overnight in the house of Zaccheus, who had been a thief and a dishonest man. The Catholic family therefore has a heart big enough to love everyone. This includes the poor, the marginalised, the hungry, the sick, the elderly and the downtrodden. But it especially includes the sinner. As a Catholic I must not despise the liar, the cheat, the adulterer, the abortionist or the homosexual. I must of course despise the sin, but how can I call the sinner to repentance and to holiness if I do not first love him? Love is the engine which drives the vehicle of evangelisation. Jesus said, "Love one another as I have loved you" (John 15:12) and "I have come not to condemn the world but to save it" (John 12:47).

Therefore, in imitation of Jesus, we are called not to condemn sinners but to save them and to love them just as Jesus did. This the family does by holiness, good example, acts of love and daily prayer of intercession for the conversion of sinners.

Being a real Catholic is not easy but it is the way to bring the world to Jesus Christ. Not only does it give us the joy of seeing others come home to their Father's house by conversion to the truth, but it is also a mighty source of grace for our own souls. "My brothers, if one of you strays from the truth, and another brings him back to it, he may be sure that anyone who can bring a sinner back from his erring ways will be saving his soul from death and cover a multitude of sins" (James 5:20). How wonderful it is for a family to realize the fruits of their love, not only in their own allegiance to the truth, but in the conversion of others who see their joy in the Lord and come to desire it for themselves. Thereby, their own sins are wiped out of the mind of God. The Word of God promises it.

The last of the charisms of the Catholic Church is that it is *apostolic,* and therefore the little church of the family must also be apostolic. This means that the family recognises it is a recipient of the teachings of Jesus and the traditions of the Church, handed down from generation to generation, beginning with the Apostles themselves. Jesus chose twelve very ordinary men to be the guardians of his truth and to hand it on to posterity, and it is interesting that Jesus chose such very ordinary men for this momentous task. He could have chosen twelve great scholars from the great rabbinical schools of Israel or he could have chosen twelve notably holy men. But he did not. The apostles were selected from very humble occupations, with little or no education and a great many human foibles and weaknesses.

Peter, the Chief of the Apostles, denied Jesus three times, Judas betrayed him for a paltry sum of money, and all of the others except John ran away when Jesus was arrested. Jesus deliberately, and with divine foresight, lifted such men up to the highest office in his Church. He wanted to teach us that our human nature is always weak and sinful and so we must not judge the Church by its leaders. They are only human beings like us. They too are capable of sin, even the Pope. We are to marvel that, in spite of the humanity of our spiritual leaders, the Holy Spirit continues to inspire the Pope and the magisterium to teach the truth, the whole truth and nothing but the truth. The Pope is infallible but not impeccable. He can and does teach the truth but he can commit sin just like anyone else.

Therefore, the members of the little church can take comfort in the fact that while they too are sinners, they can enjoy the power of the apostolic tradition, which is the ever available inspiration of the Holy Spirit. By dint of its two-thousand-year-long connection to the apostles, the Catholic family can live in the harmony of its oneness, can live joyfully in holiness, can live out the full meaning of what it is to be Catholic and can live in and perpetuate the faith of the apostles. This is the mandate of the Catholic family, the little church.

An additional attribute of the Catholic Church is that she is true. Likewise, the family is called to be true. Being true to something means two things. It first means being faithful, and second it means living in truth. As families, we are called to be faithful to Jesus Christ. We do that by being faithful to the teaching authority of the Church, which is the Magisterium. The Magisterium is inspired by the Holy Spirit and so cannot teach error in matters of faith and morals. Being faithful means being obedient to what is true and holy. Therefore, not only must a family humbly accept the dogmas of the Church as the authentic word of God, but it must live out these truths. First and foremost, a Catholic family must act upon the holy doctrine of God, which means to rejoice in the truth, to study it and learn more, to grow in wisdom, to work at becoming more virtuous, to go to war against its own sinful urges, and to love above all. A Catholic family should live in love and live for love if it is to be true. It must have a loving collective heart which prompts it not only to love the individual members within the family but to expand its love to include all the members of the human family.

A vital off-shoot of this commitment to truth is the duty to *teach* the truth to the children. They have a right to the truth and the parents have the responsibility of imparting it to them. The highest and most necessary learning for any human person is the study of God and his holy doctrine. Knowing God is far, far above any other kind of knowing and it is within the family, the little church, that it begins and is nurtured. While the big Church mothers and instructs us, nevertheless it is wrong for parents to leave the teaching of their children in the faith to the Church alone. **Paragraph 2222** of the Catholic Catechism states "Parents must regard their children as children of God and respect them as human persons. Showing themselves obedient to the will of the Father in heaven, they educate their children to fulfil God's law."

Truth then, is a priceless treasure, never to be betrayed. The little church must be a cell of truth willing to live in its light and ready to defend it against those who hate it.

The Church believes in families. She teaches, nurtures, loves them and never ceases to pray for them, interceding with Jesus through Mary for their salvation. The Church venerates Mary as the Queen of Families and so we can turn to her to mother us, to reign in our homes and to keep Satan from our door. The little church should make a solemn act of consecration to the Immaculate Heart of Mary and the Sacred Heart of Jesus whereby Jesus and Mary will watch over husband, wife and children, inspiring, guiding and protecting them. Consecration is the most powerful way by which a family gives itself over to the care of heaven, and its fruits are ever-increasing blessedness. The family which is consecrated bathes in grace and enjoys a special protection from the onslaughts of the world. Mary wraps her mantle of love around such families and guards them as her own special possession.

Pope John Paul II, in *Familiaris Consortsio*, quotes the Synod Fathers who drew up a charter of rights of the family:

1. The right to exist and progress as a family, that is to say, the right of every human being, even if he or she is poor, to found a family and to have adequate means to support it.
2. The right to exercise its responsibility regarding the transmission of life and to educate children.
3. The right to the intimacy of conjugal and family life.
4. The right to the stability of the bond and of the institution of marriage.
5. The right to believe in and profess one's faith and to propagate it.
6. The right to bring up children in accordance with the family's own traditions, religious and cultural values, with the necessary instruments, means and institutions.
7. The right, especially of the poor and the sick, to obtain physical, social, political and economic security.

8. The right to housing suitable for living family life in a proper way.
9. The right to expression and to representation, either directly or through associations, before the economic, social and cultural public authorities and lower authorities.
10. The right to form associations with other families and institutions, in order to fulfil the family's role suitably and expeditiously.
11. The right to protect minors by adequate institutions and legislation from harmful drugs, pornography, alcoholism, etc.
12. The right to wholesome recreation of a kind that also fosters family values.
13. The right of the elderly to a worthy life and a worthy death.
14. The right to emigrate as a family in search of a better life.

The Catholic Church indeed cares for the rights of all the little churches of the world. Above all things, the little church is called to give glory to the one true God. "Let there be then, no man or woman, no family, who would now turn away their hearts from the Lord our God, to go and serve these pagan gods" (Deut. 29:18). This is the supreme duty of all human families. It is the very reason why families exist at all. Not only that, without our giving the praise that is due to Almighty God, we can never hope to enjoy the one thing we need for happiness, which is an astounding and super-human love. "For this reason, I kneel before the Father, from whom every family in heaven and on earth is named, that he may grant you in accord with the riches of his glory, to be strengthened with power through his Spirit in the inner self, and that Christ may dwell in your hearts through faith; that you, rooted and grounded in love, may have the strength to comprehend with all the holy ones what is the breadth and length and height and depth, and to know the love of Christ that surpasses knowledge, so that you may be filled with the fullness of God" (Eph. 3:14-19).

This is the secret of every little church. Each family which is truly Catholic is guaranteed to be "filled with the fullness of God." The Catholic family is indeed created in the image and likeness of God himself.

CHAPTER 2

Prayer and Sacrament:
The Fuel of Catholic Family Life

> *"My house shall be called a*
> *house of prayer."*
>
> (Mark 11:17)

It is indeed a beautiful thing for the house of a Catholic family to be known as a house of prayer. It ought to be such if it is to call itself Catholic at all. Since we claim to follow Jesus Christ we must imitate his example and be in communication with his Father in Heaven. "Now it happened in those days that he went out onto the mountain to pray and he spent the whole night in prayer to God" (Luke 6:12). Jesus, in spite of being divine, **needed** to pray to his Father, first of all, to know the will of his Father for him and secondly, to receive strength for his mission on earth. We need to pray for exactly the same reasons.

Without a healthy prayer life we will stumble through our own life without divine guidance, and therefore reliant only upon our own poor human resources. It is like trying to drive a car without gasoline. Eventually, we have to get out and push and we will not be able to push it very far. Our own human strength is simply not enough. In family life, prayer is the gasoline which fuels the engine and gets us to our destination, which is Heaven.

As parents we must foster three kinds of prayer. There needs to be personal private prayer, prayer as a married couple, and family prayer. All three are vital for the spiritual health of the little church which is the Catholic family.

Jesus calls every one of his disciples to personal and private communication with God. "But when you pray, go to your private room, shut yourself in, and so pray to your Father who is in that secret place and your Father who sees all that is done in secret will reward you" (Matt. 6:6).

Even though marriage is a covenant of complete self-giving of one spouse to another, private personal prayer is still essential. We need to take our innermost thoughts and concerns to God and have a one-to-one chat with him, conveying our worries, our fears, our desires and needs to him in solitude. No matter how open a married couple may be in revealing themselves to each other, there are some things which can and should only be shared with God. This kind of prayer is akin to the Sacrament of Reconciliation. We confess our sins alone, not together, even though we are married.

As a husband and father, as a wife and mother, we need to tell God our inner secrets and to enlist his help to receive strength and wisdom. Thus fortified, a man can become a better husband and a better father. Likewise, a woman can become a better wife and a better mother. They then find their marriage bond strengthened and they enjoy God's continuing help with their parenting.

A husband in his private prayer time intercedes for his wife before God. A wife intercedes for her husband. Each prays that the other will receive the grace to grow in love, to be a better and better spouse, to be a wise parent and to achieve salvation.

The first principle of private prayer is that it is very simple. Conversation with God is not difficult or complicated. We need not seek out formulas or overly burdensome devotions. Devotions are holy and good, but they are only so for being simple. What could be more simple or beautiful than the Chaplet of Divine Mercy or the Rosary? We find it very easy to have a conversation with a friend. Surely it is just as easy with God, who is our very best friend. God loves the sound of our voice (did he not create it?) and he loves the thoughts of our hearts. So all we have to do is talk. Nothing is too trivial for God to hear. He listens attentively just like any father listens to the chatter of his child, as though it were music to his ears.

Jesus does tell us that silent prayer of few words is preferable to volumes of useless words. "In your prayers do not babble as the gentiles do, for they think that by using many words they will make themselves heard. Do not be like them; your Father knows what you need before you ask him" (Matt. 6:7-8). This is really the Lord's call to pray with full attention to the task, rather than rattling off reams of thoughtless words. Catholics are often accused of "babbling" when they say the rosary, but this is not so. The repetitive nature of the Rosary prayer is designed to help us dispel distractions and to meditate upon the mysteries of the life of Jesus. Those who simply ramble through the decades with no heart in it are of course not praying at all.

Therefore, the second principle of prayer is that our *attitude* is of extreme importance. The Pharisee prayed, "I thank you Lord that I am not like other men" (Luke 18:11), which was the prayer of vanity and therefore useless. The publican however prayed, "Lord have mercy on me a sinner" (Luke 18:13). This was the prayer of a poor man and therefore it was esteemed by God. If we are to pray with an attitude acceptable to our Creator, we must also pray in poverty of spirit. That means humility, recognizing our sinfulness and acknowledging our constant need for forgiveness and grace.

St. John of the Cross describes why we should give precedence to a prayerful attitude rather than to formulas. "The reason why it is better for the person who loves to express his needs to the beloved, rather than ask him to satisfy such needs, arises from three factors: first, because our Lord knows better than we what is proper for us; secondly, because the loved one has more compassion in seeing the need of the one who loves and is more impressed by his feeling of resignation; thirdly, because a person is less given to self-love and formality when expressing what he is lacking than in asking for what he only seems to need." Our Blessed Mother did not tell Jesus to make more wine at Cana. She merely said, "They have no wine" (John 2:3). She expressed the need and left the answer up to Jesus. We would do well to imitate her. So often we try to help God along by giving him our suggestions as to how he should solve our problems. Then if our solution is not forthcoming, we become despondent or angry. Surely God knows much better than we what is the very best solution, and we would do well to stop at stating the need and leave the rest up to God.

The third principle of prayer is never to lose heart. "Because this widow keeps bothering me, I shall deliver a just decision for her lest she finally come and strike me" (Luke 18:5). Jesus then says, "Will not God then secure the rights of his chosen ones who call out to him day and night?" (Luke 18:7). When our prayers are not answered speedily, we can become easily discouraged. We must be reminded that God's plan is still the best plan for us and for others and that he may need us to persevere even for years with our prayers. Yet no prayer from the heart is ever pointless. All good prayer bears fruit in its appointed time.

The golden key to quality prayer is the heart. "Then he told them a parable about the need to pray continually and never lose heart" (Luke 18:1). Jesus desires us to pray continually but how can such a thing be humanly possible? Certainly it would be impossible for us if prayer meant purely intellectual meditation. The Dominican priest Fr. Chevignard puts it this way: "If prayer depended upon the body, we could not pray and be occupied manually at the same time; if it were a matter of sensibility, every sensible preoccupation, sickness, emotion, would make it impossible and it would be subject to our change of moods; if it were solely in the brain, we would pray only when we would be discussing theology. But prayer is, above all, within ourselves: our 'heart' can always pray to God; even when our hands are busy, our sensibility crushed and our head burdened with worries, it can always talk about what makes its life and its love most meaningful. On the contrary, when our 'heart' is concerned about something other than God, prayer then ceases within us. It is actually our 'heart' that God listens to."

If we give God his rightful place as first in our hearts, then we will be praying continually. During our daily work and obligations we will recall God and his goodness and we will utter short prayers such as "Thank you God," "Bless me Jesus," "Glory be to God" and so on. Even when we go to sleep, we fall asleep thinking of God and our hearts will silently pray all night. This is not exclusively for saints. It is for all of us, and of course, as we progress in it we will end up by becoming saints anyway.

Couple prayer is a privilege of the married. At some point in the day, usually after the children are asleep, husband and wife should pray together for a time. Such prayer unites the couple in heart and mind as they ask God to enrich them with the graces of their Sacrament of Matrimony. It is also a time for them to give to God their concerns for their children and their well-being. It is a time to offer their children to God as a holy gift, interceding for their needs and asking for their protection. Couple prayer promotes peace in the marriage. When a couple is divided by bad feelings or differing opinions, that is the very time when they *need* to pray together, to ask God to heal their division. Without prayer the task of reuniting is much more difficult and less likely to succeed. It takes a real man and a real woman to set aside hurt feelings and to pray together, but the graces of such self-forgetting are enormous. It is beautiful to think, that while the little children are sleeping soundly and secure, mother and father are interceding with heaven for their well-being and prosperity.

Family prayer is the third form of prayer and is of immeasurable value. Time should be set aside every day, usually after supper, for the whole family to gather together to talk to God. When the children are very small, this should be a short interlude as it is not good to weary the children or have them associate prayer with boredom and restraint. But it is surprising how quickly children come to value this time since it is filled with feelings of warmth, love and togetherness. Sometimes parents are surprised at how fervent their child can be in prayer and how he or she comes to love the Rosary. A very young child, even as young as three years old, will be eager to learn his prayers and will often be impatient to lead one of the decades.

One young mother described an experience with her little three-year-old daughter. Mother was tired and wanted to forego the usual evening prayer. The child was disappointed and pestered her mother to pray with her. Mother wearily gave in but said, "Instead of our usual prayers, why don't we just sit quietly and ask God inside our hearts for anything we want." The little one sat close to her mother, closed her eyes and concentrated very hard. After a while, mother thought it was time to stop and she opened her eyes to see the child still at it with her eyes screwed shut and a look of great determination on her face. Eventually she opened her eyes and mother said, "Well, did you ask God anything?" "Yes," said the child, "I asked him what his name was." The mother smiled and asked if he responded. The little girl said, "Well, he didn't speak to me but he wrote three letters behind my eyelids. He wrote *I. A. M.*" The child had no idea that Yahweh calls himself, "I Am" but innocently reported what she had seen. Needless to say, that mother marvelled at her little one. God loves the heart of a child and we do well to pray for such a heart for ourselves.

Family prayer should also occur outside of the formal time set aside in the evening. Grace before and after meals should be said, even in a restaurant. It is surprising how other people admire a family that gives thanks to God before they eat of his bounty. It was precisely because my wife and I made the Sign of the Cross in a restaurant and said Grace that a waitress came up and asked if we would pray over her. Her husband had left her and she was finding it very difficult to raise her daughter on her own. So we laid hands on her and prayed over her right in front of a room full of diners. That could never have happened if we had not given public thanks to God as all good Catholics should. Never be ashamed to honour God, even, or perhaps especially, in public. "Everyone who acknowledges me before others, I will acknowledge before my heavenly Father" (Matt. 10:32).

The family can also get into the habit of praying together for safekeeping before going on a trip, or asking God for good weather for the picnic. In other words, the children should learn that it is good to ask God's blessing for *everything.* A child should also be encouraged to include his guardian angel in all his activities. He should be aware that his closest friend is always by his side wherever he goes and is there even when he chooses to sin. Teachers today rightly emphasize that a child should always be fair and considerate towards his friends. How much more considerate he should be towards his angel, for whom sin is a shameful thing. If I should not hurt my friends, I should not hurt my angel, who is my very best friend.

If family prayer is the gasoline for the engine, then the sacraments are the engine itself. We can put all the gasoline we want into the tank but if there is no engine, the car is going nowhere. Just as an engine provides power, the sacraments provide sanctifying grace, which we all need if we are to persevere or have the strength to resist temptation. Parents must take advantage of the sacraments if they are to be godly parents, and they need to see to it that the children come to love the sacraments also.

We Catholics baptize our children as infants and so they hold no memory of that great day, but their Baptismal anniversaries should be celebrated every year by the whole family, to give thanks to God for that most momentous occasion of the child's entire life. No other life's event is so joyfully significant. A child, however, can anticipate her first confession with great excitement. She can also, from the time of being able to walk, be allowed to accompany mother and father to the altar at Communion time. She should be taught to cross her arms over her breast as a sign to the priest or deacon that she desires a blessing. A child knows that in the blessing something beautiful and powerful is taking place, and she cannot wait till that great day when she too will receive Jesus in the Bread just like mom and dad.

Each of the sacraments signifies a special action of grace for us and each has its own external sign.

1. Baptism

Jesus commissioned his apostles to "go therefore, make disciples of all nations, baptising them in the name of the Father and of the Son and of the Holy Spirit" (Matt. 28:19). Baptism is our first reconciliation with God, and all sins both original and personal, are buried in the waters of Baptism. Baptism is irrevocable and so once a Catholic, always a Catholic, even if we renounce the Church later on.

St. Paul writes, "But you were washed, you were sanctified, you were justified in the name of the Lord Jesus Christ and in the Spirit of our God" (1 Cor. 6:11). The waters of Baptism then make us new creatures. We are transformed into members of God's heavenly family and can enjoy all of the wondrous privileges which go along with being heirs to the Kingdom. Not all of us will inherit earthly riches, but by Baptism even the poorest of the poor can inherit the priceless treasure of Heaven. What is more, the punishment which we deserve from God's justice for our personal sins is also completely cancelled out by Baptism. The Council of Trent taught that, should a newly baptised person die immediately, he would go straight to Heaven. This is why in past centuries, many people who had come to believe in Jesus would try to postpone the Sacrament, hoping for a deathbed baptism, whereby all would be wiped clean and they could go straight to Heaven. This was an abuse and was very bad theology. In effect, they played Russian roulette with their souls. I am sure many died before they could be baptised.

Jesus said to Nicodemus, "In all truth I tell you, no one can enter the Kingdom of God without being born through water and the Holy Spirit" (John 3:5). In other words, Baptism is a kind of re-birth by which we become a supernatural creation in Christ.

"For by one spirit we were all baptised into one body" (1 Cor. 12:13). Baptism therefore grafts us into the mystical body of Christ, which is the Church and we become fully fledged members with all the rights and privileges which go along with that. "It is no longer I who live but Christ lives in me" (Gal. 2:20). As a result, what divided us as profane human creatures has now been washed clean, the barriers of sin are broken down and we become branches on the vine of Jesus. We are reconciled to one another and we are marked with the indelible mark of Christ. This gives us the right to receive the other sacraments, by which we obtain more and more sanctifying grace, which is indispensable if we are to progress in holiness.

2. Confirmation

Jesus promised to send the Holy Spirit, not just to the Church as a body, but also to each individual member of the Church. Peter and John "came down and prayed for them that they might receive the Holy Spirit, for it had not yet fallen on any of them, but they had only been baptised in the name of the Lord Jesus (by Phillip the Deacon). Then they laid their hands on them and they received the Holy Spirit" (Acts 8:14-17). "It is God who establishes us with you in Christ (in Baptism) and has commissioned us: he has put his seal upon us (Confirmation) and given us his spirit in our hearts as a guarantee" (2 Cor. 1:21).

Confirmation, therefore, is a true sacrament distinct from Baptism. We are born anew in Baptism and strengthened by

Confirmation. In Baptism the external sign is the water, whereas in Confirmation the external sign is the laying on of hands and the anointing with oil. Phillip the Deacon was able to baptize but confirmation was reserved, right from the beginning, to the apostles (Peter and John) who made a special journey for that purpose. That is why Confirmation remains a function of the bishop, who is the successor to the apostles. The bishop can lawfully delegate this authority to the priest, but not to the deacon.

Confirmation marks a baptised person with the Seal of the Holy Spirit and imparts the fullness of the Holy Spirit to that Christian. Thereby, we become mature Christian adults and soldiers of Christ. As a result, we become empowered to be evangelisers, reconciling the world to Jesus, and helping in the great work of bringing souls into the Kingdom. We acquire the grace to show the right way to others, to bring people to repentance, to call fallen-away Catholics back to the Mass, to defend the rights of the Church, to honour the priesthood, to answer false accusations and to show good example to all the world.

The Catholic Catechism states, "This Seal of the Holy Spirit marks our total belonging to Christ, our enrollment in his service for ever, as well as the promise of divine protection in the great eschatological trial (the persecution of the end-times)."

St. Francis of Assisi called one of his brothers one day and said, "Brother we are going to preach." The brother replied, "Yes, father. Gladly." They set out together and walked silently along the city streets and not a word was spoken. When they returned home the brother said, "Father, you said we were going to preach, but you never spoke." St. Francis merely smiled and said, "Brother, we have been preaching the whole time, by our existence, our habit and our good example." Nothing speaks more eloquently than good example, and it is Confirmation which gives us the charism to be witnesses by example to the way of Jesus.

3. Reconciliation

By its very name, we recognize that this powerful sacrament reconciles us again and again with God. Because of our inherited sin-nature, we continue to offend God even after Baptism and

Confirmation. "If we say 'We have no sin' we are deceiving ourselves and we have no truth in us" (1 John 1:8). It is true that we are miserable, weak sinners who in spite of our best efforts keep on sinning. "So now it is no longer I who do it but sin that dwells in me. For I know that good does not dwell in me, that is, in my flesh. The willing is ready at hand but doing the good is not. For I do not do the good I want but I do the evil I do not want" (Rom. 7:17-19).

Therefore we need to be reconciled to the Lord time and time again. Jesus, knowing this, instituted the wonderful Sacrament of Confession whereby we kneel before Jesus in the person of the priest, and tell him our sins. We express not only our sorrow at having offended him, but we also assure him we will do everything in our power to avoid these sins in the future. Since atonement must also be made for having offended God, the priest will allot an appropriate penance to be performed as soon as possible. We should take this penance very seriously and do it with great reverence. After all, the penance we receive from the priest is nowhere as severe as that which we deserve from Divine Justice. Yet Jesus promised to honour the decision of his Church in such matters and by the wondrous action of his Divine Mercy, he graciously accepts the penance which his priest has meted out.

We kneel before a human priest, but we are not confessing to the priest. We are confessing to Jesus **represented** by the priest. The priest is an "Alter Christus," (another Christ) and he stands in for Jesus. That is the way Jesus commanded it to be. But many of us prefer to avoid the sacrament, either because we are embarrassed at having to recite our sins, or we are afraid that perhaps the priest will tell someone else what we have done, or might reject us later on because of what he now knows of our inner darkness. None of that is true. First of all, the priest will only rejoice that he has been allowed to hear a holy confession and he in turn, receives a blessing when he is allowed to exercise his priestly gift of absolving the sinner. Secondly, the priest can never, ever, under any circumstances whatsoever break the seal of confession. No other human being will ever hear about our private sins from the priest. Not even a court of law can force a priest to violate the confessional, even if it were to send him to prison. Thirdly, a priest can legitimately pray for the grace from God to forget our sins after he has pronounced the words of absolution. This holy forgetfulness unites the priest with Jesus himself, who also forgets our sins once we have been forgiven by him.

Blessed Sister Faustina, when she first began to receive locutions from Jesus, reported these to her superior, who scoffed at her and refused to believe. She said, "The next time you hear from your so-called Jesus, ask him what was the last sin I confessed in Confession." Sr. Faustina in obedience, but greatly embarrassed, did ask this of Jesus when next he came to her. Having received her answer she went back to her superior who asked, "Well, what did he say?" Sr. Faustina said, "He said he didn't remember." With that answer the superior believed and allowed Sr. Faustina to continue with her diary.

The Sacrament of Confession brings all walks of life together. It reconciles us all. The tribunal of penance is a truly democratic institution. There is no distinction between rich and poor, learned and simple, high and low for they are all sinners. Peace is restored to families, quarrels settled among neighbours, unjust gain restored to rightful owners and enemies brought to reconcile with one another.

4. Sacrament of the Sick

Jesus had great love for the sick. "All those who had any that were sick with various diseases brought them to him and he laid hands on every one of them and they were healed" (Luke 4:40). The institution of this powerful sacrament is attested to by the apostle James. "Anyone of you who is ill should send for the presbyters of the church and they must anoint the sick person with oil in the name of the Lord and pray over him. The prayer of faith will save the sick person and the Lord will raise him up again, and if he has committed any sins, he will be forgiven" (James 5:14-15).

The priest anoints all five senses of the sick person (the eyes, ears, nose, mouth, hands and feet, that is to say, sight, sound, smell, taste and touch), because it is the senses that lead us into sin. This strengthens us to use our senses in a holy manner and to seal them against evil influences. By means of the prayer of faith, the sick person is healed, always in his soul and often in his body. Spiritual strength is restored and, as the Council of Trent states, "The sacrament brings enlightenment and strength to the soul, by flooding it with great confidence in the mercy of God." Also, if he has committed any mortal sins, he will be forgiven and reconciled with God.

This sacrament was at one time reserved only for the dying and so was known as the Sacrament of Extreme Unction, but this is no longer the case. The sacrament is also properly used for anyone who is seriously sick and confers abundant sanctifying grace upon the invalid, eradicating all that separates him from God's friendship.

5. Holy Orders

From the first breath of our life to the last gasp of death, the priest is our sure companion and guide. He is another Christ for us, interceding for us with his priestly prayer, sacrificing for us at the Mass, fortifying us with the grace of the sacraments, shepherding us as a good pastor and constantly reconciling us to God and to one another. He calls souls not of the faith to come to their Father's house and he does this by example and by preaching and teaching. His role is that of official mediator between God and man. On one hand, he represents God's interests in the world of men, proclaiming everything which God demands of us, and, on the other hand, he represents our interests by interceding for us before God, leading souls to God by sacrifice, sacrament and prayer. Christ revealed himself as the Eternal High Priest and he gave priestly power to his apostles and their successors.

By his consecration, the priest is set apart from other men, which is both an honour and a heavy burden. He no longer belongs to himself but to his flock and to God. This is most powerfully expressed in his celibacy, by which he offers his sexuality to God not only as a personal sacrifice, but as a sign of his spiritual marriage to the entire Church. Jesus himself regarded the state of virginity to be the highest of vocations: "It is not everyone who can accept what I have said, but only those to whom it is granted. There are eunuchs born so from their mother's womb, there are eunuchs made so by human agency and there are eunuchs who have made themselves so for the sake of the Kingdom of Heaven. Let anyone accept this who can" (Matt. 19:12). It takes a very special gift from God for a man to voluntarily renounce the legitimate joys of married life. St. Paul says, "The unmarried man is anxious about the affairs of the Lord, how to please the Lord. But the married man is anxious about worldly affairs, how to please his wife, and his interests are divided" (1 Cor. 7:32-34). This is why the Church demands celibacy from its priests, because they are to lead souls to moral perfection. It is precisely because their interests are not divided that they can totally devote their lives to the flock. They must be able to say, "I have no wife and children at home; therefore I am constantly available to my flock and I am free to lay down my life for my people."

Jesus loves virginity. He willed to be born, not as the fruit of a legitimate marriage union, but from a Virgin Mother. It was into the virginal hands of Mary and Joseph that the care of Jesus was entrusted. Therefore, it is fitting that those hands which are privileged to touch him every day at the Mass be also virginal. People, many of whom ought to know better, often object that there are bad priests who violate the rule of celibacy and therefore it would be better to do away with the Church law on celibacy. But by this same flawed reasoning, we should do away with marriage also, since it is so often abused, and there would no longer be any adultery!

Even among the twelve apostles chosen by Christ there were Judas, who betrayed him, and Peter, the first pope, who denied him three times. Jesus knew the human frailty of his priests and we have a duty to pray daily for our priests that they will remain strong and true to their vocation. We must never criticise a priest. If we see some sin in him, we must encourage him and build him up. He needs the love of his bride the Church. No matter what his personal life or his personality is like, we should be grateful to have a priest who can bring Jesus to our altars. If you want a holy priest, pray for the one you already have.

6. Matrimony

"Yahweh God said, 'It is not right that the man should be alone. I shall make him a helper'" (Gen. 2:18). God then created woman and made her such that, without her, a man feels lonely and in need of help. Male and female mutually complement and complete each other, not only sexually, but psychologically and spiritually and so they feel drawn to one another in a lifelong commitment. The Sacrament of Matrimony carries with it a unique sanctifying grace which brings a man and a woman together in love and maintains that love in good times and bad, in sickness and in health and "till death do us part." In other words, Matrimony is a reconciler, giving us the power to overcome the battle between men and women, by allowing woman to be fully female and man to be fully male. God formed woman from one of Adam's ribs and this means from the inner recesses of the man's heart. Thus a man feels that his heart can never be at peace until a woman has taken that special place by his side. Marriage also reconciles us to God as well as to one another.

It is only in marriage that we can find blessing for our sexual union. It is marriage which is intended to be the setting in which new souls are created for God and we offer a pleasing sacrifice to the Father when we raise godly children for his Kingdom. Marriage is therefore the foundation of the family, which is the little church, a small trinity of father, mother and children. The Church is built with the building blocks of individual families. In fact, marital love is so powerful and so mysterious that St. Paul says, "This is a great mystery, I mean, in respect to Christ and the Church" (Eph. 5:32).

In other words, the relationship between man and woman in marriage is a symbol of the holy and sanctifying union between Christ and his Church. Just as Jesus and his Church are fused by a divine marriage, so also earthly marriage fuses man and woman into "one flesh" (Gen. 2:24).

Tertullian summed up marriage very well when he wrote, "How can I ever express the happiness of a marriage joined by the Church, strengthened by an offering, sealed by a blessing, announced by angels and ratified by the Father? How wonderful the bond between two believers, now one in hope, one in desire, one in discipline, one in the same service! They are both children of one Father and servants of the same Master, undivided in spirit and flesh, truly two in one flesh. Where the flesh is one, one also is the spirit."

7. Holy Eucharist

The greatest gift which Jesus left to us for our sanctification was the gift of his actual Body, Blood, Soul and Divinity in the bread and wine. What greater miracle has the world ever seen than this? A human priest can say the words of consecration over mere bread and wine and Jesus the Son of God responds immediately, to imbue these earthly things with his Divine Reality. Truly, when we receive the bread and/or the wine, we are receiving God into our souls. We who are sinners, who can never be worthy, are loved so much that God is willing to come to us in such an intimate way. It is a union of Christ and me which is even more awesome and powerful than the union of a man with his wife. In marriage, two human beings become one flesh, but with Eucharist, God and man become fused. Our humanity becomes, in a sense, divinised by the life of Jesus within us. "In all truth I tell you if you do not eat the flesh of the son of man and drink his blood, you have no life in you" (John 6:53). "For my flesh is real food and my blood is real drink" (John 6:55).

Could Jesus have made it any clearer? There can be no doubt that Jesus actually intended for us to consume him. He was the sacrificial lamb of the New Testament. Just as the Passover lamb was not only sacrificed by the Jews, but by God's command, *had to be eaten,* so also Jesus, who is the Passover Lamb of the New Testament, had to be sacrificed on the cross and also eaten, consumed by us for our spiritual life and growth. This is made possible by the miracle of multiplication. Jesus multiplied the bread for the five thousand as a sign that he was soon to multiply the living bread of his own Body for all generations to come and this would take place at every Mass which would ever be said till the end of time. Jesus is the New and Perpetual Sacrifice freely and generously offered. When we receive Our Lord and God in Holy Communion, our venial sins are wiped away. We become a living monstrance, carrying the true Messiah within us. We are flooded with grace and are strengthened in our battle against evil.

There is no greater reconciliation than this, that we should become one with Jesus. He is available to us sinners every day and we cannot begin to comprehend this divine generosity. We should ponder on it and rejoice in it and it should make us humble as we realize the awesome humility of God who becomes food for us. We should not rush out of church after Mass. If we truly knew the miracle which had just taken place, we would remain behind to thank God with all our hearts, to welcome him into our hearts and to express praise and adoration to the God who is within.

The Eucharist is the centrepiece of the Church. It nourishes us with divine life. The Eucharistic Bread is the greatest miracle of all time. It is the manna of the New Covenant and like the manna which was given as bodily food to the Israelites every day, so the Eucharist is available to us daily as our spiritual food. It is the daily bread we pray for in the Lord's Prayer. The Eucharist is the hub of the universe, the focal point around which dances all of creation.

The Mass is the unbloody perpetual sacrifice of Calvary. The crucifixion was not so much an event in time, although indeed it was that too. It is an *eternal moment,* and so Jesus is continually being offered as the Sacrificial Lamb to God the Father in heaven. "Worthy is the Lamb that was sacrificed to receive power and riches, wisdom, strength, honour, glory and blessing" (Rev. 5:12). The Mass is continually being offered in Heaven and continually on earth, and we Catholics are privileged to take part in this perpetual sacrifice.

We can never fully comprehend the mystery, yet we are given the opportunity every day to have a priest offer the Body, Blood, Soul and Divinity of Jesus to the Heavenly Father on our behalf. We can only marvel at such condescension on the part of God and kneel down in gratitude.

Prayer and Sacrament form the very life's blood of the Catholic family. Nothing else can sustain it and nothing else can keep the family together in love, self-sacrifice and a spirit of holiness. Let all Catholic families resolve to become families of prayer and sacrament so that the face of God can shine in their homes. As Catholics, our home should be the holy place where husband, wife, children *and Jesus* live together.

CHAPTER 3

Anger: Family War

*"Anger and fury are both of
them abominable, and the sinful
man shall be subject to them."*
(Sir. 27:30).

There are many things which can destroy the peace of family life, but nothing does this more powerfully than anger. Sinful anger is a distorted emotion which possesses the mind of the one who is angry, destroys the Mind of Christ within him or her, crushes the one on the receiving end, and terrifies the children. It never heals anything. It only leads to resentment or hurt, and even a desire for retaliation or revenge. It can even lead to murder in families where once there had been love. Anger is family war and brings about alienation, division, separation, divorce, and broken children who learn that love is not to be trusted. The angry man or woman will always justify his or her anger. But Jesus would never be convinced by their arguments. The consequences of sinful anger to the family are too evil for any justification to be plausible.

When I went through medical school in the late 1950's and early 1960's, my professors in psychiatry taught me that feelings are morally neutral, that feelings are neither good nor bad. As a young student, I accepted this without question, but I now know that this philosophy is dangerous. It does not heal. It does untold damage to our psyche and stands in open opposition to Scripture and God's Wisdom. As Saint Paul says, "For the wisdom of this world is foolishness with God" (1 Cor. 3:19).

Precisely because these so-called wise men and women believed that feelings were morally neutral, they were then forced to the absurd conclusion that it is acceptable for me to hate my father. It is acceptable for me to feel lust. It is acceptable for me to be furious with my brother. It is acceptable for me to be violently jealous of my neighbour. There is no problem. This is no sin, and therefore I need not confess these experiences in the sacrament of Reconciliation. While it is true that feelings may surface without warning, and therefore would not be immediately sinful, as soon as we engage our will in harbouring the feeling, we are now in a state of sin. Psychology, by neutralising emotions and relegating them to the simplistic level of mere animal reflexes, excuses these as being merely human, and absolves us from any moral wrong doing. But absolution is reserved to God alone, through his priests. Once again, the evil snake has slithered into our garden, and tells us we can know good and evil and we can become like God. The old sin is being re-presented to us in a bright new twentieth century package called secular psychology.

The situation becomes totally absurd when we look at how modern psychology is forced to treat anger. Many psychiatrists continue to insist that the only way to deal with anger is to encourage the patient to express it. This gives rise to a serious contradiction. On the one hand psychology says that anger is neither good nor bad, yet on the other hand it treats an angry person as though he were sick. As a medical student, I once attended a psychiatry seminar and watched the professor of psychiatry work with a poor angry patient in front of two hundred eager students. He handed him a pillow and said, "This pillow is your father. Now do to the pillow what you would like to do to your father. Express your anger." So the patient proceeded to pound the pillow and yell and scream until he was totally spent. What puzzled me at the time was that the patient looked a lot worse going out than when he came in, and yet the professor beamed with pleasure at a job well done. But now I know that the opposite is true. The therapist, by encouraging the patient to express anger, was simply teaching the man how to be more angry. He was actually creating anger with his co-called therapy rather than alleviating it.

Anger is the most common problem I encounter in my psychotherapy practice. It is also one of the most common sins brought to a priest in confession. Not only that, but it is the most poorly understood of all human emotions. It is staggering to realize just how much is taught and written about anger both by psychiatrists and by professed religious in an effort to excuse it and justify it to a modern world caught in the futile throes of denying sin.

What is anger? Anger is actually defined by the Oxford Dictionary as the **disordered** desire to correct or punish someone. It is disordered because the correction or punishment is clearly motivated by passion or fury. It is also wrong because the corrective methods used, such as mental cruelty, cursing, physical abuse or other forms of violence are sinful in and of themselves. These violate the Christian dignity of our brothers and sisters and do violence to the God of peace.

Anger displays its ugly face everywhere. Husbands and wives find themselves expressing impatience and anger toward each other. Parents react angrily toward their children, and so brothers and sisters learn to be angry with one another. Anger from within the home then leaches outside the home to be inflicted on relatives, neighbours and fellow workers. Just as a person grows in size from childhood to adulthood, so too does one's anger grow. An angry little boy grows up to find himself a slave to a man-sized anger. Unchecked, it can begin to rule a person completely.

There are two types of anger: sinful anger and just anger.

Sinful Anger

Sinful anger can be classified into four categories:

1. There is the simple emotion of anger which flares up in response to a perceived insult or hurt. It is confined, straight forward and easy to understand. It dies down almost as soon as it starts. It is directly related to the immediate event.
2. The second type is what I call "conditioned anger." It is more deeply entrenched. It has its origin deep within our past, due

to an event often long forgotten and which we have not yet brought to a healthy closure. As a result, as soon as something occurs which consciously or unconsciously triggers that past hurt, we resurrect the old pain and respond with irrational displaced anger. Conditioned anger is, in effect, the reliving of a past unresolved event.

3. The deadly sin of anger. This is much more serious, but surprisingly it is not in itself an *actual* sin; it is a *predisposition* to sin. In other words, a person suffering from slavery to the deadly sin of anger is not walking around twenty-four hours a day in a fit of anger or rage, stamping his feet and breaking things. What it means is that he is constantly and exquisitely poised to break into rage at the slightest provocation. As soon as this person perceives an insult, whether it be real or imaginary, then the angry explosion occurs. The volcano erupts. Hence, this form of anger is deadly because it is going to kill one's soul unless he is released from its bondage. In fact, it is a form of satanic oppression. Such a person has given Satan a foothold. Through his own cooperation, he has invited a spirit of anger to rule in his soul, and he is therefore under its suggestibility and power at all times. Although his will is weakened, he is still able to say "no" to the angry promptings of this adverse spirit.

4. The most dangerous and most aggravated anger manifestation of all is actual diabolical possession, whereby an intelligent evil spirit is welcomed into one's heart. Such an unhappy soul is in a constant state of anger and totally dominated by an intelligent evil spirit.

While all four categories of sinful anger are ultimately self-generated, only the first two can be helped by psychotherapy alone. The deadly sin requires both psychotherapy and prayers for deliverance, while satanic possession requires actual exorcism followed by psychotherapy for the distressing aftermath. All of the sinful angers, of course, need the sacrament of Reconciliation, not only for the cleansing of the damaged soul, but also for the grace to fight any subsequent temptation to anger.

Just Anger

Just anger, as defined by the Church, is not a sin at all. In fact it is not really anger as we understand it. It is better described as **righteous indignation.** The difference between just anger and sinful anger is simple enough. We know our anger is justified when we are angry on behalf of another person who is being violated, or in response to some serious injustice in the world. For example, we might be justifiably angry at the murder of millions of unborn babies in our world today, or we might be angry at the torture and killing of innocent people in a war zone. Just anger and sinful anger are better defined, not by the personal characteristic of what it is to be angry, but rather by the object on behalf of which I am angry. Just anger is always in right proportion. The actions which arise out of just anger are always moderate. For example, if we feel anger at the plight of children caught up in the horrors of war, we might legitimately respond by collecting food and clothing and sending these to the war-torn region. We could never legitimately respond by picking up a machine-gun and killing the perpetrators of the injustice. In other words, just anger never results in sinful action. As Saint Paul says, "Be angry but sin not" (Eph. 4:26).

Sinful anger, on the other hand, is almost always on behalf of myself. I feel unfairly attacked or hurt or used. My anger is always out of proportion, and my thoughts, words and actions are immoderate, destructive, and offensive to man and to God. You only have to look into the face of an angry person to know that you are not looking into the face of Jesus, who is meek and humble of heart.

Many people who are troubled by their human angry emotions try to justify these by pointing to Jesus and the cleansing of the Temple. However, if one examines all four Gospel accounts, the word anger is never used to describe Jesus' strong action. There is simply no basis from which to assume that Jesus was experiencing the same kind of anger to which we give in so frequently. On the contrary, it is certain that, even if Jesus was angry, it must have been of an entirely different variety from sinful anger, for the reason that Jesus was incapable of sin. We can surmise that Jesus was not reacting on his own behalf. In fact Scripture tells us that Jesus shouted, "My house shall be a house of prayer but you are making it a den of thieves" (Matt. 21:13). This is the key to Jesus' reaction. He was acting purely on behalf of his Father and his Father's house. He was indignant at the incredible offence being given to God by the profanation of God's holy temple. Jesus was displaying the *holy anger of God.* As the perfectly pure one, he had the right to purify the temple. You and I, as human creatures, are not pure enough to be purifiers. We cannot and must not equate our petty human self-centred anger with the righteous and just wrath of God. God's anger is holy. But apart from a truly just anger, ours is never holy. "His disciples recalled the words of Scripture, 'Zeal for your house will consume me'" (John 2:17). In other words, Jesus was displaying a righteous indignation or zeal for the temple, not giving in to a self-indulgent rage.

As humanity lives through the dying years of the twentieth century, it has come to believe that we live in an era of scientific enlightenment. This predominately pagan society now regards psychology as its new religion. Science has become our god and we worship at the feet of technology, labour-saving devices, a mindless dependency on computer information, and an uncritical acceptance of the lie that science will solve all of our planetary problems. Humanity is content with its voracious consumerism and no longer feels it needs God. A little thought, however, soon explodes this misplaced confidence in human technology. Because the greater part of humanity has rejected God and has elevated science to the status of an idol, God leaves us to our own unaided intellect. But intellect without God's intimate and wise guidance and blessing becomes disordered. It makes unholy decisions, and so we reap the whirlwind. The planet is in grave jeopardy. Pollution is destroying our ecology, the ozone layer is depleted and we thereby suffer a huge increase in cancers of all kinds. By destroying the rain forests, we are killing more than one hundred species of plant, animal and bacterial life forms every twenty-four hours, with the result that potential healing medicines are lost forever. By killing fifty-five million unborn babies a year, we are exterminating the very people who, had they lived, might have solved the insurmountable problems we face today. We are blind to the fact that a holy people will have holy leaders, will be inspired by the Holy Spirit and will find holy solutions to our practical problems.

Twentieth century science is so blind it fails to recognize that all it can do is observe what God has created. It can only measure and define what God has put in place. Where science disagrees with revealed truth, it is simply wrong. Man, the creature, cannot know better than the Creator what he has made. And never was this more obvious than in the fields of psychology and psychiatry. Secular psychology is fundamentally opposed to the basic doctrines of our Christian faith, not the least of which is the role of the Cross in our earthly journey.

Any psychology which contradicts true theology is a lie. The only valid psychology is one which is in full harmony with the truth as revealed by Jesus Christ, the Son of God. Jesus, who is Truth itself, told us that "the truth will set you free" (John 8:32). So how can a secular, pagan psychology pretend to free us from emotional bondage? It cannot. Only a holy psychology can heal the human soul.

There is a printed handout distributed by a pregnancy centre in the United States which teaches the following erroneous ideas about anger:

1. Anger brings about needed change — good change.
2. Anger can make an impression for truth — we get honest.
3. Anger is a strong motivator — it makes us move.
4. Anger can be used to rebuke or correct — Jesus got his point across.

I do not agree. As a Christian I reply that the emotion of anger is a sin. Therefore:

1. Anger does bring about change, but never good change.
2. Anger never makes an impression for truth, because the thoughts which generate our anger are always distorted.
3. Anger is indeed a strong motivator. It makes us want to hurt another person.
4. Anger can be used to rebuke or correct, but it always over-rebukes and over-corrects. Jesus did get his point across, but it was not with sinful anger.

So what do the Scriptures have to say about anger? It is impossible to appeal to a higher authority than Jesus himself. His actual words are above any challenge and we are obliged to give them our total obedience. Jesus states, "You have heard it was said to those of ancient times, 'You shall not murder,' and 'whoever murders shall be liable to judgement.' But I say to you that if you are angry with a brother or sister you will be liable to judgement. And if you insult a brother or sister you will be liable to the council. And if you say, 'you fool,' you will be liable to the hell of fire" (Matt. 5:21-22).

Jesus links anger with murder. This is very serious indeed. In the same discourse, he says in verses 27-28, "you have heard that it was said, 'You shall not commit adultery.' But I say to you that everyone who looks at a woman with lust has already committed adultery with her in his heart."

According to Jesus, just thinking lustfully is in the same category as actual adultery. Likewise, being angry is akin to murder. As lust is the precursor to adultery, so anger is the precursor to murder. Anger, therefore, is not a neutral emotion; it has powerful moral implications and Jesus warns us sternly against it.

"Keep this in mind, dear brothers, let every man be quick to hear, slow to speak, slow to anger, for a man's anger does not fulfil God's justice" (James 1:19-20). Anger, therefore, is a sin against justice.

"You must put all that aside now, all the anger and quick temper, the malice, the insults, the foul language" (Col. 3:8).

Even the Old Testament holds anger to be a grave sin: "The hot-head provokes disputes. Someone in a rage commits all sorts of sins" (Prov. 29:22).

There is, however, a very common misinterpretation of Scripture which many people, priests included, use to justify anger. It is found in the words of St. Paul, "If you are angry, let it be without sin" (Eph. 4:26). This is often taken to mean that it is acceptable to be angry as long as one does not sin with it. However, Paul is not suggesting that it is permissible to be *sinfully* angry. In the original Greek, Paul uses the word *orgizesthe.* This form is only used once in the entire Bible and it refers specifically to an inner attitude of *indignation* towards a person or an injustice. In other words, Paul is talking here about righteous indignation or just anger. He is not referring to sinful anger at all. In fact the same passage goes on to say, "Get rid of all passion and anger" (Eph. 4:31). On the one hand, Paul says "be angry," yet on the other, he says "get rid of *all* anger." He clearly means something very different from the popular modern interpretation, since he would most certainly not contradict himself.

There is, then, a powerful theological foundation for regarding anger as sin, and thus it should be combatted by means of our will and by means of God's grace. We should not excuse it, but rather confess it.

Nevertheless, I have great compassion for those Christians who still struggle with anger and feel impotent against it. This chapter is not meant to inflict guilt on those who suffer with the problem. On the contrary, it is designed to bring them good news: there is freedom from anger if you want it, and that freedom will be found in truth, for as Jesus promises, "The truth will set you free" (John 8:32). We need not buy into the satanic lie that we cannot help it, because that merely sets us up to have a lifelong problem with anger, and therefore with sin.

Consider someone whose temper flares up instantly. It can occur so fast that the anger appears to be an uncontrollable reflex reaction. Many, indeed, would even conclude that this person simply can't help himself, thereby absolving him from all responsibility for his anger. But this is an error. If a video were to be taken of the onset of the anger, and if it were to be replayed at slow speed, one could discern several stages in the development of that anger. Firstly, some person or some event presses that man's button. Secondly, the subject recognises that his button is being pressed. Thirdly, there is now a window of choice, a time interval during which the person chooses how he is going to react. He chooses anger, but he could just as easily choose to respond with humour or humility. The fourth stage is, of course, acting out the choice. This man has, in fact, practised his anger so much over the years that he has become very good at it, and he has shortened his window of choice to the point that the anger appears to have become irresistible. This is the deadly sin of anger referred to at the beginning of this chapter.

One point must be emphasised at this stage. Because of original sin, we have inherited a fallen nature. Consequently, our disordered natural instinct is capable of flaring into anger as an involuntary response, without the consent of our will. This is not an actual sin. Actual sin occurs if, when we recognize the anger, we then fuel and savour the feeling by *willfully* entertaining angry thoughts. This is comparable to the phenomenon of sexual arousal, in which our animal instincts can be unconsciously triggered and we become sexually alert. There is no sin in this unless we choose to use our minds to derive and maintain pleasure from the arousal. That is the sin of lust. Likewise, reflex anger is not a sin, but as soon as we engage our will to fan its flames then we are sinning. In short, original sin is our inheritance; actual sin is our choice. We can learn to unlearn our angry choices. We can learn to expand our window of choice so that instead of choosing anger we give ourselves time to choose Jesus, that is to say, the option for peace. It is really nothing more than what my father used to tell me when I was a boy. "Son," he said, "always count to ten before becoming angry, then you'll find there's a better way." When I became a clever medical student, I "knew" he was too simplistic. But then I only had knowledge. My dad had wisdom. There is a major difference between knowledge and wisdom. Knowledge is only stored information, but wisdom is inspiration. It comes from the Holy Spirit, and it comes to holy hearts. The beauty of it all is that the simplest of uneducated people can possess wisdom. Knowledge, no matter how great, can only bring one up against the mystery of God and no further, while wisdom, no matter how little, can allow one to penetrate it.

There are some basic truths about anger which can be very helpful if taken to heart:

1. Anger leads to family war. It violates justice. It submerges love and eventually love can be destroyed. An angry person is compelled by his anger and so family violence is inevitable, leading to wife abuse, husband abuse and child abuse. War between nations is nothing more than a collective manifestation of a personal anger between individuals.

2. Anger is always easily justified in one's own mind. I am not disputing one's reasons for becoming angry. I too can always give good reasons, but that still does not change the fact that anger is destructive, harmful and sinful. If I want to be angry,

I have the power to think it, I have the power to do it, and I have the power to justify it. I could provide some very good reasons for robbing a bank, but these could never justify such action.

3. Anger is painful, it is paralysing, and it prevents a person from getting what he or she wants. It blocks healthy psychological functioning. Certainly, it might crush your victim and you may think you have won a victory, but in fact, your victim will likely harbour resentment, hurt or fear. He is damaged by your anger, and your short term gain will be lost in the long run. The most likely consequence is that you have now made an enemy who may wreak vengeance upon you at a later time.

4. Nobody makes you angry. The events of this world do not make you angry. You do not catch anger like you catch a virus from someone with the flu. The truth is that you generate your own anger and you do it by what you are thinking. In other words, your angry response occurs from what you are telling yourself about another person's bad behaviour. All emotions, anger included, are secondary to the thoughts in your head. If you think angry thoughts, you will soon feel anger in your body. The feeling will tend to trigger angrier thoughts and so you feel more angry. This spiral of anger culminates in rage or fury, but it all begins with what you choose to think.

5. The thoughts which generate your anger and which make your anger worse are always distorted thoughts. They are lies which become more and more irrational, the angrier you get. Suppose my wife insults me. I think, "How dare she! She has no right to be my judge." So I start to feel angry. Then the next thought might be, "She doesn't love me or she would never say such a harmful thing." Now I am more angry. "Why did I ever marry such an unfeeling person? I can't stand her any more." I am now approaching a rage. "That's it. I should call a lawyer and get a separation. Oh, I have been betrayed!" Now I am in a fury. I am not thinking straight. I am holding on to crazy thoughts, and so I decide to do crazy things. I am out of control, and now I might find myself

striking her and violating the temple of the Holy Spirit, the body of the woman God gave to me as my life's companion. And if my children happen to be watching, then I am teaching them anger by example. They are learning from me that anger and violence are valid ways to solve a problem.

6. Anger often occurs because we think another person is being unfair, but if you try to see the world through that other person's eyes, you will be very surprised to find that he does not think he is being unfair at all. We behave as though there is a kind of universal standard of fairness, but there is no such thing. There is a universal moral law, but that is far above any vague notion about fairness. Other people rarely believe that they are being unfair. On the contrary, they are more likely to think that you are being unfair with your anger.

7. Much of our anger is due to poor self-esteem. A poor self-image makes us very vulnerable to anger because the slightest negative remark strikes us as a major attack. But it is irrational to blame someone else for my own poor self-esteem or my own feelings of unworthiness. If someone really is attacking me, that is actually his problem, not mine. He is responsible for his anger, not me. I am only responsible for mine.

8. As mentioned before, many therapists believe that a person must give vent to his anger in order to gain relief. But this is not so. Anger is not a release of pressure. It is an increase in pressure. The angrier one gets, the longer it takes to recover. If you don't get angry in the first place, you have nothing to recover from.

9. Anger is mostly an habitual response when a person loses his bearings or is feeling insecure. People who have their bearings have more understanding of another's behaviour. They say, "Oh, he doesn't mean it" or "He doesn't know what he's doing." In this way, they are more likely to opt for a compassionate attitude rather than irrational anger.

10. Anger is usually learned from one's family of origin. If dad or mom got angry a lot, then the children probably have learned anger by imitation. A child is not born angry.

11. If a person gives up anger, this does not mean that he says goodbye to a rich emotional life. On the contrary, he will

still have strong feelings, but they will be positive feelings such as compassion, humility and humour.

12. Giving up anger is not the same thing as pretending not to be angry or suppressing it in an unhealthy way. The whole idea is that a person experiences a provocative situation and understands it. The instinctive reaction is one of compassion, which displaces any temptation to become angry in the first place. For example, if you see a parking space and you make for it, and then, just as you are getting close, someone else backs into it, you now have a choice. If you lose your bearings you might think, "Look at that inconsiderate jerk. How dare he steal my space!" If you keep your bearings, you are more likely to think, "Oh well! He must be under a lot of pressure, to do a thing like that. I've done the same thing myself in the past. I'll find another spot." Understanding neutralises anger.

When it comes to the management of anger, there are two types of intervention which can prove helpful: psychotherapy and spiritual intervention. Spiritual intervention is the real key to all true healing. Psychotherapy is the less important of the two, but it will be dealt with first.

Psychotherapy

Before talking about how to combat anger it would be helpful to understand the concept of moods. Everybody has moods. In fact, our moods go up and down like an elevator, many times in a day. Imagine that this mood elevator is in a building with one hundred floors. When it is up above the fiftieth floor, the building is bright and nicely decorated. When we look out the window we can see clearly for miles and miles. But when the elevator goes down to the ground floor, the building is dark and depressing and the windows are dirty, so what we see out there looks threatening and distorted. Because it looks that way to us, we believe that this is how things really are. In other words, in a low mood we believe in our distorted perception of the world around us.

Therefore, when our elevator is up, we are in a high mood, and we know it because we experience warm feelings, such as joy, peace, gratitude, compassion, hope, and humility. Our thoughts are positive and they are in perspective. We can see clearly, and so what we see is the way the world and our problems really are. We can trust our thoughts, and we can trust our decisions and we can trust our perception of reality.

In a low mood, however, we risk generating negative feelings like anger, fear, jealousy, guilt or shame. Our thoughts are negative and most importantly, our thoughts are distorted. The lower the floor we are on, the more distorted our thoughts become. Therefore we are not seeing reality as it truly is, and we should not trust our thoughts when we are in this state. It is our low mood thoughts which generate our negative feelings; but these thoughts appear real to us, and we are tempted to believe in them and to act upon them, with often disastrous results.

Don Quixote was a fictitious medieval knight who was very brave, but not very bright. He thought he saw huge giants in the distance and he feared they would kill the people in his town. So he drew his sword, rode out against them and set about trying to kill them. But what he never seemed to realize was that they were not giants at all. They were only windmills! It is the same with our minds. When we are in a low mood, we think we see all kinds of giants out there, but they are not there at all. They are only our own thoughts. They are only harmless windmills. Don Quixote must have been in a low mood that day.

Healthy people relate to their low moods in a wise way and refuse to be fooled by their distorted thoughts. Unhealthy people believe in their own distorted thoughts, so they act on them and do all kinds of damage, both to themselves and to others. There is not much that can be done to avoid having moods. Moods are a fact of life, but we can learn to act in a wise way when we find ourselves in a low mood:

1. Get into the habit of recognising a low mood as early as possible, and when you recognize it, tell yourself, "It's only a mood. I don't have to do anything. It will pass." Ask yourself "Which floor is my elevator on?" If the answer is below fifty, then remind yourself that you cannot trust your thoughts right now, nor can you believe in the way reality looks to you.

2. Never make major decisions when in a low mood. For example, if I am upset with my kids, it would be ridiculous for me to put them all into a foster home! If ever I did such a thing I would soon regret it. As soon as my elevator went back up, which it always does, I would wish I had my children back. I would wonder how I could ever have been so stupid.

3. Never ever try to analyse a low mood. Never look for its cause. This flies against all modern notions of how to deal with a low mood. After all, it seems reasonable that if I don't try to find out what is causing my low mood, then I will never know what to do about it. But this is precisely what should not be done and the reason is very simple: Imagine that my elevator is at the fortieth floor. I am feeling a bit despondent and anxious. So I say to myself, "I'm not feeling one hundred percent. I wonder what's causing this." At this point, my conditioned thinking will never fail to come up with a distorted reason. "Oh, I know what it is. It's my job. I sit for hours all day listening to people's problems and I'm exhausted at night. Not only that, but some of my patients don't seem to get any better. That must mean I am a poor therapist. Maybe I'm not cut out to be a therapist. Maybe I should quit and look for another job altogether." So where is my elevator now? I was at the fortieth floor to begin with, but now I'm down somewhere around the fourth floor. I am much worse off. Analysing my mood only made my elevator go down farther.

It would have been better if I had remained on the fortieth floor. All I had to do was wait until my elevator went back up, which it will always do. Once I am back into a normal mood, I might be thinking something like this, "You know, I'm lucky to have such a good job. I meet all kinds of beautiful people and they share their intimate problems with me. That is a privilege for me. It certainly feels good when a patient gets better. Of course, there are some who take a long time, but that's all right. I can journey patiently with them." What happened here? Did my job suddenly change? Of course not. My mood was the only thing which changed and so my thoughts changed with it. My job did not change, but my attitude towards it did. As Dr. George Pransky, a practising psychologist, once said, "In a low mood, my car is a clunker, in a high mood, my car is a classic."

4. Never try to solve problems when you are in a low mood, because they will look entirely different when you come back into a high mood. For example, consider an argument between a husband and wife. He is in a low mood and he is thinking, "We had a terrible fight last night. The things she said to me! They were terrible things. That must mean she doesn't love me any more. Oh, no! My marriage is breaking up. Maybe I should protect myself and call a lawyer. My whole world is coming apart."

If he could just recognize that he is in a low mood, if he refused to believe his distorted thoughts, and if he refused to act on them, soon his elevator would go up. Now he may think to himself, "Boy! We had a real good one last night. She was so mad at me, but then I can't blame her. I was being so unreasonable. She was feeling really insecure and threatened and she did not mean what she was saying. I know she still loves me, so I know what I'll do. I will call the flower shop and send her some roses. And I'm going to apologize for my self-centred behaviour." When I am in a low mood, I think it is being caused by my problems. But it is the other way around. It is my low mood which makes me think I have the problems. Even if I do have some problems, my low mood thinking will make them appear larger than they really are, just like Don Quixote's giants.

5. Be silent. If you speak out of a low mood, then the words which come out of your mouth will simply be your distorted thoughts, and since these thoughts are not true you will do untold harm. "Oh, you don't care about me. You don't love me any more. I wish I'd never married you. I should have married Susan Jones. She understood me better than you do." This is crass nonsense. When you come back up into a higher mood, your thoughts will be back on track, and you will know that your wife loves you and that she understands you better than anyone else on the planet. And perhaps you might remember that Susan Jones was not interested in marrying you anyway. Perspective and sanity will have returned. Therefore

when you know you are in a low mood (and you know by asking yourself frequently where your elevator is right now) then resolve not to do any harm with it. All you have to do is patiently wait and your elevator will come up again. Then, and only then, can you trust your thoughts and ideas.

Anger usually arises out of a low mood. If a person is in a low mood and he starts to entertain angry thoughts, then the feeling of anger is sure to follow. He does not have to be a slave to these impulses. Strangely enough, it is much easier than he might think to become a person of peace and to receive the gift of peace which Jesus promises. Here's how:

a. Decide to give up your anger. Make the decision that you are tired of being an angry person.

b. Take responsibility for your own angry feelings. See your anger as only a thought, generated in your own head, as merely a habit in response to losing your bearings. Do not insist that your anger comes from outside of yourself. That only justifies it. As soon as you say, "Insults make me angry" then you are locking yourself into anger. Thereafter, every time you are insulted, for the rest of your life, you will immediately become angry. But your anger is not linked to the outside world; it is only in your own mind. The cause is your thoughts and the effect is your anger.

c. Try to stop seeing so much malice in what other people are doing. The imputing of motive is arbitrary and occurs in your head. You do not know what another person's motive really is. Even allowing for the fact that someone is acting out of malice toward you, it is still your mind which decides how you are going to respond. The imputing of motive is a habitual suspicion of others, and this is not the mind of Christ. Blaming others is a function of the ego, and *the size of the ego is the measure of the distance between the self and God.*

A violent husband and father is just such a person. He sees malice where none exists. In order to counteract this tendency within us, we must cultivate the habit of seeing more innocence in what other people do. As Jesus said on the cross, "They do not know what they are doing" (Luke 23:34). People are more often negligent than malicious. Understand this and you will feel more warmly towards people. It helps to remind yourself that whatever is being done to you, you have probably done the same to someone else at some time in your life.

d. Discount your thoughts. Accept that they are distorted and coming from your low mood and not from your life. Angry thoughts and feelings will grow according to the attention you give them. So disengage your mind. Do not dwell on your thoughts, but rather say to yourself, "So it's only a low mood. Things are not as bad as they appear to me right now. I'll wait until I'm in a better mood."

When I'm in a good mood, my spouse is a well-meaning angel. When I'm in a bad mood, my spouse is an out-to-get-me devil. How can she be an angel yesterday and a devil today? The answer is *moods.* Once this is understood, then life becomes a lot less frightening. It is scary to have to fight monsters, but when you know they are only your own thoughts, life is a lot less intimidating.

e. Early recognition is the most valuable tool in eliminating anger and violence. As soon as you recognize you are a little off balance or somewhat low, then it will not get any worse. The anger is stopped in its tracks. "Aha! This is the way my spouse talks to me which gets me going." In other words it is much easier if you can see you are about to get angry, than if you wait till you actually are angry. My dad said, "Count to ten!" He was right on.

6. You never have to give in to a low mood. To give in is to say yes to your negative emotions and this always leads to sin. Jesus, on the other hand, asks us to rise above our low mood, to refuse to be ruled by our feelings, to exercise our will and to do what is right. Everyone has low moods, but we are quite able to set these aside whenever there is a call to love. I may be feeling sad or hurt or defeated, but when I see the elderly lady next door struggling to take out a heavy garbage bag, am I not able to go and help her? The mystery and the miracle is

that when I do so, my mood is likely to disappear. Dying to self is not just good theology. It is also very good therapy.

Spiritual Healing

Naturally, this involves prayer, to call upon the healing grace of a loving God and to call forth repentance from the angry person.

1. In prayer, lay on hands as Jesus commanded through Saint Paul. Husbands and wives can do this for each other and for their children.
2. Ask the person to renounce the idol of anger. Then ask him to embrace and accept Jesus as his only God.
3. Pray with him to forgive the perpetrator, the person or persons who hurt him in the past.
4. Have him repent of his past sins of anger and beg God the Father for his forgiveness.
5. Ask him to pray out loud, seeking forgiveness for the sinful effects of his anger upon others.
6. Have him fill the space which the idol occupied with the powerful personal presence of Jesus. This is not the same as prayer for deliverance from an evil spirit or an exorcism. These should be reserved for the ordained ministers of the Church, but the vacuum left behind by the anger must be filled by the Love of Christ, in order to prevent a relapse.
7. Finally, I will share with you a wonderful and infallible suggestion which is guaranteed to eliminate any low mood, no matter how bad it is: *Spend fifteen minutes praising God.* Praise him in words and in song. Really praise him. Give him the glory for his creation. Tell him he is the most high God. There is no other. Praise him for all his works. Praise him for creating you out of love, for the gift of your eyes, your ears, your limbs, your spouse, and your children. Sing a hymn of praise to him. Pray in tongues if you have the gift. I guarantee, that after fifteen minutes, your low mood will have vanished like snow melting in the sun. In its place, you will have joy, peace and gratitude to the God who gave you so much.

I used to be puzzled by the idea that God demanded praise from his creatures. It did not make much sense to me that he could need anything at all, let alone something from us, but like so many things, it took a little child to teach me one possible reason. When my son Rob reached his sixth birthday, he had already asked me to buy him a tent for the big occasion. He was delighted with his new treasure, but unfortunately the weather was so bad we could not put up the tent that day. Worse than that, winter really set in and there was no way Rob could enjoy his tent until the spring. He patiently waited, never let out a complaint and always lovingly took the tent to bed with him every night. Then, after a seemingly endless winter, the blessed day arrived when it was warm enough for us to put up the tent in the back yard. So Rob and I went out to sleep together and enjoy the big father-son adventure. As I read him a story by flashlight, I was aware of something very special going on. I stopped reading and I looked down at my son. He was gazing up into my face with a look of sheer delight. I asked him what was happening and he softly said, "Gee dad, you're my hero!" My son was **praising** me and I can confidently state that at that moment I would have given him **anything** he asked for. I am certain that our Father God responds in just the same way when we praise him. He cannot resist it. His Fatherly heart simply melts when we praise his holy name just as mine did for my own son.

A wise man once said, "Forgive those who have wronged you or upset you. Nothing cools off anger quicker than a forgiving heart." A forgiving heart is vital to a life of freedom from anger, and we acquire a forgiving heart by learning to say from our own cross, "Father, forgive them. They do not know what they are doing" (Luke 23:34). Our God is a God of peace. As Christians we are called to be instruments of peace in the world, to be reconcilers, and to mediate the peace of Christ to our unhappy brothers and sisters. That can only happen when we realize that we can and should renounce our anger for ever.

CHAPTER 4

Forgiveness: Family Peace

"Forgiveness is the fragrance
the violet sheds on the heel that
has crushed it."

(Anon.)

Just as anger is the engine of war in a family, so forgiveness is the dove of peace. Without radical, self-denying forgiveness, we cannot call ourselves Catholic at all.

A marriage takes place when a man and a woman from two completely different family experiences come together before God and set about the awesome task of becoming "one flesh." Each brings a lifetime of conditioning from his or her family of origin and so has his or her own assumptions, opinions, habits and memories. It would be astounding if these were identical for both. Yet is that not what the newlywed couple expects? They are so much in love that they often fail to appreciate these separate realities. Later on, when they realize the truth about one another, this often leads to division, arguments, harsh words and a determination to prove that "I am right and you are wrong." The result is, of course, hurt feelings or a smouldering resentment. There is only one antidote to this sinful conflict and it is the antidote given to us by Jesus Christ through his own perfect example. It is called *forgiveness.* Forgiveness is the soothing ointment which, gently rubbed on our marriage wounds, produces healing. Love is the greatest commandment of all and when love is wounded, it needs medicine like any other wound, and forgiveness is that medicine.

St. Francis of Assisi once said, "As surely as you love the Lord and me, see to it that no brother in the whole world, no matter how badly he has sinned, is ever allowed to go away from you without forgiveness, if he ask for it. And if he does not ask for forgiveness, then ask him if he does not want it. And if he comes a thousand times with sin, then love him altogether more than you love me, so that you may draw him to the Lord. And be always merciful to such persons."

At the ordinary human level, this may sound far too lofty an ideal. It seems far above our ordinary human ability. Yet, St. Francis was talking to you and to me. He knew it was not as difficult as we might think, but he also knew that we make it very difficult for ourselves.

When I began to do my research for this chapter, I went through every single psychiatry and psychology text book and paper in my possession looking for some reference to the notion of forgiveness as a tool for healing of persons and relationships. To my amazement and deep disappointment, I found only one, and that was from a good Jewish psychologist. This initially struck me as very strange, but the more I thought about it the more I was able to understand why.

In these times, we are easily fooled into believing that modern psychology and Christianity are both in agreement with one another. After all, both claim to want happiness for every individual. Both strive for inner peace and harmony and self improvement. But that is as far as the similarity goes. The truth is, modern secular psychology could not be further from the basic dogmatic truths of our Catholic Faith.

The prevalent psychology of the twentieth century is a humanist philosophy which denies original sin, despises the cross of Jesus, and insists that we can and should live a life without suffering. That is to say, we do not need God, and furthermore we can be gods ourselves. It extols and worships the human mind and concludes that we, not God, are the final deciders as to what is right and wrong. "If-it-feels-good, it-must-be-good" is its diabolical motto, thus denying the concept of sin. Is this not a reminder of a very old story? The story of Adam and Eve is about the very first married couple, who wanted to become like God and to decide good and evil for themselves. Secular psychology is nothing more than the original sin of Adam and Eve repackaged and dressed up all over again. It is simply an apple of a different colour, but living in it is the same old ugly worm. Modern psychology teaches that we can be our own god, and we will become like him when we swell our ego and "realize our full potential." It also scorns the notion of forgiveness as a necessary path to emotional health.

Our Catholic Faith, on the other hand, tells us that we are a fallen people. We are born under the damaging effects of original sin and we stand in need of redemption. We must take up our cross if we are to find peace. We accept that suffering cannot be avoided, that it is foolishness to even try, and that it is only by embracing it that we can find true peace and true joy. God also wants us to "realize our full potential" but that cannot be done by pursuing the path of self-centeredness and conceit. It can only be done by way of the cross and dying to self. "The wisdom of men is foolishness to God" (1 Cor. 3:19). It is only by imitating our gentle master Jesus that we can enjoy the "peace that surpasses all understanding" (Phil. 4:7). This is a peace which endures within us, in spite of all kinds of disturbing events in the world around us. It is not by deciding for ourselves what is right and wrong that we will find happiness. It is by being obedient to *God's* standards of right and wrong that we find true happiness.

We have an unfortunate tendency to think of God in our own image. We believe that God is "mad" at us for sin that we commit, but the fact is that God's love never changes. His love does not depend upon our virtue, although our happiness does. God simply goes on loving us no matter what we have done to him. We do well to imitate God and to go on loving others no matter what they have done to us. The reason Jesus gives for forgiving our enemies is that "you may be the children of your Father in Heaven, who makes his sun to rise on the good and the evil and sends rain on the just and the unjust" (Matt. 5:45). If becoming children of God is not sufficient reason to forgive, then there is no reason good enough. But we must remind ourselves that becoming children of God is not the same thing as becoming god. Jesus asks us to learn from him for he is "meek and humble of heart" (Matt. 11:29). Satan, on the other hand, asks us to become our own gods and to learn from him for he is arrogant and proud of heart. The terrible truth is, that in pursuing our own illusion of divinity, we end up being enslaved to Satan. Too late, we discover that our conceit is an option for eternal humiliation at the hands of the evil one. In fact, life is a choice between two slaveries. We can be slaves of God or slaves of Satan. Slavery to Satan is bondage. Slavery to God is freedom.

It is a good and holy thing to imitate Jesus in all things, even to forgiving those who have hurt us, who have offended us, or rejected us, even to forgiving those who would murder us. Jesus did. Our Dear Lord went through a terrible and dreadful passion and it is easy for us to forget how unspeakable it really was. Sometimes we look at a crucifix and we find it difficult to relate to the agony of the God-man on the cross. It all looks like a pretty tableau. The crucifix is meant to remind us of the supreme agony which Jesus voluntarily suffered out of love for us. The gaping breach between us and God could not be repaired without an infinite sacrifice, and the infinite is only possible to God, not to man. Yet the sacrifice had to come from man, since we were the ones who had sinned, so God the Son decided to become a man to do what was impossible for man. He, as God, could make the perfect sacrifice and, as man, could represent all men. The breach was healed, and we now can · lay claim to the kingdom of heaven as sons and daughters of God the Father. But the price was terrible.

On Holy Thursday, Jesus went into the Garden of Gethsemane. There he experienced his greatest agony. This agony was far, far greater than the physical torment he would face the next day. That night, he saw and took on all of the sins which had been committed in the world up to that time, all of the sins which were being committed at that very moment, and all of the sins that would ever be committed in the future. He saw my sins and all of our sins in their fullest horror, and he allowed himself to be covered by them. Is it any wonder Jesus sweated blood?

Doctors know that for anyone to sweat blood, a person must be in the most extreme agony of physical and emotional pain. Not only must the suffering be intolerable, there must be no prospect of relief. The capillaries on the surface of the skin dilate and throb, the walls of these blood vessels become stretched and thinned out and then blood oozes out of the vessels and into the sweat glands. Luke, the Evangelist, was a physician and he understood. He writes, "In his anguish, he prayed even more earnestly, and his sweat fell to the ground like great drops of blood" (Luke 22:44).

During the unjust mockery of a trial before the Sanhedrin, a trial which was illegal since it was conducted at night, contrary to Jewish law, Jesus was beaten. His nose was dislocated and bruised. He was dragged before Pilate, who ordered him to be scourged and a Roman scourging was a dreadful torture. The instrument used is called a *flagrum.* This is a short thick stick which has up to three leather thongs hanging from one end. Attached to the tips of the thongs are lead dumbbells or sometimes pieces of bone. A soldier skilled in scourging would strike the prisoner's body, the lead would embed itself in the skin, then with a flick of the wrist, he would pull the flagrum back with a ripping motion, and bring with it pieces of flesh. As far as can be told from the Shroud of Turin, Jesus received approximately one hundred and twenty lashes from two men. By the time the beating was over, there would have been very little skin left on his adorable body. In effect he was flayed alive. Meanwhile, because of the impact of the blows on the chest wall, Jesus' lungs were filling up with fluid, which made him increasingly short of breath. His heart was going into failure and that caused fluid to build up in his feet and ankles and lungs, which added to his struggle for air. The bruising around his kidneys resulted in kidney failure and so his blood urea was rising with every minute. As a result, he was dehydrated, experiencing a raging thirst, his tongue was swollen, his mouth was dry, and he had a burning fever.

To add to the cruel torture, the soldiers then fashioned a cap of thorns for his holy head. These thorns are about two inches long, and they are green and succulent with a sap which is like acid. This was cruelly pressed down so that the thorns pierced the skin of the scalp. Some lodged in the skull, but others tracked along under the skin to come out through the skin further on, releasing a burning acid along the way. Careful examination of the Shroud shows a probable exit wound over the right eyebrow. This is precisely at the point where the supraorbital nerve leaves the skull to come to the surface. If that point is pressed upon, any person will experience acute and severe pain. This wound must have caused Jesus great agony right up to the moment of his death.

After such a brutal and sadistic beating, something of the order of one hundred and fifty pounds of wood was roughly placed on his shoulders. It is impossible to imagine the pain of that weight on skin that was lacerated, bruised and torn to shreds. Jesus had very little lung capacity left with which to gasp for oxygen and this, combined with his heart failure and his kidney failure, called for a superhuman effort to drag that cross to Calvary. It was only half a mile or so, but every step must have been excruciating. It is little wonder that he fell three times. A lesser man would have collapsed completely.

At Calvary, the soldiers threw the cross onto the ground and made Jesus spread himself upon it. The cross piece is called the *patibulum* and a Roman carpenter would already have drilled two holes in the wood to receive the nails. Roman nails were not as sharp as we are accustomed to today. They were thick and rather blunt spikes, so it made things a lot easier if they were being driven into holes already prepared. The first spike was easy enough for the soldiers. They held Jesus' wrist over the hole and then pounded in the spike. The wrist and not the palm of the hand was used, because a nail through the palm would not be able to hold the weight of a human body hanging on the cross. It would simply tear through. So the spike was hammered through the Space of Destot in the carpal area and in doing so, it severed the median nerve. The agony of the nail piercing the nerve was beyond description. As a result the thumb was paralysed and it curved over onto the palm of the hand.

The second nail seems to have been more of a problem. The Shroud of Turin clearly shows that the left shoulder is inexplicably lower than the right. It is a plausible theory that when the soldier stretched out Jesus' right arm, it would not reach the hole in the wood. Given that this would not be a rare occurrence in the soldier's experience, it is reasonable to imagine that he would simply pull viciously on the arm till Jesus' shoulder was dislocated and then he would be able to complete the job. This could explain the curious disparity of the shoulder position. His feet were then nailed to the cross and the cross lifted up and dropped into a hole with a bone-jarring thud.

Jesus is now "lifted up" as he himself prophesied, and he is hanging in a state which doctors call "total body pain." This is impossible for us to imagine, who have never experienced it. Every single cell in the body is screaming with pain and it is relentless and extreme. Anyone in such a state is unable to think of anything else but the pain. Yet Jesus, in the midst of his agony, was able to muster power from deep within and he cried out to his Abba, "Father, forgive them, for they know not what they do" (Luke 23:34). Unbelievable though it seems, our Jesus loved us so much, he was able in the midst of unspeakable agony, to utter a word of forgiveness for his murderers. And we too are his murderers. My sins on their own were sufficient to demand this death from my loving Jesus.

The reader might well wonder why I have described the passion of Our Lord in such vivid detail. I have done this not only that we should better appreciate the terrible reality of Jesus' suffering, but also that we should ask ourselves a very serious question. Have I ever been hurt by someone as severely as Jesus was hurt by me? This is crucial to the understanding of forgiveness. Jesus forgave me on the cross. Can I ever point to the worst hurt I have ever received and say that it is comparable to what Jesus suffered? No matter if my spouse has yelled at me and insulted me, no matter if my spouse has beaten me, no matter if my spouse has been unfaithful to me, can these things ever compare with the hurt given to our gentle God? They do not even come close and even if they did, they could never exceed it. Therefore we cannot excuse our refusal to forgive, even in the face of the most heinous of crimes against ourselves. Yet, in our human weakness we try to do just that. We feel perfectly justified in saying that some hurt or other is unforgivable. Jesus does not agree.

We are to put on Christ, to become Jesus for others, and so, like him, we must forgive. Jesus did not ask us if we would like to forgive others. He did not ask us to forgive only if we felt like it. He did not say, "try your best to forgive and that will be good enough!" He *commanded* us to forgive others and to do it without imposing conditions.

"Then Peter went up to him and said, 'Lord, how often must I forgive my brother if he wrongs me? As often as seven times?'

Jesus answered, 'Not seven, I tell you, but seventy times seven'" (Matt. 18:21-22). Peter here was being just a little bit sanctimonious. He expected the Lord to admit that he was being excessively generous. The Jewish Law only demanded forgiveness to be offered to an enemy three times. After that, one had the right to denounce that enemy and have nothing more to do with him. Peter thought he was being very magnanimous in offering to forgive a man seven times, to go so far above and beyond the demands of the law. Imagine the look on his face when Jesus said, "Not seven times, but *seventy times seven.*" In other words, there is to be no end to our forgiveness of one another. No one can hurt us enough, or frequently enough, that we can be excused from the duty of forgiving him or her.

Elsewhere, Jesus says, "I tell you therefore, everything you ask and pray for, believe that you have it already and it will be yours. And when you stand in prayer, forgive whatever you have against anybody, so that your Father in heaven may forgive your failings too" (Mark 11:24-25). It is no accident that Jesus places effective prayer and forgiveness together in the same statement. He is telling us quite clearly, "Don't bother asking God for a favour if you are refusing to forgive a brother or sister." Jesus has bound up effective prayer and forgiveness in the same package. He is saying to us, "You only love God as much as you love your worst enemy." It is by how much we forgive others that God knows how much we love him.

So it is good to ask God in prayer for something dear to our hearts, but our hearts must be free of any grudge or hatred towards another. Our forgiving invites God's giving. For a Christian therefore, the catch phrase might be "forgive and *get*." This makes much more sense than the old cliche, which tells us to "forgive and *forget*." It was Don Quixote who first said that, but it is a most destructive untruth. The idea of forgiving and forgetting has caused more undeserved guilt among people than almost anything I know of. How is it possible to forget? To forgive is mandatory, but to forget is impossible. Any doctor knows that memories are stored in the brain for life. It is impossible to erase a memory. Apart from a disease which damages the brain, the only way to make someone forget a past hurt is to surgically cut out the part of the brain which holds that memory. Therefore, if any of us believe we have forgiven someone, and yet are still troubled by the memory of that hurt coming back to mind, we should not feel guilty. This is a perfectly normal phenomenon and should merely prompt us to quietly and peacefully pray for that person once more. The experience of the past hurt is locked in our memory banks and we cannot forget it no matter how hard we try. Jesus does not say, "forgive and forget." He merely says, "forgive."

To find the perfect example of forgiveness, aside from Jesus, one only has to look at a child. Jesus asks us to be like little children: "Let the little children come to me, and do not stop them, for it is to such as these that the kingdom of God belongs" (Luke 18:16). Many years ago I remember coming home one evening after a very trying day at work. I was angry at a colleague and I was still brooding on my hurt when I walked in the door. My little four-year-old daughter, Deirdre, came to greet me and started to go on and on about something she wanted. I wasn't listening to her. I was too caught up in my own low mood. So I yelled at her to keep quiet. She immediately collapsed on the floor, sobbing her little heart out, hurt to the quick by my totally unreasonable response. Seeing her hurt, I felt like a heel and I lifted her up into my arms and I said, "Daddy is sorry for yelling. Do you forgive me?" Immediately, she threw her little arms around my neck and she said, "Yes, Daddy, I forgive you." And she cheered up instantly, wriggled out of my arms and ran off to play. My thought was, "If my little daughter can forgive me so readily, can I not also forgive my colleague who has hurt me?" She had taught me a Jesus-lesson. She did not ask for explanations. She did not ask for retribution. She simply forgave without hesitation. As a child she was a little forgiveness machine, refusing to hold on to a grudge. True forgiveness does not ask for explanations. Forgiveness is eager to show mercy. Forgiveness simply obeys the demands of love, and a truly forgiving heart forgives instantly and joyfully.

Why would Jesus command us to forgive those who have hurt us? While the theological reasons are very compelling, there are also excellent psychological reasons for us to forgive our neighbour. Jesus loves us so much that he wants us to have peace of mind. Being God, he knows that when we refuse to forgive, we suffer terribly, often without even knowing it; and not only do we suffer, but the person who needs our forgiveness also suffers. Refusal to forgive weighs heavily on our hearts. It lies there like a lump of wet cement, dragging us down, indigestible, robbing us of the lucidity of our souls and thereby damaging our relationship with God and with our brother or sister.

Anne White, who has a powerful Christian Healing Ministry tells about her five-year-old son, who for three long years had suffered from dreadful asthmatic attacks. Nothing seemed to be of help. Neither wonder drugs, nor vaporizers, nor changes of climate brought any relief. One awful day she was told by her doctor, "There is really nothing more we can do medically." She was devastated, and seized with an overwhelming hopelessness and helplessness. That very night, at two in the morning, she again heard her little boy's laboured breathing. She went into the bedroom feeling nothing but despair. She said to herself, "There is nothing I can do." Suddenly, she sensed a small still voice within her saying, "Yes, there is. You can kneel down and pray." She was so startled that she immediately did kneel and pray, and then she heard the voice again. "It is not my will for an innocent child to suffer. It is your *bitter resentment* which is the block, and you must forgive the person who has hurt you." By the grace of God, she was immediately able to know who that person was and to say, "Lord, I forgive her," and to mean it with all her heart. Then the voice said, "If you have true faith, then you will thank me before you see the results." She uttered a heartfelt thanks. At that very moment, her son took a deep quiet breath and has never had an asthmatic attack since.

This story demonstrates the great mystery of how we are all connected. Her lack of forgiveness was holding her little boy locked in his illness, and it was only when she forgave that God could bring his healing grace to bear on the child. The innocent child was suffering for her sin. However, this story must not be taken to mean that all children's illnesses are due to some lack of forgiveness on the part of a parent. This is an extraordinary case but it helps to illustrate the important principle that we are indeed all connected as children of Adam and Eve. No wonder Jesus, who is all love and wishes only healing and wholeness for us, commands us to "Love one another as I have loved you" (John 13:34), and likewise to "forgive and you will be forgiven" (Luke 6:37). He knows that by refusing to love and refusing to forgive we create our own hell, and a troubled marriage is hell indeed.

Human beings are tri-partite or trinitarian beings. That is to say, we are made up of three components: body, soul and spirit. This is attested to by St. Paul when he says, "May the God of Peace make you perfect in holiness. May he preserve you whole and entire, body, soul and spirit, irreproachable at the coming of our Lord Jesus Christ" (1 Thess. 5:23). All three of these components are hurt by our lack of forgiveness.

1. The Body:

Refusal to forgive causes us to hold a grudge in our hearts and this leads to a smouldering resentment. Prolonged resentment eventually causes the body to undergo chemical changes, which attack our organs and our immune system. Thus we run the risk of developing such diseases as migraines, stomach ulcers, bowel disorders, high blood pressure, angina, various psychosomatic complaints, and even arthritis and cancer. This does not mean that all of these disorders are only caused by lack of forgiveness, but it is one of the more important factors, usually neglected by the medical profession. In refusing to forgive, we are, in fact, refusing to love the temple of the holy spirit, which is our own body. Our lack of forgiveness is meant to hurt our enemy, but it ends up hurting ourselves as well.

2. The Soul:

The soul consists of our mind, our will, and our emotions. As previously stated, lack of forgiveness always causes us to harbour resentment in our hearts, that is to say, in our soul. Resentment can be directed a) outwards or b) inwards.

a. Outwards:

Outward resentment never stops at resentment. It swells into anger and anger becomes rage, and that can progress into a dark desire for vengeance. A spirit of vengeance leads us to plot actual punishment on our enemy. And so we set out to harm him by slander, destroying his reputation, to hurt him financially or socially or physically. The end point, of course, is to ultimately entertain a death wish for our enemy and to even plot his murder. In this way, by refusing forgiveness, we refuse to love our neighbour and so we refuse to love the body of Christ.

b. Inwards:

Inward-directed resentment very quickly becomes hurt, which leads to self-pity, which leads to grieving, which can then precipitate depression. Depression in this case can progress to the self-inflicted hell of despair, and that will precipitate withdrawal from family, work, friends, the church, and may even lead to a preference for death over life, and finally suicide. Refusal to forgive then becomes a refusal to love ourselves, and this places us in defiance of the second of the Great Commandments, which is "to love your neighbour as yourself" (Matt. 22:39). It is important to understand that not all cases of depression are caused by inward-directed resentment and refusal to forgive. There are many forms of depression, most of which are not in any way the responsibility of the sufferer. It is most often a chemical disorder outside of a person's control.

3. The Spirit:

Lack of forgiveness puts us out of right relationship with God. Whenever we say the "Lord's Prayer" we pray, "Forgive us our trespasses as we forgive those who trespass against us." If we refuse to forgive, then we are inviting God to refuse to forgive us and to treat us in exactly the same way as we treat others. At the same time, we can pray as fervently as we like for something dear to our heart, but if we haven't forgiven an enemy then our prayer is likely to go unanswered. Jesus himself said, "So when you are offering your gift at the altar, if you remember that your brother or sister has something against you, leave your gift there before the altar and go; first be reconciled to your brother or sister and then come and offer your gift" (Matt. 5:23-24). Because our prayer is unanswered, we often begin to resent God. We no longer believe he cares for us and so we start to lose faith. We move more and more deeply into our resentment of God and more and more deeply into our unjust anger at him. Thus a refusal to forgive is also a refusal to love God.

It can now clearly be discerned that withholding forgiveness is an all-embracing sin. It is a refusal to love ourselves, our neighbour, and our God.

Two very good questions to ask ourselves are, "Have any of my prayers gone unanswered lately? Could there be an area of lack of forgiveness in my life which I have not attended to?" If I am not able to recall any obvious incident which demands my forgiveness, then I should ask the Holy Spirit to bring to my mind anything which I have forgotten, which as yet remains unhealed.

Jesus, understanding all these consequences, is eager to prevent us from becoming both sick and unhappy. Therefore, he tells us to forgive one another. It is not unlike myself watching my little two-year-old at play. She wants to stick the nice house key into the nice power socket. I sternly say "No," and she responds with hurt disbelief. She cannot understand why daddy would stop her from doing something which looks perfectly logical and safe to her. She does not understand about electricity and she has no idea that she could be killed. But I, as her loving father, know better, and I want to keep her from hurt. Jesus knows better too. He knows the deadly danger we risk by not forgiving. My daughter could suffer a shock to her body, but we could risk a deadly shock to our souls.

Many people misunderstand what forgiveness is. They think it is a feeling, but that is not so. Forgiveness doesn't have anything to do with feelings, except indirectly. This can be better understood by using the example of love. Love also is not a feeling. Certainly the first stage of love between a young man and a young woman is a state of intense feeling. It is so unique that there is a special word for it. It is called infatuation. However, it cannot and does not last. The passion inevitably subsides and should be replaced by a life-long, more spiritual relationship, which we still call love. In fact, it is a deeper and more enduring love. It is a love of one soul for another, not just a union of two bodies. The passion gives way to an ever deepening regard and admiration for the other, and an ever clearer vision of the other as an image of God. For example, let's say that my wife crunches her toast loudly at breakfast every morning and that it gets on my nerves. Is she going to think that I love her if I criticise her? I doubt it! I may not feel very loving when she does this, and I may even feel justified in attacking her, but that is not an act of love. Judging is God's job, not mine. The fact is that I do have a holy alternative. I can refuse my own resentment and perform an act of love. I can prove my love for her by making the toast for her! That is dying to self. That is real love and, in doing so, I am *deciding* to love her. Love is not a feeling. It is a *decision* to act in a loving way, even when I do not feel like it. So it is with forgiveness. I choose to forgive or I refuse to forgive. To refuse is to refuse mercy. To refuse is to refuse love. To refuse is to become a judge, and when I judge I am stealing from God, who alone reserves the right to judge.

Most people who are having trouble forgiving say, "But I can't forgive. I'm too angry, or I hurt too much or I'm too depressed." In other words, "I'm going to wait until the anger or the hurt goes away and then I might feel like forgiving my enemy, but otherwise, it's impossible." Modern humanist psychology agrees with that sentiment, but it is all wrong. In fact, it is backwards. It is only when we *choose* to forgive that the feelings of anger and hurt will start to subside. We cannot be free of anger and hurt until then. A non-believer is likely to wait till the feeling of resentment goes away before forgiving, but he will wait till the moon turns to blue cheese. A Christian, however, forgives in spite of his feelings, and then to his great joy the feelings melt away.

One day, St. Francis found a man bitterly cursing the employer who cheated him, literally wishing that God would damn him. St. Francis begged him to find forgiveness in his heart, so that the man could free himself. That man was in bondage to his lack of forgiveness. And for as long as he refused to show mercy to his employer, he was condemning himself to a life of bitterness and misery, and risking his immortal soul. If only he had known as St. Francis did that he was creating his own living hell.

At the purely psychological level, lack of forgiveness is nothing more than contamination from memory. This contamination closes off our access to the present moment, because we choose to dwell on the pain of the past. These memories pollute our minds and prevent us from enjoying the present moment. Yet the truth is, this pain is self-inflicted. It may appear to me that the pain is coming from the person who hurt me, but this is not so. The painful event is in the past and so it is over. The person who hurt me is no longer hurting me so why would I keep resurrecting the memory and relive it over and over again? The pain is coming from my own mind and my own choice to dwell on the memory. It is like the pass receiver in a football game. Once, when he caught a long pass from the quarterback, he was hit hard from behind by the running back. It really hurt. Now today, when he is about to catch another pass, he thinks he hears footsteps behind him, his mind is distracted from the ball and so he fumbles it. But there are no footsteps at all. It is all in his mind. His thought of being hit convinces him that he is actually going to be hit. He believes in it and so he takes his eye off the ball and misses the catch.

A memory only has power over us if we allow it to frighten us. But a memory is only thought. Once we grasp that, it becomes a lot less frightening. As thinking beings, we have the power to recognize a hurtful memory as merely a thought in our heads. It has no power unless we give it power. Therefore, we also have the power to un-think it. We can clear our minds of the disturbing thought and come back into the joy of the present moment. The present moment is a Sacrament. It is a gift of God. There is no need to squander it by living in the past. Digging up a corpse can never bring it back to life.

There are three reasons people give for not forgiving.

1. Some people believe that by holding on to a grudge, they can avoid getting hurt ever again. But not only is this person continuing to feel the pain, he is using energy to focus on it, thereby losing the joy of the moment. Such people live in the past and are still screaming inside for revenge, or justice or retribution. Yet the pain is only being caused by thought, not by the perpetrator. Once we realize that, we can start to experience the pain differently. True freedom lies not in *remembering* the past hurt, but in merely *recalling* it. There is a big difference between remembering and recalling. When

we remember something, we bring the memory back to life, we re-enact the memory and so we resurrect all the feelings that went with that hurt. In effect we are re-traumatising ourselves by reliving the pain of the past event. We are in bondage to a memory when we remember. Recalling, on the other hand, is healthy in that we see the memory as though we were watching a movie. We are aware of what took place, but we are not pulled into the movie and so we do not re-experience the old feelings.

The antidote to the pain is forgiveness. It is much simpler than you might think. Decide that you do not want the pain anymore. Go ahead and simply make an act of forgiveness as best you can. Jesus will accept it. Understand that the pain blocks your access to wisdom. Get in touch with wisdom and you will have insight and will respond spontaneously to life and to the present moment. Wisdom, of course, is the quiet voice of the Holy Spirit, and he can only be heard in the soft gentle breeze, as Elijah discovered. An unforgiving mind is a storm in your head, which drowns out the voice of God. Only a quiet mind can hear him. Therefore, stand back from your thoughts of the past, distance yourself from them, refuse to let them have authority over you, refuse to believe in them and you will be able to calm your mind, quieten it down, and so hear the voice of wisdom in your heart.

2. People often think that if they forgive a person who has hurt them, they are somehow *condoning* the sin of the perpetrator. This is not so. By forgiving, the only thing being condoned is mental and spiritual health. One is *not* condoning the sin. Mistakes, sins, and evil acts are a fact of life. People do such things. This may as well be faced. The only effective response to such evil is forgiveness and prayer for the perpetrator. It is hard to go on hating an enemy when you are praying for him. When you pray for the well-being of the person who has hurt you, Jesus honours you in turn and sets you free from your bondage. This might seem very difficult to do at first but, amazingly enough, it gets easier and easier. The miracle is that, in doing this, your feelings of resentment or anger rapidly become displaced by a rising feeling of compassion for the

person who has hurt you. You focus, not on your own pain, but on the sorry state of your enemy's soul. Do you really want your enemy to go to everlasting torment in hell? When you truly think about it, you should recoil at such a thought. Therefore, your poor enemy is in desperate need of your prayers. Who better to pray for him than the one whom he has hurt? Should this not be even more compelling when your "enemy" is your own spouse, the one whom God specially chose for you? "Do not repay evil for evil or abuse for abuse, but on the contrary, repay with a blessing" (1 Pet. 3:9). Do we ever think of returning a blessing for an insult? I am convinced from experience that when we do, we foster our own mental and emotional health and we bring grace down upon the head of our enemy. After all, who needs a blessing more than one who is sinning his soul by hurting another?

3. Some feel that if they let go of their pain, they will not care anymore about injustice in the world. Again, this is not so. The truth is that we will deal with injustice much more effectively out of a spirit of peace and serenity than we ever could out of vengeance or anger. Evil is not neutralised by evil. Evil is merely compounded by evil. The pro-life movement will wonderfully transform the abortion mentality if it acts out of forgiveness, love and prayerfulness, rather than out of angry self-righteousness. The abortionist will be more effectively stopped by a prayer than by a bullet. In fact, justice will be more wonderfully realised, because, not only will the abortions stop, but the abortionist's soul might also be saved. Once more, a blessing will realize the kingdom of God far more readily than a curse.

It is good to remember that not only are we victims of a perpetrator, but we too are perpetrators. While we are struggling to forgive an enemy, someone else is struggling to forgive us. This thought brings us to humility, and it is humility which opens the door to forgiveness.

All I have to do is to *decide* to forgive. I can decide that I do not want to go on feeling badly. I have the choice. I can choose to remember that I am a rape victim and to let that poison the rest of my life, or I can allow the memory to become just another memory in my mind along with the billions of other memories, which do not bother me at all. This is not to imply that it an easy thing to do and so often it takes years of therapy. But I *can* let it go. It is like putting the memory back into the floppy disc of my computer instead of keeping it constantly up on the screen. It is still present on that disc, but it is no longer running my life. It has lost its power over me and has become simply another stored event in my mind.

Lewis B. Smedes, the theologian, once said, "Forgiveness has creative power to move us away from a past moment of pain, to unshackle us from our endless chain of reactions, and to create a new situation in which both the wrong-doer and the wronged can begin in a new way."

The perfect formula for success is to make the forgiveness decision into a prayer. Every time you think of the perpetrator say quietly, "Jesus, I *choose* to forgive him or her." Never mind whether you "feel" like it or not. Simply do it as an act of will and Jesus will do the rest. Jesus taught us that the force which obtains God's forgiveness for a sinner is for us to forgive the sinner's offense. This is a holy inversion of the Lord's prayer, where we pray, "Father, forgive us our trespasses as we forgive those who trespass against us" (Matt. 6:12). For a merciful soul, it becomes rather, "Father, forgive those who trespass against us, for we have already forgiven them for everything." In other words, our forgiveness frees our enemy to be forgiven by God in turn.

Any offence which we give others, or receive from others, is a sin against charity, a sin against love. Lack of love strips us of God. So he who offends becomes spiritually naked, and only the forgiveness of the offended person can put clothes back on such nakedness. Why? Because he brings God back into the relationship. God forgives us if we forgive our neighbour, and he forgives the neighbour who repents. It is indeed a sin to hurt another person, but it is also a sin for that person to refuse to forgive. It will be done unto you as you do unto others. "Put away from you all bitterness and wrath and anger and wrangling and slander, together with all malice and be kind to one another, tender-hearted, forgiving one another as God in Christ has forgiven you" (Eph. 4:31-32).

When God creates, he creates in his own image and likeness, and since he is a Trinity, creation also displays trinitarian qualities. Likewise, *perfect* forgiveness is also trinitarian, since it is the imitation of God. Perfect forgiveness is actually a triangle of forgiveness. Firstly, the perpetrator needs to ask for forgiveness from his victim. Secondly, not only does the victim eagerly offer his forgiveness, but he in turn asks the perpetrator to forgive him! This may seem ridiculous at first glance, but it is only just. The victim must ask for forgiveness for harbouring anger at the perpetrator and also for not forgiving him sooner. Thirdly, both the perpetrator and the victim then turn to God and beg his forgiveness for offending him by their sin. This is the true trinity of forgiveness, which reconciles the two persons with each other and reconciles both with God.

Pope John Paul II writes, "We have already called attention to the fact that *he who forgives, and he who is forgiven,* encounter one another at an essential point, namely the dignity or essential value of the person, a point which cannot be lost and the affirmation of which, or its rediscovery, is a source of the greatest joy" (*Dives In Misericordia,* Chapter 14). Can we imagine any act of forgiveness more powerful than that of our good Pope John Paul II entering the prison cell of Ali Agca and offering his forgiveness to the man who had tried to assassinate him? That was a Jesus event. That was the kingdom of God present among us.

God will forgive us in the same measure that we forgive others. Then, and only then, will all our hurt feelings go away and we will be restored to right relationship with him. He will answer our prayers. We will give up our resentment and so will have peace. Our body chemistry will normalise itself once more. Relationships will be healed and so the body of Christ will also be healed. Jesus was indeed a wonderful psychiatrist and a wonderful healer. He said, "Learn from me, for I am meek and humble of heart" (Matt. 11:29). It was his humility which led him to forgive even at his crucifixion. We therefore should also pray daily for the grace of humility, so that we too can enjoy the blessings of a forgiving heart, that we too can forgive our spouse and our children and bring peace to our families.

When husband and wife forgive each other for hurts received, no matter how devastating they may be, even the mortal wound of infidelity, they are leaning on the power of God and not on their own weakness. Sometimes a hurt will appear to be much bigger than our capacity to forgive, but it is never bigger than the grace of God, and we must pray for that grace every day. Moreover, when our children witness the forgiving action of their mother and father, they learn the secret of family peace. They too, learn that no sin is too great that it cannot be forgiven by God, and no offence against themselves is too great that they cannot forgive in turn.

An anonymous wise man once wrote, "Forgiveness is the fragrance the violet sheds on the heel that has crushed it." Let us choose, then, to shed that same fragrance on all who would crush us. Forgiveness is family peace.

CHAPTER 5

Trust: Family Security

"Trust in the Lord and do good
that you may dwell in the land
and live secure."

(Ps. 37:3)

According to the Oxford Dictionary, trust is defined as "A firm belief in the reliability, honesty, veracity, justice, strength, etc. of a person." But while that is true, trust has a much deeper connotation for us as followers of Christ. Trust is intimately connected with the great theological virtue of hope. "Hope in God: For I shall again praise him, my help and my God" (Ps. 42:11). Hope is one of the three theological virtues; faith, hope and charity. And hope is, not without reason, placed between faith and charity. Without hope there can be no faith and without hope, charity dies. Faith presupposes a constant hope. How can we believe in God if we do not hope in his promises? If we do not hope in eternal life, how can we believe that God's word which promises eternal life applies to us? Likewise, how can charity be alive in us if we have no hope? Hope precedes charity because a person needs to hope in order to love. Those who have lost all hope cannot love, because loss of hope is despair, and despair paralyses all good works, especially the supreme work of love of God and neighbour.

The three virtues are like the patibulum or cross-piece of the cross of Jesus. Faith is at the right wrist of the crucified Jesus, the power of the right hand, faith which can "say to this mountain, 'Be taken up and thrown into the sea' and it will be done for you" (Mark 11:23). Hope is at the head of the crucified one, the mind of the master, or the master-mind, if you will, connecting faith on the right wrist to charity on the left. "If I have all faith, so as to remove mountains, but do not have love, I am nothing" (1 Cor. 13:2). "Faith by itself, if it has no works, is dead" (James 2:17). That is to say faith without the fruit of love in action is dead. Therefore, faith and love need a connecting link to bring them to fruition in our lives, and that link is hope. Faith and charity nail my wrists to the cross, but it is hope which elevates my eyes towards heaven and makes the cross bearable. Another way of describing hope is trust in God.

Adam and Eve were our first parents and God had given them everything in the Garden of Eden. He gave them life, and food and all that they could desire and he gave them each other. But after they sinned, Adam and Eve forgot all that. They lost their trust in God, and their trust in each other, they lost hope, and so when they heard God's footsteps in the garden, they "hid themselves from the presence of the Lord God among the trees of the garden" (Gen. 3:8). Their thoughts were now distorted by their lack of trust; they believed in these distorted thoughts and convinced themselves that God would never forgive them. To this day people are still hiding from God, believing that he could never be so loving as to forgive them for their sins. Much of what I do as a therapist is to convince broken people that they are loveable and therefore forgivable, to lift them up out of distorted thinking and into the love-filled truth of a forgiving God. This is not the despair of St. Peter, when in shame he cried, "Go away from me, Lord, for I am a sinful man" (Luke 5:8). Rather, it is the humble trusting prayer of the tax collector who prayed, "God, be merciful to me a sinner" (Luke 18:13). It takes real trust in God's love to acknowledge the raw reality of who we are as God's creatures.

It would seem that one of the most difficult things for us to do is to face the truth that we are sinners. Our pride likes to tell us that we are really not all that bad. "If we say that we have not sinned, we make Jesus a liar and his word is not in us" (1 John 1:10). So we cannot even get to first base in the spiritual ball game if we do not fully and firmly accept the indisputable fact that we are indeed sinners.

If we really could see sin for what it is, we would know that even a venial sin is a monstrous affront to God's goodness. We would embrace humility and accept that we are dreadful sinners in God's eyes. It is a relief for me to acknowledge that I am the worst sinner who ever walked on the planet because I can then get on with my spiritual journey, renounce all pride, which is the greatest obstacle to my spiritual growth, prostrate myself before the infinite good God, and beg for forgiveness and grace. I can beg for his forgiveness because I have hope — because I *trust* in the Lord.

So many people today live without trust in the Lord. Those who take the birth control pill do not trust in the Lord. Those who abort their children do not trust in the Lord. Those who kill their suffering elderly do not trust in the Lord. Politicians who vote for legislation which violates the justice of God do not trust in the Lord. Husbands who become violent do not trust in the Lord. Wives who constantly complain do not trust in the Lord. Children who fall into drugs or promiscuity do not trust in the Lord.

The strange paradox is that we are out of control, and yet we insist that we are the masters of our own lives. We believe this lie so profoundly that we now defend assisted suicide as a legitimate option. "It is my life, so I can end it if I choose." But that is another satanic lie. "No one lives as his own master and no one dies as his own master" (Rom. 14:7). The epidemic of suicide and the epidemic of divorce in today's world is at root an epidemic of lack of trust in the Lord. We are indeed sinners, caught up in doing it our way instead of God's way. We seem to be driven to control our own lives in a frantic effort to avoid pain, but as we shall see, it is far better to hand over our puny human control to the perfect and loving will of God our Father.

The Good News is that Jesus came for sinners. He is the divine physician for those who are soul-sick. The problem is we refuse to acknowledge that we are soul-sick. In fact we do the opposite. We justify our sins, especially the sins of anger and lust. "After all I'm only human. Sorry, God. You made me this way, so you will just have to put up with it. It is your fault I am so weak." We deny our most precious gift, which is our free will, in order to excuse our very worst actions.

God did not initially design us to be the way we are. We are the way we are because of Adam and Eve and their rebellion against what God intended in his creation. God created us for sainthood — to be a holy people. But people are afraid to be holy because that would mean giving up their favourite sins and exposing themselves to ridicule from their friends. They do not want to rock the boat. Yet we must rock the boat, because we must challenge the sin within ourselves. In fact, we are sailing on a boat which is being constantly rocked, and the boat is the barque of Peter, the Catholic Church, but it will never be sunk. "And the gates of hell will not prevail against it" (Matt. 16:18). So there is no need for fear when we and the church are persecuted. God has promised us the victory. Do we trust in that promise? Do we believe God will keep his word? Sadly, many of us do not.

What then is the opposite of trust? Many of us would simply reply "distrust," and that is true. But how can we know that we are living in distrust? There is one sure sign that we do not trust God, and it is that we *worry*. We worry and worry and worry. Worry is a lack of trust in the fatherhood of God. It will therefore be profitable to spend some time on the whole question of worry, and to do that I would wish to acknowledge the monumental work of Fr. John Hampsch, C.M.F., who is both a priest and a psychologist.

The Oxford Dictionary defines worry as "giving way to anxiety." Worry and anxiety are therefore synonymous and both these words will be used interchangeably in this chapter. Most worries are unfounded and usually concern the future. So often we are anxious about what might or might not happen, but as one wise man said, "I wish I knew what to worry about because everything I worry about never happens." Another chronic worrier, for whom worry had become his daily bread, joked, "I'm worried because I've nothing to worry about." In other words, worry is needless suffering. It is true that suffering is a part of the cross, but worry is a cross that we hammer together for ourselves. It is not the cross that God asks us to carry. In fact, many people are so busy carrying crosses they build for themselves that they are too burdened and exhausted to carry the true cross which Jesus wants to give them.

Our self-inflicted cross is very, very heavy, but the cross of Jesus is light. "My yoke is easy and my burden light" (Matt. 11:30).

In the original Greek of the Gospel, the word used for worry is **merimnao,** which means, "to divide the mind." This means that when we worry, the mind is being pulled in two directions. The mind is divided between worthwhile interests and damaging thoughts. And so our thoughts go round and round in a circle and never come to any resolution.

Yet Jesus, in the gospel of Matthew, orders us *five* times not to worry. It would be enough for us if Jesus were to say something only once but if he took the trouble to repeat himself five times, then he must have desired to make a very critical point.

"That is why I am telling you *not to worry* about your life and what you are to eat, nor about your body and what you are to wear. Surely life is more than food and the body more than clothing! Look at the birds in the sky. They do not sow or reap or gather into barns: yet your heavenly Father feeds them. Are you not worth much more than they are? Can any of you, however much you *worry,* add one single cubit to your span of life? And why *worry* about clothing? Think of the flowers growing in the fields: they never have to work or spin; yet I assure you that not even Solomon in all his royal robes was clothed like one of these. Now, if that is how God clothes the wild flowers growing in the field which are there today and thrown into the furnace tomorrow, will he not much more look after you, you who have so little faith? So *do not worry*: do not say 'what are we to eat? What are we to drink? What are we to wear?' It is the gentiles who set their hearts on all these things. Your heavenly Father knows you need them all. Set your hearts on his Kingdom first and on God's saving justice and all these other things will be given to you as well. So *do not worry* about tomorrow: tomorrow will take care of itself" (Matt. 6:25-34).

Has worry ever brought me to a healthy decision? It is not very likely. "For that person must not suppose that a double-minded man, unstable in all his ways, will receive anything from the Lord" (James 1:8). That means that a worrier is double-minded which is to say he is of two minds about everything so that his emotions, his convictions, his understanding and his reasoning are all unstable. Worry is therefore a waste of time. It is a disordered frame of mind because Jesus commanded us not to worry. Jesus repeated that command five times, reminding us first of all not to worry, and secondly to trust in his Father and his loving providence. Jesus is stating that when we worry we are refusing to trust in God. When we worry we are saying to God, "I do not believe in your promise to care for me." Is this not the same thing as calling God a liar? Therefore worry is a disorder and it requires remedial action.

God gave us a promise and he will keep his promise, but only if we give him permission to do so. When we worry we tell God to back off. We tell him that we do not trust him and that we prefer to trust ourselves. God has given us free will and if we choose to fret and worry, then he can do nothing because he refuses to violate the gift of free will which he gave us. He will allow us to try and control our lives if that is what we insist on doing, but he is saddened, because he knows we will only go from bad to worse. He patiently waits for us to become miserable enough to admit that we are helpless to control our lives, and hopes that we will turn back to him. He is there waiting to keep his promise to us, waiting to be asked. Is it not awesome to ponder upon the humility of God who respects our right to choose even when we choose to offend him?

Worry cannot be excused as being uncontrollable. Worry is distrust in the truthfulness of God. It is a sin of self-destruction because it leads to sickness of the body, the temple of the Holy Spirit. It is a sin because we cannot worry and pray at the same time, unless it is a worrisome prayer, which is not prayer at all. It is a sin because of what it does to family life. Have you ever tried to live with a worrier? It is a sin because it undermines our Christian witness. It blocks our spiritual journey. "But my righteous one will live by faith. My soul takes no pleasure in anyone who shrinks back" (Heb. 10:38). That is to say God derives no pleasure from one who falters in his trust and shrinks back. Worry always causes us to shrink back from our Christian purpose. The truth is, we can choose to refuse to worry. This does not mean that one should not care about life's problems, but there is a vast difference between a *morbid anxiety* and a *holy concern.* Morbid anxiety leads to a futile self-preoccupation. Holy concern leads to a humble reliance on divine providence.

When we come up against a difficult situation we should first of all ask ourselves if we have any control over it. If we see that we do, a prayer should be offered up to Jesus, that we make a right decision, and then go ahead with confidence. If on the other hand, the situation is clearly out of our control, then it is not our job to deal with it. It is God's job. "Father in heaven, this situation is beyond my power. Therefore I know it is your problem and not mine to solve. I place it confidently into your loving hands, knowing and trusting that you will work it out for my good and the good of all. Thank you Father."

"To those who love God, all things work together unto good" (Rom. 8:28). Do we really believe that? *All* things, without exception, work together unto good, for those who love God. If we love God, we will trust him, and if we really trust him, we will love him all the more, and accept all things as for our own good, even things which appear evil to our human way of thinking.

Father Hampsch tells a wonderful story of trying to get to Los Angeles airport to catch a plane to a nearby city. He was to give a talk there to three hundred nuns! He drove onto the airport freeway, which of course is notorious for being the longest parking lot in the world. The traffic was bumper to bumper and nothing was moving. He found himself becoming agitated and he started to fret. "I'm going to miss my plane! I'll never make it to this talk." Soon he realized that he was worrying, and doing exactly what he told his parishioners not to do. So he instantly switched off his worrisome thoughts and turned to God saying, "This situation is out of my control. Therefore it is your job, Father. I give it over to you." He then sat back, put some music on the car stereo and relaxed. Slowly he inched his way into the airport, too late for his plane time. He went up to the desk to ask if there was a later flight and was told, "Your flight was delayed, sir. If you rush through the gate now, you might just make it." So he dashed through the gate and made it into the aircraft just as they were closing the door. But of course, he was still going to be late for his talk. He again handed it over to the Father. When he finally arrived at the hall, he found to his horror that it was empty. He thought, "Oh, no! After all that, the nuns have been and gone." There was one solitary sister in the hall puttering about at the podium. He went forward to her and said,

"I'm so sorry sister to be late. I have let you all down." She looked puzzled and said, "Oh no, Father. We don't start for another half hour yet!" Ever since that day, Father Hampsch has wondered how God managed to do it!

Trusting in God does not mean that we are to become apathetic. Quietism and indifference are sins also. On the contrary, we should work for the kingdom of God but always with a totally calm trust in the Lord. We must believe that he will take care of it. "The Lord is my shepherd, I shall not want. He makes me lie down in green pastures" (Ps. 23:1-2). "Fear not, for I have redeemed you; I have called you by name. You are mine" (Isa. 43:1). This is a profound truth. The Almighty God has called *you* by name. He claims you as his own. In truly believing this promise of God, it becomes impossible to ever think of worrying. Surprisingly enough there are three hundred and sixty-five "Fear nots" in the Bible, one for each day of the year. How many times does God have to tell us that there is no need to worry?

Jesus says, "Do not fear, only trust" (Mark 5:36).

"Draw near to God and he will draw near to you" (James 4:8).

"Give us this day our daily bread" (Matt. 6:11).

"Trust in the Lord and do good: so you will live in the land, and enjoy security" (Ps. 37:3).

"The oath that he swore to our ancestor Abraham, to grant us that we, being rescued from the hands of our enemies might serve him *without fear* in holiness and righteousness, before him all our days" (Luke 1:73-75).

God kept the oath, the promise he made to Abraham and so will he not also keep the promises he made to us? Now we too can worship and serve him without fear, that is to say, without worry. God is trustworthy. He made promises to us and since he is a promise-keeper, we can and should confidently trust in him. Trust means to be worry-free. To be worry-free means to be at peace and everyone desires to have an abiding inner peace.

Worry has many more serious consequences than we might realize at first glance. A few years ago, a major U.S. government study concluded that eighty percent of all serious illnesses are adversely influenced by worry and by anger. Science has now proven that worry causes the release of chemical transmitters in the nervous system which affect the thymus gland, located in the chest, and so the secretions of the gland become pathological. This gland is the most important organ in the body for the regulation of the immune system. As a result of chronic worry, the T-cells from the thymus become defective and are not activated by the presence of cancer cells in the body. As a result the T-cells ignore growing cancer cells, which now become free to proliferate and cause a malignant tumour. This does not mean that all cancers are caused by worry but it is a significant factor. Not only cancer, but also heart disease, strokes, digestive disorders, bowel disorders, migraines, back pain, and many other diseases are initiated or made worse by relentless worry. God created our bodies in this way. He knows how our bodies work and out of his holy concern for our well-being, he took great care to command us not to worry. He tells us this five times in the gospel of Matthew, and three hundred and sixty five times throughout the scriptures, precisely because he does not want us to become needlessly sick. Medical scientists have only recently discovered that God was right all along!

Apart from the bodily consequences of worry, there are also psychological and spiritual consequences. At the mind level, people who worry have a faulty perception. Worry is a low mood, it constantly lowers our mood further and further, and causes our thoughts to become more and more distorted. When we worry, we cannot and should not trust or believe in our thoughts. Worry is mental static. Our judgement becomes faulty and therefore our decisions are going to be faulty. Worry easily becomes fear and fear paralyses the mind completely. There is a word for this condition. It is called *abulia,* which means that we are so paralysed we cannot make a choice on anything, not even a menu. Spiritually of course, chronic indulgence in worry can eventually lead to oppression by an evil spirit of worry, and no psychotherapist can talk that spirit away. Only prayer of deliverance can heal it.

So we worry and worry and worry, about money, the kids, the economy, about disease, about dying, and it is all so futile. Ask yourself, "What was I worrying about one year ago?" You probably cannot even remember. And if you do, you know today that it was all for nothing. Things still worked out regardless of your worrying. Worry is futile and it is a sin against God's desire to care for us. Worry means we are not habitually putting on the Mind of Christ.

St. Augustine once said, "Leave the past to the mercy of God; leave the future to the providence of God; leave the present to the love of God." Does that not sum up for us the secret of inner peace? The past is gone. It cannot be recovered. Leave it to God's mercy for he wants to take care of it. He has given us the Sacrament of Reconciliation, and by its grace we are forgiven. As John Rice said, "Never put a question mark where God has put a period." In other words, leave the past where it belongs, in the past. As to the future, it is pointless to worry. It has not even been born yet. God is in charge of the future. His providence will work all things to our good in the end. All we have to do is to love him and to trust in his perfect plan for our lives. With regard to the present, if we trust our Heavenly Father, we will live in the midst of his tender love. If only we believed that, no matter what is happening to us right this minute, we are wrapped in his loving arms. We are being taken care of. Our God is the God of the past, the present and the future and he can heal all of it. "Jesus Christ is the same yesterday and today and forever" (Heb. 13:8). "Cast all your anxiety on him because he cares for you" (1 Peter 5:7).

We can *choose* to *refuse* to worry in the same way as we do with anger. Like forgiveness, trust in God is a decision. Decide right now that you are going to trust the Father in Heaven and you will find your worries beginning to calm down. This is inevitable since by making such a decision, you are beginning to hand over control to your God instead of neurotically holding on to your own will. In other words, "You let go and let God." You will be amazed to find that you are learning to catch yourself right at the beginning of a worry party, and you will joyfully cast it upon the Lord, who will take care of it for you. He has promised it and he will do it.

Blessed Taulerus in the fourteenth century tells the story of a great theologian who for eight years prayed to God to show him someone who would teach him the way of truth. One day God answered him and said, "Go to the temple and there you shall find him." So he went and, as he was going in, he saw a poor beggar on the church steps, half-clothed with a few rags and covered with sores. Moved with compassion he said, "May God give you a good day." The beggar looked up cheerfully and said, "I have never had a bad day." "Then God give you good fortune," said the theologian. The beggar replied, "I have never experienced any misfortunes." The theologian was astounded and asked how this could be. The beggar gently said, "I will tell you. I have cast myself wholly upon the divine will, to which I conform my own, so that whatever God wills, I will it also. So when hunger, thirst, cold, heat, or sickness molest me, I do nothing but praise God, and whatever happens to me, whether it be prosperity or adversity, whether it be pleasing or unpleasant, I take all from the hand of God with great gladness, because it can only be good, coming as it does from a cause which can produce only what is best." The theologian had met the man God wanted him to meet.

St. Francis of Assisi never worried. He lived a life of total abandonment to divine providence. He had complete trust in God no matter how bleak or impossible things may have looked. As St. Bonaventure wrote of him, "Francis' poverty was so well supplied that it provided miraculously for the needs of those who come to his aid, procuring food and drink and a house, when money or any other means could not be found. Poverty such as that will certainly never be left short of the necessities which God gives to everybody in the ordinary course of divine providence."

Again St. Bonaventure writes, "At another time ... while on a missionary journey from Lombardy to Treviso, they were overtaken by nightfall and enveloped in pitch darkness. The road was dangerous in the dark because of the river and the marshes, and his companion said to him, 'Father, pray that we may be kept safe from all danger.' The saint replied confidently, 'God has power to banish the darkness and give us light, if it pleases him in his kindness.' The words were scarcely out of his mouth, when a brilliant light shone about them with a heavenly radiance and they could see their way clearly and for quite a distance around. They finished their journey safely, singing hymns of praise to God." St. Francis loved God above all, casting his cares upon him whom he trusted totally, and so the providence of God was free to act fully on his behalf.

Jean Baptiste de la Salle said, "The more you abandon to God the care of all temporal things, the more he will take care to provide for all your wants. But if, on the contrary, you try to supply all your own needs, providence will allow you to continue to do just that, and then it may very well happen that even necessities will be lacking, God thus reproving you for your want of faith and reliance in him." Mother Frances Xavier Cabrini wrote, "I have started houses with no more than the price of a loaf of bread and prayers, for with him who comforts me, I can do anything."

Father J.P. de Caussade, a Jesuit mystic who wrote a wonderful treatise called *Abandonment to Divine Providence,* wrote about a convent of Poor Clares in the town of Albi, in Italy. These Franciscan sisters were totally cut off from the world. They entered religion without any dowry and they lived only on alms from day to day. He says this: "Struck by their great austerities, I asked them one day whether the hardship of their life did not greatly damage their health, and shorten their days: they replied that they hardly ever had invalids among them, that very few died young and that most of them lived till past eighty. They added that their austerities and fasts contributed to fortify their health and to prolong their lives which a too plentiful regime would shorten." These Franciscan sisters, daughters of St. Clare, had abandoned themselves totally to divine providence. They trusted in God so absolutely that they never worried. As a result, they rarely had serious illness in the community, and they lived to a joyful old age.

At Guadalupe, Our Blessed Mother had these words for Juan Diego: "Hear, and let it penetrate into your heart — let nothing discourage you, nothing depress you. Let nothing alter your heart or your countenance. Also, do not fear any illness or vexation, anxiety or pain. Am I not here who am your mother? Are you not under my shadow and protection? Am I not your fountain of life? Are you not in the folds of my mantle, in the crossing of my arms? Is there anything else that you need?" What a beautiful guarantee of help and love from our Blessed Mother. She is constantly watching over all of us, ready to rush to our aid whenever we need her. As Catholic families, we should ask daily for the help of Mary, who understands all families and their needs. She is the Mother of Our Lord and he can refuse her nothing.

One could quote saint after saint and all of them would testify to such a hope in God, that they simply gave up all useless anxiety. They lived with the peace which surpasses all understanding and we, who yearn for that same peace, can have it too. Worry is the disease and God has given us the prescription for it. Hand over all your cares to him and choose to refuse to worry.

How is God's trustworthiness manifested? Is it only in practical matters like food, clothing and drink that we are to know? That would be absurd since God is not only the God of the body, but is also the God of our soul and our spirit. The most beautiful and most compelling proof of God's trustworthiness is his Divine Mercy. The Apostle of the Divine Mercy, chosen by Jesus to propagate this devotion, was Sr. Faustina Kowalska, a Polish nun beatified by Pope John Paul II. In 1931 on February 22, Sr. Faustina wrote this in her diary, "In the evening, when I was in my cell, I saw the Lord Jesus clothed in a white garment. One hand was raised in the gesture of blessing, the other was touching the garment at his breast. From beneath the garment, slightly drawn aside at the breast, there were emanating two large rays, one red, the other pale. After a while Jesus said to me, 'paint an image according to the pattern you see, with the signature: Jesus I trust in you. I desire that this image be venerated first in your chapel and then throughout the world.'"

Clearly in our era, Jesus has inaugurated a time of mercy upon a sinful world. He promises that we are graced every time we say, "Jesus, I trust in you." By this unwavering trust in Jesus, we can lay claim to his infinite mercy. Many do not appreciate what God's mercy is really like. We tend to limit it because we cannot imagine something that is infinite.

It may help our understanding to relate a true story about a little boy many years ago, who was like any other little boy in that he was often late for his meals. One day his mother, who had finally had enough, let him know very clearly that if ever he was late for a meal again, he would be punished by receiving only bread and water. The boy nodded in assent and went off to play. Sure enough, he got so totally caught up in his play that he forgot the time, and that evening he came home late for supper. To his horror, his mother and father were sitting down to his very favourite food, but at his place there was only a glass of water and a plate with a simple slice of plain bread upon it. The boy knew he could not complain, so he sat down at the table with his head bent in remorse. As he looked at this uninviting meal before him, he suddenly was aware of his father's big hands coming forward and removing the glass and the plate from him. The father then took his own plate of appetizing food and placed it in front of his son. Father then said, "I will take your punishment for you." That boy will never, ever forget his father's act of mercy. Justice demanded that the boy be punished, but his father in mercy took upon himself his son's punishment. That boy grew up to be a fellow student of mine at the Seminary, and is now also a permanent deacon.

Is this not a wonderful human example which reflects the perfection of the divine mercy? God took the punishment for our sins upon himself. No greater act of mercy has ever been seen in history than the freely accepted death of Jesus upon the cross of Calvary. We disobey and Jesus dies. We sin and Jesus saves. We fall and Jesus forgives.

Pope John Paul II in his Encyclical, *Dives in Misericordia,* (Rich in Mercy) states:

1. God is mercy itself.
2. His mercy is the only answer to our human condition.
3. Now is the time to turn to his mercy, repenting, trusting and pleading.

It is vital for us to lovingly nourish our trust in the divine mercy. Jesus tells Sr. Faustina that we can do this in four ways:

1. By proclaiming the mercy of God.
2. By praying and begging for God's mercy.
3. By glorifying his mercy. As he said, "At three o'clock, immerse yourself in my mercy, adore and glorify it, invoke its omnipotence. I claim veneration for my mercy from every creature."
4. By deeds of mercy.

To those who take this to heart, Jesus promises that their names are written in the Book of Life.

There is, in a sense, a circle of mercy which, like a coin, has two sides. On one side we receive mercy from God and on the other we give mercy to our neighbour. This is nurtured and brought to perfection by means of yet another coin. On one side is the saying of the chaplet of Divine Mercy and on the other is the prayer of Praise of God's Mercy. In the chapter on anger I wrote that praise could dispel a low mood, but praise is worth even more than that. It makes us recipients of torrents of divine mercy poured out on us from the heart of Jesus.

This image of the Divine Mercy is a visual reminder of Jesus' presence in our hearts. "Abide in me as I abide in you" (John 15:4). He asks us to say over and over again, "Jesus, I trust in you" because it is lack of trust in him which is leading families and the world to conflict and division. Our trust in Jesus is our continual and complete "yes" to him. This *fiat* is our declaration of faith in his benevolent intention for our welfare. By our trust we glorify him, and he in turn, glorifies us.

This cry, "Jesus, I trust in you," can and should be on our lips day and night. It is a way of responding to the indwelling presence of the Lord within us. It is a way of living in the circle of mercy. Trust transforms our lives from self-reliance, to Jesus-reliance; from exercising a stifling control over our world, to opening our arms to whatever God wishes to do in our world. Jesus says, "Mankind will have no peace until it turns with trust to my mercy." As Catholics we should also remind ourselves that Mary, Our Mother, is called the Mother of Mercy because she is the mother of Jesus, who is Mercy itself. She understands our poor weak human hearts, and if we turn to her in trouble, she will joyfully mother us. She will protect us and calm our worry and our fear.

Families which are plagued by worry are dysfunctional families. When a family member gives in to morbid worry, he or she is trying desperately to exercise control over his or her life. The problem is that control is a fool's paradise, or more accurately, it is a fool's hell. By insisting on control we are actually insisting on solving all things with our very poor and limited human intellect, instead of solving it in the divine mind of God. That is the foolish choice we make when we are "hell-bent" on keeping control of our lives.

This can become so diabolical that inevitably, in order to keep control of our own lives, we have to control the lives of other people. Adolf Hitler was so obsessed with controlling his own little terrifying world, that he was ultimately driven to try and control the entire world and to annihilate the Jewish people. On a smaller scale a husband, who insists on rigid control of his life, will soon force his wife to conform, by shouting and even violence. A wife who insists on rigid control of her life will soon force her husband to conform, by complaining, by making unreasonable demands or squandering his earnings on trinkets. Parents who insist on control will stifle their children and poison their initiative, thereby stunting their growth into spiritually and emotionally wholesome adults.

The perfect antidote to worry and control is trust. First of all, trust in God, secondly, trust between husband and wife, and lastly, trust between parents and children. Trust is one of the foundation stones of a happy and a holy family.

When a Christian couple learns to trust God, they will automatically trust one another. This trust in the other will be sustained *even when there is no good reason to trust.* In the face of the greatest betrayal of all, which is infidelity, a holy spouse will cast his or her pain on to the Lord, forgive the terrible offence, and move on in peace. We are the undeserving recipients of divine mercy, and so we in turn are empowered to extend that same mercy to our spouse. In human relationships, trust is a function of the truster not the trustee. In other words, we trust regardless of the trustworthiness of the other. This is the proper response of one who claims to love. Love continues to love even when it is betrayed. In the divine relationship, trust is a function of God, who is trustworthy regardless of whether we trust him or not. "He remains faithful — for he cannot deny himself" (2 Tim. 2:13). Therefore we can only trust our spouse in so far as we have trust in God himself. We must believe that "all things work towards good" (Rom. 8:28), even things which hurt deeply and do not make sense to our human reason.

Likewise parents must foster trust in their children. But this is not the same as the trust between husband and wife. The difference is that children are only children and while we should trust them, we should also protect them from harm, which they may not be able to resist. I might trust my two-year-old that she does not want to die, but I wouldn't let her play in traffic! Likewise, I may trust my teenager that he wants to be good, but I would not let him go to a party where drugs were being passed around. Teenagers may find this difficult to swallow, but parents have the mandate and the duty before God not only to trust their children, but also to protect them. Parents should impress upon their teenager that they trust his good will and integrity, but that they cannot yet trust his judgement. They should trust him or her as a person but in a complex and often confusing world, teens can easily be misled into making wrong choices. A teenager, nevertheless, needs to *believe* that his parents *believe* in him. Christian parents must demonstrate that they themselves are trustworthy. This, more than anything, convinces a child that he too should be trustworthy. It also leads the child to believe that God can be trusted too.

There is a golden rule of Catholic life which is well worth putting into practise, beginning right now. Whenever something good is happening, a Christian should be quick to say, "Thank you, God." God loves and rewards a grateful heart. If something negative or painful is occurring, the Christian response should be, "I trust in you, God!" This is the secret of acceptance of the holy and perfect will of God. Our salvation is hidden within the events of our daily lives whether these events are good or bad in our own estimation. "The Lord gives and the Lord takes away, blessed be the name of the Lord" (Job 1:21). Job understood this secret and God restored him greatly. If these prayers would spring to our lips in all the circumstances of our daily lives, we would enjoy a life free from worry and free from fear.

It can now be concluded that worry, control, and distrust are disorders, and that God's prescription for these is total trust in him. The problem is how to come into that holy trust in our Heavenly Father.

Psychologically, there is a simple technique which is remarkably effective. Some time ago, I realised that the subconscious mind can be used as a servo-mechanism in addition to its many other functions. That is to say, I can give my unconscious mind certain commands and it will obey. This discovery is not described elsewhere in the psychological literature, but I have put it to good use in my practice and in my own personal life. It is really very simple. Whenever I catch myself in a worry party, I immediately give my unconscious mind an order. I say to myself, firmly and convincingly, "Clear my mind, now!" Believe it or not, my subconscious immediately responds by clearing away all worrisome thoughts. This clearing effect lasts for about three seconds, during which time, I then move my mind onto some harmless activity. The mind-clearing response is something like putting the mind into neutral gear or, as Dr. George Pransky describes it, "Going into a free-fall."

However, since I am a habitual worrier, it probably won't be long before my mind falls back into its old worry pattern once more. If this happens, simply re-issue the command. As you do this easy exercise repeatedly, your subconscious will finally get the message that you no longer wish to be troubled by worrisome thoughts. Within a remarkably short time, you will discover to your great delight that you are catching yourself earlier and earlier, until you even become aware of yourself *before* a worry session can get started. This technique has put an end to a lifetime of worry for me personally, and it has helped numerous patients in my practice. I was able to give up worrying completely in a matter of only three weeks.

Relief from worry also takes prayer, and for this kind of healing I recommend that someone pray over the worrier by the laying on of hands. This can be done by an individual or by a prayer team. "They will lay their hands on the sick and they will recover" (Mark 16:18).

1. The minister invokes God's presence into the room, into himself, and into the person being prayed over. The Sign of the Cross is made on the person's forehead with holy water.
2. Ask the Father to show the person where he is *bent towards the creature,* in other words, where he is worshipping a created thing or person instead of God. Ask God to reveal to him where he has embraced false gods or idols, and to name them. Is it worry, control, money, power, sex and so on?
3. The person then forcefully renounces his idols and chooses only Yahweh as his God.
4. Ask the Holy Spirit to show the person where he needs to forgive others, especially those who gave him his idols. For example, one's parents may have passed on their worry habit to their child.

5. Then he is asked to forgive these people with all his mind, heart and spirit.
6. Ask the Holy Spirit to show the person where he needs to ask others to forgive him, especially for hurt he has inflicted on them by his idols. For example, he may have hurt his wife by his obsession with control. He may have damaged his children by rigid, excessive punishment.
7. Then in prayer, ask forgiveness from these people.
8. Next the person repents of the sins he has committed against God by means of his idols, and begs God's forgiveness and his mercy.
9. The person convincingly thanks God for forgiving him.
10. Now the person must open the door of his heart. "Father, I choose from this moment on to do only your holy will. I renounce all that is not pleasing to you."
11. The minister now asks Jesus to fill in all the spaces left behind by the discarded idols. This leaves no room for the spirits to return. "For when an unclean spirit has gone out of a man it goes and brings seven other spirits more evil than itself and they enter and live there: and the last state of that person is worse than the first" (Luke 11:26). So it is vital to in-fill the vacuum with the living presence of Jesus. "I welcome the indwelling Christ to grow within me. Maranatha! Come Lord Jesus! Stay with me always. You must increase while I must decrease. Give me the grace to know you are within me every moment of my day and every moment of my life."
12. The minister now anoints the person with blessed oil on the forehead, the eyes, the ears, the nostrils, the mouth and the hands so that his mind and all his senses are sealed against the return of his idols.

The healing session can be closed with a prayer of thanksgiving. "So I tell you, whatever you ask for in prayer, believe that you have received it and it will be yours" (Mark 11:24).

So be healed of morbid worry and sinful control and you and your family will live together in peace, confident always in the loving providence of God the Father in heaven. Trust in God is emotional, mental, physical and spiritual gold. It dispels worry, anxiety and fear so that we can begin to walk in the peace of Christ, accepting each moment in holy detachment. It is Jesus' way. It leads us to his truth and it gives us his life. Learn this lesson as husbands and wives. Teach it to your children, and your family will be always immersed in the peace that is not of this world.

CHAPTER 6

Love: The Master Key

*"I love my master and my wife
and children. I do not wish to be
freed."*

(Ex. 21:5)

Ultimately, everything that is good in a Catholic marriage can be summed up in one word, **LOVE.** If we are to become free from anger, if we are to ask for and freely give forgiveness, if we are to abandon ourselves totally in trust to the Lord, then we must become lovers. If we learn to love, then all these other ideals will fall into our hands like windfall from a fruit tree. Love is the fire which gives warmth to our homes and without it, we can hardly speak of family at all.

"If I speak in the tongues of mortals and of angels, but do not have love, I am a noisy gong or a clanging cymbal. And if I have prophetic powers, and understand all mysteries and all knowledge, and if I have all faith, so as to remove mountains, but do not have love, I am nothing. If I give away all my possessions, and if I hand over my body so that I may boast, but do not have love, I gain nothing" (1 Cor. 13:1-3).

These are very powerful words from St. Paul. I can appear to men to be a very holy person. I might even perform miracles, but if I do not have a loving fire burning in my heart, then all my good works count for nothing before God. Love then, is vitality and life. It gives life and it sustains life.

Lack of love, on the other hand is mere existence and being a living spiritual death, will eventually lead to certain eternal death. "Whoever does not love, abides in death" (1 John 3:14). For a Christian, love is easily defined and it is reducible to one single word: God. Love is God and God is love. "Whoever does not love does not know God, for God is love" (1 John 4:8).

How beautiful that thought is. We creatures are only capable of love "Because God first loved us" (1 John 4:19). In fact, it would enhance our understanding of true love if we were to read all of this passage from the first letter of John. "Beloved, let us love one another because love is from God: everyone who loves is born of God and knows God. Whoever does not love does not know God, for God is love. God's love was revealed among us in this way. God sent his only Son into the world so that we might live through him. In this is love, not that we have loved God but that he loved us and sent his Son to be the atoning sacrifice for our sins. Beloved, since God loved us so much, we also ought to love one another. No one has ever seen God: If we love one another, God lives in us, and his love is perfected in us. By this we know that we abide in him and he in us, because he has given us of his spirit" (1 John 4:7-13). Accordingly any love we might enjoy can only come from God himself, and we can only grow in true love according to the spirit of God working in us. God, therefore, is the source of all love on the face of the earth, while we are merely very small reflections of that same love.

In the light of the gospel, it is possible to discern six different categories of love. The first and the highest is love of God. Love of God is the most sublime experience of love because it is totally a spiritual love, a love which is not blemished by anything carnal or profane. There simply is no other way to love our creator God. It is a love which is unselfish. It is a love devoid of any sensual rewards. It is a love of God which we enjoy for himself and himself alone. Such love accords to God his rightful place as our creator, and recognises that we are undeserving recipients of his divine and eternal love.

The second type of love is the love between husband and wife. "So God created humankind in his image, in the image of God he created them, male and female he created them. God blessed them" (Gen. 1:27-28). The love between man and woman then, is a blessed thing, a holy thing, and God saw that it was good. We must also bear in mind, however, that before the fall, the love which existed between Adam and Eve was a completely innocent phenomenon. They loved naturally, though not naturally as it is understood today, but naturally as to the nature of innocent children of God. Adam saw Eve as "Bone of my bone and flesh of my flesh" (Gen. 2:23). He saw her as truly a part of his own self, and as the helpmate who dispelled his loneliness. Eve, coming from the side of Adam, saw herself as an extension of Adam, having her origin from Adam, and so there was no battle of the sexes. She was truly his helpmate. There was no male domination and no female rivalry for power. As a result, although they were husband and wife with full marital rights, they gazed upon each other with totally innocent eyes. They were even naked, but their nakedness was childlike and not disfigured by lust. "Now, both of them were naked, the man and his wife, but they felt no shame before each other" (Gen. 2:25). The Original Sin distorted that innocent vision, and from that moment on man and woman were tempted to look at each other with an unnatural lust which we now mistakenly call natural. But lust is not natural, in that it does not emanate from the nature of innocent children of God. The Book of Genesis relates that the first thing Yahweh did for Adam and Eve after the fall was to make clothes for them. He knew that the human race would now struggle with lust and immodesty and that their former innocent nakedness now needed to be covered.

Pope John Paul II in his wonderful book, *Love and Responsibilty*, shocked the secular world when he stated that it is sinful for a husband to lust after his wife. He was calling all mankind with authority, to aspire to the holy and innocent love of Adam and Eve before the fall. He understands the Scriptures very well and that lust is a consequence of the sin of Adam and Eve, a consequence that all of us have inherited.

The third type of love is love of a mother and a father for their child. Before the original sin, everything in the Garden of Eden was regulated by and based upon love. The love of parents for children was a specific command of God, who on the sixth day of creation said, "Be fruitful and multiply and fill the earth" (Gen. 1:28). Bearing children was to be a holy, pure and powerful love. As parents, we have the sublime duty to teach our children how to love in a holy way, and we do that, not only by loving them without reservation, but very importantly by the example of the love between mother and father, and between parents and God. When children see how mother and father love each other and how they love God, they bathe in the warmth of that love and they learn what true love is. They learn by imitation and, if their home is filled with love, they too will learn how to love in a godly way.

The fourth love type is the love of our neighbour. Love of our neighbour would be impossible were it not for the first three forms of love; love of God, spousal love and parental love. We need to know that God loves us, that our parents loved each other, and that we are loved by both God and our parents, in order for us to perfectly love the stranger who is our neighbour. In other words, the more perfectly we are trained in the love of the family of God, the more we can embrace the family of man. More than that, we need this love in order to learn to love the neighbour who is our enemy.

The fifth category of love is love for knowledge, but it must be love for *holy* knowledge, which is the science of God. There is no higher knowledge for the human mind than to know God and his Word. Learning about earthly things is in itself good, provided it is humbly placed at the service of the kingdom of God, and leads to a sense of wonder at God's marvellous creation. But this must never be confused with a lust for knowledge as an end in itself, which is an unholy thing and which is really only idolatry. So many people spend hours of study in schools, in colleges and universities, acquiring knowledge for the purpose of an earthly career. Yet how many hours have we spent acquiring knowledge of God and our Catholic faith? This may not further our climb up the corporate ladder, but it will propel us up the rungs of Jacob's ladder to our heavenly promotion, which is eternal.

The sixth love is love of work, in the holy sense of work as imitation of God's six days of creative work, when he established the universe and blessed it with abundant life. This holy love of work stands in opposition to the workaholic, who runs away from life, wife, and strife by plunging himself into futile endless work.

He may justify his disordered priorities, but addiction of any kind usurps God's rightful place as the god of his heart. For such a man, work has become god. True work is done for the glory of God, for the proper provision for family, and as a service to the community. A holy love of work must also include a holy love for the Sabbath, the seventh day of creation, when God rested. God expects us to set aside one seventh of our lives, one day a week, to give it over to him as a day of prayer and adoration. "Remember the Sabbath day and keep it holy" (Ex. 20:8). Unnecessary work on Sunday is a violation of God's right to a day of prayer and recollection by which we should take time to dwell on him and the blessings of his creation.

All other loves are really not loves at all. Rather, they are hungers or even lusts. They are negations of love, which deny the supremacy of God and deny the dignity of man. I can like my car and I can enjoy my car, but I must never love it. If I do, then I have placed a false god before the One True God. Many women today "love" the television "soap operas." Many men today "love" sports. Many children today "love" cartoons. These appetites or desires are disordered and soul destroying, if they usurp our duty to love one another and to love God above all.

Unfortunately for us, the English language makes it difficult to talk about love. The reason for this is that we only have one solitary word for it. The Greeks are much more precise in their language and so they wisely have three words to describe the various aspects of love. *Eros* means sexual love, hence the English word, erotic. *Philos* means the love between friends. *Agape* means a selfless, self-giving love towards all people, the kind of love a Christian should have for everyone. When a Greek speaks of love, he can never be misunderstood; his precise meaning is clear. But when I say to a man in our western culture, "I love you," how does he know what I mean? Am I addressing him as my close friend *(Philos)*, am I expressing a homosexual desire *(Eros)*, or am I embracing him as my brother in Christ *(Agape)*? It is very sad that the most important and life-giving virtue in the universe is reduced to one four letter word. It is a pitiful fact that our English-speaking culture is so distorted in its thinking that whenever we hear the word love, we immediately connect it to its erotic, sexual meaning.

Another aspect of love which is seriously misunderstood is the idea of loving oneself. Jesus gave us the two great commandments, "You shall love the Lord your God with all your heart, and with all your soul and with all your mind and with all your strength. The second is this, 'You shall love your neighbour as yourself'" (Mark 12:30-31).

Therefore we can only love our neighbour to the degree that we love ourselves. In a sense, Jesus is really giving us three commandments here; to love God, to love our neighbour *and* to love ourselves. He is demanding that we love ourselves, not so that we can love ourselves for our own sake, but so that we can more purely love our neighbour. If I hate myself, as so many broken people seem to do these days, then I really cannot claim to love other people. As followers of Jesus, we must learn to truly fall in love with ourselves. But this love of self must not be misunderstood. Obviously Jesus would never recommend that we become self-centred, or conceited or vain. That is the suicidal anti-love of Narcissus, who, while admiring his reflection in a lake, fell in and drowned. Jesus is talking about something else entirely. *To love myself means to see myself with the eyes of Jesus.* My eyes become opened to see the awesome miracle which I am, thanks to the gentle, creative act of a loving Father God. Billions of years before I was conceived, God was planning me. He was conceiving me in his divine mind and he "saw that it was very good" (Gen. 1:31). "The Lord called me before I was born" (Isa. 49:1).

When I was about nine years old, we lived in a small apartment. We were quite poor. My mother only had a short length of kitchen counter top and an old cracked enamel sink. She had no ironing board and so she painfully had to do her ironing on the kitchen counter. My dad worked a hard twelve-hour shift on the railroad, often in dreadful weather, and so he would come home exhausted every evening. After his meal, he would sit down in the kitchen and promptly fall into a deep sleep. One evening as usual, dad was sound asleep on the chair. I was playing on the floor with my little sister and mom was trying to iron some shirts. She accidentally placed the iron down too close to the edge of the counter, and of course, it toppled off and landed on the floor, burning a hole in the linoleum, linoleum which we could not afford to replace. Poor mom burst into tears and started to complain. "I can't stand it any more. I don't even have an ironing board." Dad opened his eyes, and although he was still half asleep he took in the situation. Instead of getting angry as he could have done, he got up, put his arms around mom, and said, "It's alright, Ina. I'll make you an ironing board." So the next day, dad went off to the lumber yard and bought some cheap spruce and since he had no place to work in the apartment, he rolled up a rug in my bedroom and got down to the job. It took him two weeks, working in the evenings after a gruelling work day, to finish the task. Then the great day came when he proudly presented the ironing board to my mother. She was as thrilled as if he had given her a diamond necklace. From that day on, every time my mother took out the ironing board, I looked on it and my heart filled with a great love. I loved it then, and I still love it to this day. Why? Because it was something my father made and it was made out of love.

That is exactly what Jesus sees when he looks at you and me. He sees someone made by his Father in heaven and someone made out of love. So he too fills with love when he looks at us. If we could see what Jesus sees, we would stop complaining about our imagined defects. "I'm too fat. I'm too thin. I'm too tall. I'm too short." We would stop complaining about our flaws. "I'm no good. I'm worthless. I'm a nobody." Instead we would rejoice in awe and wonder at the incredible artwork of the creator, the God who fashioned us out of nothing at all. We can legitimately fall in love with ourselves, and this holy self-love leads us to such a gratitude to God that we become empowered to see Christ in all others, and so to love them as Jesus commanded. Learn to love yourself in the right way, and you will soon learn to love God and men. Not only that, but when we see ourselves with this new clarity we become fully whole, fully alive, and fully adult, so that when we meet the one we will marry, we can offer him or her a totally integrated person, capable of a more complete self-donation. Marriage then, becomes a real prospect for success and life-long love, if both partners can give to each other a new creation in Christ. When I marry, I do so not because you will meet my needs or solve my broken-ness, but because I wish to give you myself.

So many marriages take place because two wounded people expect the other to meet all of their needs, but that is not humanly possible. When they come to realize the truth, as they must, that their partner cannot do this, they become angry or hurt, depressed or defeated, and the marriage may totally break down. Nothing will kill love more insidiously than false expectations of what marriage will provide. My office is filled with un-met expectations and I spend a lot of time re-educating couples to love themselves and to place all their expectations onto *God*, not onto their spouse. Once I see myself with the clarity of Jesus, then my eyes become fully opened, and I can now also see my spouse as he or she truly is. Therefore, I can truly love, and the love I bear for my spouse becomes wide open to new life, the new life which is the God-given product of our love. Love welcomes new life and loves it. Not only that, but love welcomes that other life which is not of my flesh: the orphan, the beggar, the widow and the oppressed. But if I do not love myself with the mind of Christ, then true love is dead, with the result that it now becomes easy to put on the abortion mentality. Self-love becomes self-adoration and so my ego becomes my god. Now I can kill without conscience. Indeed, I must kill my unborn child, because even life itself must be sacrificed for my selfish needs, which are money, sensual pleasure or power.

True love transforms our ponderous human nature into a supernatural nature. A man refusing to love becomes corrupt of himself and corrupting of others. But love makes him live in the atmosphere of God, and so he lifts up his neighbour. Love is the great driving force of the universe, while all the misfortunes of the earth come from lack of love, beginning with disease and death, both of which were caused by Adam and Eve's refusal to love Yahweh.

True love is actually obedience. Jesus loved his Father perfectly and he proved his love by obediently leaving heaven, coming to earth and taking on our humanity. He obediently led a life of poverty for thirty-three years, and obediently allowed himself to be slaughtered on the cross. That is perfect obedience and that is perfect love. "But when anyone does obey what he has said, God's love comes to perfection in him" (1 John 2:5). In other words, if we are obedient to God, God in turn fills us with his love and that kind of love is more and more perfected, the more we obey.

St. Paul expands on the theme of love when he states very clearly what love is and what it is not. "Love is patient; love is kind; love is not envious or boastful or arrogant or rude. It does not insist on its own way; it is not irritable or resentful; it does not rejoice in wrong-doing, but rejoices in the truth. It bears all things, believes all things, hopes all things, endures all things" (1 Cor. 13:4-7).

Husbands and wives who love are always patient with each other. They show kindness and generosity at all times. Many couples are stingy with each other and fight over what is yours and what is mine. But there is no room for this kind of exclusive possessiveness in marriage. Marriage is a covenant, whereby everything you have and everything I have are held in common. Money and things are "ours," not yours and mine. In the old marriage ceremony, the husband used to vow to his beloved, "with all my worldly goods I thee endow." It is a tragedy that this was ever removed. The only things in the home which should be "his" and "hers" are the bath towels!

Then there is rudeness. So many spouses fall into the habit of being unbelievably rude to the one given to them by God. They would never dream of being rude to a complete stranger, but feel quite justified in being rude to their life's partner. This is unacceptable and ignorant behaviour, unbefitting a marriage covenant. We may disagree about something, but that does not justify bad manners. We are entitled to our own opinions on everything except the truths of our Catholic Faith. People so easily become self-centred, and insist on their own way no matter what their partner may think. This applies not just to strongly-held opinions, but also to important family decisions. "We are moving to Timbuktu, and that is that." Love never behaves in this way. Instead, it listens to the other's point of view, tries to understand it, respects it, and looks for a way to become of one mind and one heart. Perfect love, of course, dies to self, abandons its own opinion and is willing to accept the opinion of the other, provided it is not a question of morality.

St. Paul says love is not irritable or resentful. It is not, but I see many couples who vent their irritability and resentment on one another in my office. It can sometimes be very difficult to get them to see that this is doomed to fail, and that before they can ever hope to rediscover their love for one another, they must start by renouncing resentment, which is the same thing as saying they must forgive one another. In "bearing all things" love allows the lover to forgive the other, no matter what he has done and no matter how often he has done it. True love is perpetual forgiveness. People do not want to hear that message today, because they will only allow their egos to be bruised just so much. A real lover, however, simply goes on and on, obeying the demands of perfect love, and by doing so, he or she "hopes all things and endures all things." Fr. Gaston Salet, S.J. summarised this very well when he said, "Love is union but not absorption." In other words, by enduring all things, we need never fear that we will be annihilated as individuals. In fact, it is by learning to love more perfectly that we discover our true selves. For this reason, husbands and wives should strive to "out-love" one another.

Thomas A Kempis, in the *Imitation of Christ*, expands on St. Paul's theme. He says, "Love is swift, sincere, pious, pleasant and beautiful, strong, patient, faithful, prudent, long-suffering, manly and never seeks itself. For when anyone seeks himself, there he falls from love. Love is guarded, humble, upright, not soft, nor light, nor reaching for empty things, sober, chaste, steadfast, quiet and self-controlled in all the senses. Love is subject and obedient to all in authority, base and despised in its own eyes, devoted to God and thankful, trusting and hoping always in him, even when God is not a sweet savour to him, because without sorrow, there is no living in love."

We should not be misled by Thomas' description of love as "manly." That is not a sexist comment. He is merely referring to the manly love of Jesus as the perfect model for us to imitate, for we know that Jesus embodied all of the perfect features of both masculine and feminine love. If we could only begin to practice the ideas of St. Paul and Thomas into our model of loving, we would have holy families. Such families would reflect the humble and pure love of the Holy Family of Nazareth. Some might argue that this is too idealistic, and that no one could ever reach such dizzy heights of selfless love. I have not climbed to such altitude either, but without the ideal, how would I know what to reach for? I need a vision of the "perfect" in order to more accurately assess my "imperfect" and to strive to go higher.

I recently heard about a Catholic mother who was dying of cancer. She loved her husband and her children with a totally unselfish love. She would call her children around her every evening and she had them pray with her, begging God to send them a good mother after her death. Not long afterwards she did die, and about one year later her husband met and married a woman who turned out to be the perfect loving step-mother to the children. How many of us could love our spouse so much, that we would pray to be replaced in his or her heart by another after we die! That is sacrificial love. That is the love which imitates Jesus, who was meek and humble of heart and who laid down his life for his friends. We are his friends, and he asked us to imitate him by laying down our lives. Love is a laying down of life in sacrifice and service. That Catholic mother did not think perfect love was beyond her. She reached for it and embraced it wholeheartedly and we can too.

Modern psychology has gone off at a tangent when it comes to counselling married couples. Instead of focussing on love as it ought, it has distilled all marital dysfunction down to a "communication problem." It has brainwashed our society into believing that we have a universal communication breakdown, as though there was an epidemic of some kind of linguistic dyslexia. For today's therapists, therefore, the answer is very simply to teach couples communication skills and presto, instant marriage recovery. They persist in this philosophy even though the results of their interventions are abysmal in terms of subsequent divorce rates. The reason for this is, simply, that communication is not the problem in troubled marriages. The real reason is that couples so often lose their "warm feelings" for each other and so they drift further and further apart, until they come to believe that their love is truly dead. That is when they develop a problem, not before. When they were young and in love and were filled with warm feelings, there was never any hint of a communication problem. On the contrary, they knew that they communicated perfectly well and not only in speech, but in the body language of love, loving glances, touching hands, and in love-filled smiles. Years later, when they had allowed their loving feelings to slowly leak away, they began to feel rejected and unloved. These feelings soon gave way to anger, frustration, hurt, disappointment and anxiety. Now they communicate *these* feelings to one another, and they do a very good job of it. They still do not have a communication problem. They are communicating very well indeed, but instead of communicating love as they did earlier on, they are now communicating their negative feelings. So what should couples do who have gotten into trouble? An analogy might help to reframe the problem away from the idea of communication breakdown and into the concept of communication of warm feelings.

Imagine a young married couple, very much in love, who are in a beautiful log cabin in the mountains. It is forty degrees below zero outside, but they are snug and warm, sitting on the chesterfield, holding onto each other and sitting in front of a big log fire. Everything is perfect for a while, but unfortunately the husband happens to glance around and he notices that a window in the far corner of the cabin is slightly open. He thinks to himself, "That window is letting in cold air, so I'd better go and close it." He gets up, leaves his wife and the fire and he goes to shut the window. But it is stuck! So now he has to go down to the basement and get a hammer, a chisel, and a saw, and he starts to work on the window. After about an hour he finally gets it to shut properly. He starts back to rejoin his wife, but in doing so, he passes the cabin door and he feels a draught coming in because the door is not fitting well. So he gets to work on the door. Two hours later the door is fixed, but to his dismay, the cabin is now freezing because the log fire has gone out. The warmth has gone. He had tried to fix it and ended up losing it. The answer was not to go weather-proofing the cabin, but to throw another log on the fire! Then the young couple would never have gotten cold in the first place.

Marriage is like that. As long as we fuel our warm feelings for each other and focus on the good things about each other, our marriage will never grow cold. But as soon as we start weather-proofing our marriage, we are automatically getting colder and colder. If we do not stop, the fire of our love will seem to go out. When we are in love, we see only the beauty in each other, and we love what we see. But as soon as we begin to mentally dissect our spouse, we are in trouble.

For example, I'm saying to myself, "Susan is a wonderful person. But she would be perfect if only she would be more tidy around the house. So I better get her to work on that." Meanwhile Susan is saying, "Bill is such a great guy. But I wish he would wipe his muddy boots before he comes into the house. Then he would be just perfect. While I am on the subject though, it would be nice if he would stop chewing his food with his mouth open. And another thing, I hate the way he always says, 'yes' to his mother." Meanwhile, Bill is adding to his list of flaws, and so both Bill and Susan have started weather-proofing. They are now determined to transform each other into their own idea of the perfect spouse, instead of accepting the other just as they are, which means seeing one's partner as a gift from God. They forget to nurture their love as their most precious possession. They start to accuse each other of being imperfect, and then both react by feeling unaccepted and unloved. A deep hurt takes over, and the fire is slowly going out in the log cabin. Love and warmth have been abandoned. The answer is to stop weather-proofing. Whenever we become aware of an irritating habit in our spouse, we should simply overlook it. Deliberately tell yourself, "I could be really bothered by what my spouse is doing right now, but I refuse to be bothered. I choose to overlook it." I guarantee that if you do this, you will be filled by a surging feeling of tenderness and compassion and love for your spouse. You will be overtaken by the warmth of the big picture. You will recall your spouse as he or she was when you were courting, and you will whisper a prayer of gratitude to God for the gift of this treasure. Suddenly the perceived flaw will seem very insignificant and not worth your irritation. It is that simple.

Couples who "work" at their marriages are making a fatal mistake. They are more likely to work their marriage to death than to save it. Far better to recover their good feelings, and then the so-called problems in the marriage will look very much smaller, because the couple will feel close and united. They will discover that together they can take on anything, together they are a team, and together in the Holy Spirit, they can again be of one mind and one heart.

A couple of months ago, a patient of mine told me of a very wise lady lawyer in Ontario. She worked in family law, and one day a very angry lady of about thirty came in and demanded an immediate separation from her husband. She also said, "I'm so angry with him, I want to hurt him as much as I possibly can, within the law." The lawyer thought for a moment and said, "Well, I can certainly arrange for a legal separation, but it will take about a month for me to prepare the documents." The lady looked disappointed, but then said, "Well do you have any suggestions as to what I could do between now and then to really get back at him." The lawyer said, "Sure. Why don't you go home and drive him nuts. Go home and serve him. Make him his favourite meals, iron his shirts perfectly, keep the house spotless, put on your most attractive clothes, be utterly charming and I guarantee he will really come to know what he will be missing when you leave." The lady thought that was a perfect idea and off she went. One month later she and her husband walked into the lawyer's office, smiling and holding hands, and the lady said, "I want to thank you for saving our marriage. I thought I was going to drive him nuts by serving him, and I did. But I saw the look of deep love and hurt and longing in his eyes. My heart remembered the love I once had for him, and I could not stop it from coming back again. Not only that, but he responded by starting to serve me, and I loved it. We don't need that separation now and we never ever will."

The secret here, and the wise lawyer knew it, was that it does not have to take "two to tango." If only one partner becomes the best and holiest spouse he or she can be, as God intended, then very often the other will respond wonderfully. The goodness of one spouse usually brings out the very best in the other.

St. Francis certainly embraced the sublime perfection of love and lived it. As St. Bonaventure wrote, "Loving compassion made him regard everything with affection, but especially the souls which Jesus Christ redeemed with his Precious Blood. If he saw one of them being stained with sin, he grieved with such heartfelt pity that he seemed to be in travail over them continually, like a mother in Christ." How many spouses grieve over the sin of their partner? If they did, they would pray for their partner's soul and gently call him or her to greater holiness. St. Francis wrote a poem for the friars entitled *The Praises of the VIRTUES*, and in it he said this: "Holy love puts to shame all the temptations of the devil and the flesh and all natural fear." St. Francis understood perfectly what we are told in Scripture, "There is no fear in love, but perfect love casts out fear. For fear has to do with punishment, and whoever fears has not reached perfection in love" (1 John 4:18).

St. Francis loved with a powerful generosity. As St. Bonaventure said, "He was kind and gentle by nature and the love of Christ merely intensified this. His soul melted at the sight of the poor or infirm and where he could not offer material assistance, he lavished his affection."

As Benedict Joseph Labre said, "To love God you need three hearts in one, a heart of *fire* for God and a heart of *flesh* for your neighbour and a heart of *bronze* for yourself."

Jesus himself told Catherine of Siena, "The important thing is not to love me for your own sake, or yourself for your own sake, or your neighbour for your own sake, but to love me for myself, yourself for myself, and your neighbour for myself. Divine love cannot suffer to share with any earthly love."

St. Joseph Cafasso said, "We were born to love, we live to love and we will die to love still more."

The greatest of modern Franciscan saints, St. Maximilian Kolbe, said, "The knight of the Immaculate does not confine his heart to himself, nor to his family, relatives, neighbours, friends or countrymen, but embraces the whole world, each and every soul, because, without exception, they have all been redeemed by the blood of Jesus. They are all our brothers. He desires true happiness for everyone, enlightenment in faith, cleansing from sin, inflaming of their hearts with love toward God and love toward neighbour, without restriction."

Often we forget that men and women are somewhat different in their love needs. Dr. John Gray, in his book *Men are from Mars, Women are from Venus,* beautifully describes the *primary* love needs of men and women. There are six primary needs for men and six for women. Actually both men and women ultimately need all of these but if the primary needs are not met first, then neither can be fulfilled by the other six.

WOMAN	MAN
1. Caring	1. Trust
2. Understanding	2. Acceptance
3. Respect	3. Appreciation
4. Devotion	4. Admiration
5. Validation	5. Approval
6. Reassurance	6. Encouragement

1. *Caring versus Trust.* When a man shows heartfelt caring for his wife she feels loved. So she is confident in trusting him. When she shows trust in him, she shows that she believes he is doing his best. When he feels trusted, he responds by being more caring.

2. *Understanding versus Acceptance.* When a man listens without judgement and shows understanding of her feelings she learns to accept him. When she takes him as he is without trying to change him, he feels accepted and so he finds it easier to listen to her and show more understanding.

3. *Respect versus Appreciation.* When a husband acknowledges his wife's rights, wishes and needs she feels respected and so will find it easy to appreciate him. When she does this he knows his efforts are valued by her and so he learns to respect her more.

4. *Devotion versus Admiration.* When a man conveys his complete fidelity to her as a wife she thrives because she feels cherished and special. When she feels she is number one in his life then she admires him. In admiring him she regards him with wonder and delight and so he feels that admiration. In being admired he feels secure enough to devote himself even more to his wife's well being.

5. *Validation versus Approval.* A wise husband accepts and validates his wife's feelings. He does not argue with her feelings or discount them. She is then able to give him the approval he needs. Her approval acknowledges his goodness and his competence. Approval does not mean she always has to agree with him. Approval means she sees the good intentions behind what he says or does. When he enjoys her approval, he finds it easy to validate her feelings.

6. *Reassurance versus Encouragement.* If a husband shows he cares, understands, respects, validates, and is devoted, she then feels secure in his love. This reassurance needs to be given by him over and over again. Her reassurance battery needs constant recharging. If she does feel reassured, she will delight in giving her husband encouragement. This gives him hope and confidence in his abilities as a protector and provider and so he happily gives her the reassurance she craves for.

This is a very perceptive summary of Dr. Gray's clinical experience working with couples. It fits with the kind of loving which Jesus asks of us as Catholic married couples.

Jesus said, "You will know them by their fruits" (Matt. 7:16). Likewise, we recognize love in a person by its fruits. The fruits of love are also visible in the family which lives in love. It does not take a genius to know when a husband and wife love each other with a holy love. This couple exhibits deep affection, high regard and patient acceptance of each other. The name of the Lord comes quickly to their lips as they bless his Holy Name both for their joy and for their sorrow. There is a cheerfulness about them in all their circumstances, and a solidarity even in their misfortunes. They welcome the graces of the sacraments as often as they can, daily if possible, and they refuse to tolerate serious sin in their souls, but rush to confession to make things right with the Lord. They welcome Jesus as the unseen guest in their house, and they welcome him in the person of strangers.

The children in such a home know they are loved. They behave as though they are loved. They are secure in their own uniqueness, because their parents affirm them. They believe in the love of God for them because they witness their parents' love in action. Love is real for them. They know their prayers and they love the Eucharist and the stories of the saints. They are confident in their relationships with each other and with their friends, able to give love and to receive it. They are never robbed of their holy innocence by being given adult knowledge while still only children. They know how to play.

Fr. Ken Roberts tells a wonderful story of an encounter he had with little Johnny at his First Communion. He asked him whom he loved most in all the world. "My dog" the boy replied. "How much do you love your dog? Can you show me?" Johnny extended his arms and said, "This much." Father Ken asked him to look at Jesus on the large crucifix behind the altar. Jesus had his arms outstretched too. "Do you love your dog that much, Johnny?" Johnny looked up at Jesus and nodded, keeping his arms outstretched. "If you really do love your dog that much, I can tell you how to prove it. Why don't you give up your friends, your family, your nice clean bed and everything and in fact, give up even being a little boy. I'll wave a magic wand and you can become a dog just like yours. You can live in a kennel and eat bones and dog biscuits." Johnny shook his head, "No. I don't love my dog that much." He lowered his arms. Fr. Ken then said, "But Jesus loves you that much. He loves you enough to become a boy, to talk like a boy, to eat like a boy, to play like a boy and to die like a man."

What Fr. Ken was saying is that the cross is the greatest sign of Jesus' love for us as human beings. He became one of us and died as one of us. "No one has greater love than this, to lay down one's life for one's friends" (John 15:13). But Jesus is God and he can show even greater love than that. If little Johnny didn't love his dog enough to become a dog, he certainly did not love his dog enough to become a dog biscuit! The greatest sign of God's love for us is that Jesus became our food, our daily bread, the food of our bodies and the food of our souls.

The ideal Catholic family moves, lives and breathes in a bubble of love. Its members absorb it and exude it. Love is the log on the fire which keeps the home fire burning brightly. It gives off warmth to the entire family, husband, wife and children, and gives off warmth in hospitality to all who come into their home. Love makes room for Christ, gives him his rightful kingship of the home, and it consoles him.

Love, indeed, is the home fire burning in God's human family. Parents must gather their children around them and sit close to that fire, basking in its warm glow. It will sustain a family no matter how cold the world outside may become.

As Solzhenitsyn wrote in his book *The First Circle,* "The simple words 'Do you love me?' and 'I love you,' said with glances or with murmuring lips, fill the soul with quiet rejoicing."

"So faith, hope and love remain, these three, but the greatest of these is love" (1 Cor. 13:13).

CHAPTER 7

Sexuality: Playing in the Garden of the Lord

"I belong to my love and his desire is for me."
(Song of Sol. 7:10)

This chapter is not for children since they are not ready for adult things. It is intended for teenagers and for mature Catholic adults only. "When I was a child, I spoke like a child, thought like a child, reasoned as a child, but when I became an adult, I put an end to childish ways" (1 Cor. 13:11). It may surprise some that this chapter is not about sex, but rather is about our holy sexuality, which is a very different thing. Sex is simply biology and human beings have never had problems with knowing how to do it. Sex is an instinct and so we come to it naturally. *It does not need to be taught.* The focus here is on the principle that our sexuality, like all other things, is only properly fulfilled when we place it at the service of God's perfect plan for us. Understanding sexuality means understanding what it means to be fully male and fully female, and an appreciation of this sexuality influences everything we do and share together as man and woman. Seen in that light, sexuality *does need to be taught*.

Some of us labour under the misapprehension that "It's my body and I can do what I like with it." But that is like saying, "It's my car and I can drive it into thirty people standing at a bus stop if I want." Just as we have to behave responsibly and obey the rules when we drive a car, so we have to understand what God intended when he created us to be sexual beings. He gave us our sexual nature and he designed it. Surely, he has the right to tell us how to use it in a holy way. Sadly, many of us misuse this wondrous gift, and that is a disorder.

The first thing to understand is that it was God's idea to create us as male and female. "And God saw everything that he had made, and behold, it was very good" (Gen. 1:31). God was pleased with his miraculous work, which separated humanity into two distinct sexes. He intended man and woman to complement each other. Notice that Scripture does not say that he created us to be male and male, or female and female. There was never any same-sex or homosexual intention in God's creative plan for our sexuality. He decreed that only male and female should have the right and the privilege to come together in sexual relationship. As one good priest put it, "God created Adam and Eve. He did not create Adam and Steve!" "God **blessed** them and said, 'Be fruitful and multiply and fill the earth'" (Gen. 1:28). God's blessing on sexual love was therefore only given to male and female in marriage, signified and sacramentalised by God's blessing. No other variations are deserving of God's blessing.

Prior to the Fall, Adam and Eve lived perfectly in the Will of God. They were naked but, being totally innocent and pure of heart, they looked at each other without any trace of lust. After the tragedy of the Fall, they lost that childlike innocence and became "aware" of their nakedness. Now they were ashamed. "Then the eyes of both of them were opened and they realised they were naked" (Gen. 3:7). For the first time, Adam and Eve experienced the sadness of lust and they tried to cover themselves with fig leaves. After God had pronounced the dreadful outcome of the Original Sin upon all of the human race, the very first thing he did was to make clothes for Adam and Eve. "Yahweh God made tunics of skins for the man and his wife and clothed them" (Gen. 3:21). God understood their new propensity for lust, and in making clothes for them he was teaching them the great value and necessity of modesty as a God-like virtue.

We too suffer the consequences of the Original Sin to which we are heirs, and so we are always vulnerable to lust. As husband and wife we must lovingly embrace modesty and we should never dress in such a way as to provoke or invite lustful thoughts from another person. Our nakedness is intended for our spouse and our spouse alone.

Scripture leads us to a second conclusion. Our sexuality is not simply the satisfaction of a basic animal instinct. Human sexual relations are never meant to be reduced to the mindless copulation of cattle in a field. God created our sexuality to be holy, and love-making is intended to be a sacred act which fulfils God's perfect plan for humanity. Therefore we need to come to a knowledge of how we can enjoy our sexual relationships in a manner pleasing to God and which cooperates with his plan. We also need to know what violates that plan and offends our good God. It is clear that, just because we get married, we cannot assume that we are allowed now to do anything we please with our bodies or with our spouse's body. Like all of the other gifts God has given us on this earth, we can use our sexuality for good or for evil.

It helps to clarify what is good and what is evil to take a look at God's purpose in giving us a sexual nature. He designed our sexuality for two vitally important objectives which we must never deliberately nullify.

Firstly, it is intended to be the means by which we and God create a new life. God has wonderfully chosen to give to us, mere creatures, the power to create in cooperation with him, to share in the awesome miracle, which by rights is reserved to him alone. Together, a couple forms their child's body, and God honours that by breathing an immortal soul into this little body at the very moment of conception, a soul destined to live forever. Therefore, anything we do to frustrate that design of God is a violation of God's primary purpose for our sexuality, and is a very serious matter indeed. Chapter 8 will discuss the whole question of contraception and why it violates this primary purpose of our sexual nature in the sight of God.

Secondly, God wants our sexual union to be a powerful expression of our deep love for one another: "and the two shall become one flesh" (Gen. 2:24). Therefore, when I get married, my body is no longer mine. My wife's body is no longer hers. But at the same time, I do not own my wife's body, and she does not own mine. Our two bodies become one flesh. Our bodies become united in a mysterious and beautiful melding which is symbolic of God's love for himself and for the world. It is a solemn matter of union, not a trivial matter of who owns whom.

In Scripture, God explains his covenant with us in the language of marriage. Jesus refers to the Church as his bride. Jesus himself sanctified marriage as a Sacrament at the marriage feast of Cana. St. Paul tells husbands to love their wives in the same way as Christ loves his Church. Sexuality, then, becomes so much more than mere erotic satisfaction, more than mere genital stimulation, and much, much more than mere orgasmic climax. It is a holy privilege, lovingly provided by a loving God. Marriage is a vocation, held in the highest esteem by God, and thus our sexual union is so sublime to God that he conveys his eternal agreement with humanity in the language of sexuality. Solomon's "Song of Songs" in Scripture is a passionate love song which uses the powerful images of human love. God's love for us is so all-consuming, that he speaks to us with the passion of a bridegroom to his bride. "As a young man marries a virgin, your Builder shall marry you. As a bridegroom rejoices in his bride so shall your God rejoice in you" (Isa. 62:5).

As has been pointed out before, marriage is not a contract, nor is it between two people only. It is a covenant between three people: husband, wife and God. Therefore any sexual act, indeed any sexual act, which cuts God out of the agreement violates the covenant, and is a serious disorder. In other words, it is a sin. This is why sex is intended by God to be reserved for marriage and only for marriage, because in this Sacrament the couple makes a covenant with him, one by which God, husband and wife become co-creators. God has given our bodies a *nuptial purpose,* and that nuptial purpose can only be legitimately fulfilled, in the sexual sense, in a truly permanent bond of total commitment of man to woman and woman to man and both to God. This bond is Sacramental Marriage. Sex outside of marriage is so sinful, precisely because it is not a permanent commitment. In fact, it is no commitment at all. It rejects the original intention of God and excludes him from their sexual interaction.

We can begin to understand and accept what is holy and what is not holy in a Catholic marriage if we keep in mind these two principal aspects of human sexuality:

1. Procreation
2. An expression of mutual love between husband and wife.

PROCREATION: Every act of sexual intercourse must be open to the *possibility* that God may choose to bless it with the conception of a new human being. Therefore, any contraceptive interference, whether it be by means of the barrier methods, such as condoms, diaphragm and vaginal foam, or the birth control pill or the "morning-after pill" or sterilisation or *coitus interruptus* (unnatural ejaculation outside of the vagina), is a deliberate violation of God's design. If we use these artificial means, then we cut God entirely out of our sexual union. We buy out his share in the covenant. Actually it is more like a hostile takeover. I am telling God to back off, that this is an affair between me and my wife, and that there is no room for God in our sexual lives. Not only that, I am making a statement to my wife, and she in turn is making the same statement to me: I am saying that my erotic sexual satisfaction comes before all things, especially children. I am only interested in sex for the sake of sex, and my spouse is only there to please me. I no longer see my spouse as a temple of the Holy Spirit, whom I must love and serve. I am blind to the wonderful truth that it was God himself who brought us together. I am telling my wife that I refuse to give her my entire self in love. I am withholding my life-giving seed from her. She, in turn, is telling me that she is refusing to give her entire self to me. She is withholding her life-receiving and life-nurturing self from me. Our loving is a sham. I am no longer thinking of her and her joy. I am only thinking of me and my own selfish orgasm. She has now been reduced in my mind to a mere sex toy, that is to say, only a body which I use for my own pleasure. I no longer see her as God's specially selected gift to me. I no longer envision her as a sacred temple of the Holy Spirit and she is no longer a potential mother in my eyes. Such a man as much as says, "I want it and I want it now and you will give it to me." He has lost all sense of what true love means. His idea of love is merely animal, and it no longer has room for tenderness or self-donation, and certainly not self-sacrifice. This couple is cheating itself of the greatest joy of sex, which is to forget oneself and to enter into the soul of the other.

Some people try to excuse contraception by saying that the earth is overpopulated. By contracepting, they believe they are being "responsible." That is far from true. If all of the people currently living on the planet stood shoulder to shoulder, they would only fill the state of Maine in the United States. All of them could live in the State of Texas and have a detached house with its own front and back yard. God asked us to multiply and fill the earth, so is it not reasonable that he would provide the earth with adequate resources for feeding his children? The truth is that the wealthy nations of the world spend enough money on armaments in two weeks to feed the entire planet for one whole year. If there are children starving today, it is not God's fault. It is our fault for refusing to share our food with the poor. As a sinful race, we prefer guns to food.

MUTUAL LOVE: There is no doubt that our sexuality is a wonderful way (not the only way, of course) by which to express love between husband and wife. This mutual love, if it is to be authentic, demands self-giving. It only has its true meaning when two people give themselves totally to the other, not when one "takes" the other. True love does not sexually exploit the other, or dominate the other, nor does it use or abuse the other for one's own selfish satisfaction. It never demands that the other do something which he or she finds immoral or distasteful.

Sexual foreplay and climax can be a glimpse of paradise, if they are focussed on one's spouse. However, if these are centred on self, then they become the worst kind of immaturity, deforming my spouse from a beautiful person to be cherished, into an object for my own gratification. The human body is a temple of the Holy Spirit, a holy vessel for the indwelling of God, and a sanctuary for the immortal soul. Thus if your body is holy it is possible to sin against it, and since your spouse's body is holy, it is possible to sin against it also. Therefore, if I am to be a true lover, I must discard the notion that anything goes. God has a right to tell us what we can and cannot do with our bodies, and indeed he does. It is not fair to accuse the Church of interfering when she teaches us what to do or not do in our bedrooms. The Church is only carrying out its mandate from God to consistently teach his truth. It can do no less.

Many men think that their spouses must do whatever they want them to do. They justify this by saying that it gives them pleasure, as if pleasure was the deciding factor when it comes to right and wrong. A little thought will show us that this is absurd. If sin did not give pleasure, why would anyone bother committing it? It is precisely because we so often derive pleasure from a sinful act that Satan is so successful in tempting us. Human pleasure is not the deciding factor. God's pleasure is. Just because it feels good does not make it good. What makes our loving good is if it is pleasing to our loving Father in Heaven, who made our bodies for a holy purpose. Anything less means, once again, that I reduce my spouse to an object for my own use and pleasure. The other is no longer seen as having dignity, as being worthy of my total giving, as being someone to treasure or cherish. Satan tempts us with fleeting pleasure, but we often forget that God also "tempts" us. He tempts us with joy, everlasting joy.

If I gave someone a new coffee table as a gift and that someone proceeded to scratch it and disfigure it with a penknife, would I not have a right to feel hurt? God gave us a beautiful body. If we disfigure it with unholy acts, does God not also have the right to feel hurt? I think he does.

It is important to understand that men and women are different, not simply in their physical, sexual appearance, but also in the nature of their needs when it comes to sexuality. By that I mean that when a man expresses a sexual desire, he needs to feel desired by his wife. If she seems to make too many non-sexual demands on him and then withholds sexual loving from him, he feels used and abused. A woman, on the other hand, links her sexuality to her need for security, protection and intimacy. If her husband does not provide these things, then she feels used and abused by his sexual demands. In my practice I often hear a man say to his wife, "I feel hurt when you dodge me or reject my sexual advances." Likewise, I often hear a woman say, "Well, I feel angry and used when you ignore me all day and then grab me at bedtime." The answer to this problem should be fairly obvious.

Men need to know that if they keep the romance alive in their marriage, the sexual life will take care of itself. A man should do all kinds of little things every day to let his wife know that he loves her. Of course, he should tell her he loves her, over and over again. He should buy her flowers, not just on her birthday, but for all kinds of occasions, sometimes for no other reason than to tell her that he loves her. He should touch her, hug her, and kiss her without it having to end up in bed. Very importantly he should spend time listening to her. A wise man always accepts his wife's feelings even if he does not always understand them. Most important of all, they should pray together and ask for God's grace in their Sacrament. Do all of this, and I guarantee you a happy and fulfilling life together, part of which will be a happy and fulfilling sexual life together. I once knew a couple who were so filled with gratitude to God for his gift of sexuality to them that they prayed to him for grace before every act of love, and then together they thanked him afterwards. That couple truly understood their relationship with the Lord and believed that they owed everything to him, especially their sexual joy. They knew, that in the sexual act, three people make love, not just two. God delights in this holy union, and as a man and woman make love to one another, he is also loving both of them.

Most couples go into marriage with different degrees of sexual sophistication. One probably wants more than the other understands or is willing to go along with at first. This is perfectly natural and should never be taken to mean that they are sexually incompatible. Both partners are *teachers* for each other in the sexual area. They must listen to each other. They should be eager to learn about each other. They should joyfully teach each other about what makes them feel good, and what makes them feel loved. When they learn to delight each other, their sexual life will be always new and gratifying, and God will be pleased in their Sacrament.

We live in a world of sexual obsession. We teach sex education to little children, who are not ready for adult things. We extol recreational sex and reduce real love to insignificance. We portray sex without shame on television, movies, and in magazines. We regard virginity as a sign of inhibition or neurosis, as though it were something to be rid of as quickly as possible, if we ever hope to be "normal." If the sinful world had its way, the entire planet would be in a state of permanent sexual arousal. Infidelity is no more remarkable than having a cup of coffee, and perversion is simply a matter of harmless sexual preference. Sterile sex is applauded, while pregnancy is regarded as a failure of responsibility.

Compare the above scenario with the purity and chastity of the Christian sexual ethic. A young man and young woman are to rejoice in their youthfulness. They are to value their virginity as God's greatest gift to them. They jealously cherish that state and guard it as the perfect wedding gift, which will be lovingly donated to their spouse on their wedding night, the night of nights, which has been solemnly blessed by God in a Sacrament. As the young couple exchange their gifts of virginity, they enter deeply into the mystery of one another and into the mystery of God. These two mysteries can never be fully explored. The first takes a lifetime, while the second takes an eternity.

However, each sexual act is a unique encounter in itself. Some lovemaking will be so sublime it will be beyond words. Some encounters will be filled with humour and laughter. This is sexual play, and no doubt God laughs with us in such happy moments. Some acts will seem like a failure. Accidents do happen. With all the best control in the world, a husband may ejaculate too early, or a wife may not be able to have a climax. Some couples make the mistake of treating these events as major world-shattering tragedies. That is a mistake. The world of sex is a constant learning experience and by far the best response is to lighten up, laugh at the mistake and learn from it. There are no pass or fail grades being handed out.

Many women, contrary to what the world of pornography would have us believe, are simply not able to have an intra-vaginal orgasm. That is to say, they cannot reach climax during actual intercourse. This is due to the fact that the thrusting action of the penis in the vagina is not causing adequate friction of the woman's clitoris. In such instances, a woman can only experience her own climax through manual stimulation of the clitoris by her husband. This is not a forbidden thing to do. In fact, it is a necessary thing to do since, by having an orgasm, the woman is relieved of the considerable pelvic congestion (swelling of the pelvic organs with blood) which has built up during foreplay. Failure to provide that release can leave the wife with a deep, uncomfortable, and even painful pelvic condition, which can take hours to subside. The loving husband who has taken the trouble to learn about his wife will see to it that she achieves this release. This can be done before or after intercourse, which is where the husband must *always* reach his own orgasm. He must always release his semen into his wife's vagina. No other form of ejaculation is acceptable to God. The semen is a man's seed and the seed must be planted in the right soil, not discarded. God will decide whether the seed will bear fruit or not.

Foreplay is often fraught with problems for some couples. Basically, foreplay is the time of sexual play, when a couple rejoices in arousing one another, stimulating one another and elevating the level of arousal higher and higher, until both are prepared for intercourse itself. A selfish and utterly thoughtless man dispenses with foreplay and simply launches himself into immediate intercourse. Such a man is only obsessed with his own selfish orgasm and rushes to achieve it as quickly as possible and get it over with. He never spares a thought for what this does to his wife. The problem is that, since his wife is not anywhere close to being aroused, her vagina will not be lubricated by her natural secretions, and so the intercourse becomes a "dry" encounter, which is very painful for her. Of course, the even bigger problem is that he obviously does not know how to love, and he thinks his wife is there only for his own relief.

Spouses always have different levels of sexual sophistication. One may want to indulge in some type of foreplay which the other finds unsavoury or maybe even a bit disgusting. The rule here is simple. In bed, no one should be made to do what he or she does not want to do. Otherwise, this is coercion, and coercion violates one's spouse. Some foreplay falls into the category of perversion, and this is absolutely forbidden, no matter if even both partners desire it. For example, sado-masochistic acts are sinful, as is bondage, group sex, and many other activities. We must never forget that our sexual loving is meant to be holy and should always be governed by what is pleasing to God and by a never-failing respect for the dignity of our partner. Apart from that, we are allowed and entitled to enjoy our foreplay. The human body has not been marked off into zones which are acceptable and zones which are forbidden, as in green for "go ahead" and red for "do not touch." We can touch what we want, caress what we want, and kiss what we want. All God asks is that the husband's climax must always take place inside his wife's vagina. The reason for this is simply that God is thereby given permission to decide whether to open the womb or not. This is a privilege reserved to God and God alone.

Many couples expect that, once married, they can indulge in sex as often as they want. This is an unrealistic expectation. As with all good things in life, there has to be a sense of balance and proportion. What if one of the partners is sick? It would be cruel to insist on sex at such a time. What if the wife is in the early stages of recovering from childbirth? What about when a couple is apart for any reason? Each would expect to save himself and herself, until they were reunited, thereby demonstrating both fidelity and self-control. Not only that, but when a couple is planning their family and using Natural Family Planning (N.F.P.), there is an unavoidable fertility period of a few days each month. Abstinence will need to be observed during these days, if the couple has prayerfully discerned that there are grave reasons for not conceiving a child at this time. Abstinence need not be a burden. On the contrary, it is an opportunity for the couple to love each other in non-sexual ways. It is a chance for the husband to learn, with awe and reverence, the wonderful rhythm of his wife's hormonal cycle, to rejoice in the miracle of her womanhood, and to show his true love for her by his willingness to sacrifice mere sexual gratification in the interest of a greater love. Through abstinence both husband and wife demonstrate to each other that their love for the other is greater than their love for themselves.

In today's society, pornography is everywhere. There are many, especially men, who justify the use of erotic material by saying it helps them to get aroused. There is no room whatsoever in a Catholic home for pornography. Pornography is, in and of itself, a disgusting abomination to God, and it is always sinful. When a man or woman buys erotic magazines or watches so-called adult movies, he or she is contributing to the exploitation of both women and men. Again, it reduces the human person, the image of God, to a mere sex object. The sexual act is a totally private encounter between a husband, his wife and God. It was never intended by God as a public spectacle. Anyone who watches such displays is always going to be illicitly aroused, and that is a grave sin. Pornography brings the image of another person into the exclusive relationship of husband and wife, and as such constitutes an act of adultery in the mind.

Pornography instills in your mind the lie that you have a right to dominate. It encourages masturbation, which is a solitary sexual sin. This is particularly true about television shows. Their erotic images imprint deeply on your mind and can rush up to the surface to arouse you even many years later. The dirty movie is not over when it is over. It is replayed again and again in your mind, and it is waiting to grab you in an unguarded moment. By looking at these things, you are really saying to your spouse that she is not enough for you.

By the same argument, there is no place for indulging in illicit sexual fantasies when you are making love to your spouse. Some people will appear to be making love to their spouse while at the same time fantasising that they are making love to someone else. This is nothing short of mental adultery. Jesus himself said, "Whoever looks at a woman with lust in his heart has already committed adultery with her in his heart" (Matt. 5:28). So Jesus is very clear on this activity. It is very displeasing to him. It is indeed a mortal sin, and it is a betrayal of your wife, who believes that you are making love to her, when in fact, you are making love to a fantasy in your own head.

"The husband should give to his wife her conjugal rights and likewise the wife to her husband. For the wife does not rule over her own body, but the husband does; likewise the husband does not rule over his own body, but the wife does. Do not refuse one another except perhaps by agreement for a season, that you may devote yourselves to prayer; but then come together again, lest Satan tempt you through lack of self-control" (1 Cor. 7:3-5). This is a very important observation made by St. Paul regarding the sexual privilege of marriage. We are *not* to regard our body as our own, but rather, we should be generously available to our spouse if she or he expresses a need, even if we do not feel like it. This is a call to charity and self-donation. Our God-given gift of sexuality, like all other gifts, carries with it a burden of responsibility towards one another. Many spouses cruelly withhold sexual favours as some sort of punishment, but where both partners are healthy, this is a sin. Just as love is a decision, so also is lovemaking. Certainly, a couple can abstain, but it must be by mutual agreement. I realize this is a very contentious issue these days, but St. Paul is very clear on the point. Not only that, but by refusing to give my spouse his or her legitimate sexual rights, I am exposing my spouse to the temptation of finding satisfaction in sinful alternatives, such as masturbation or, God forbid, adultery.

Many people take exception to the Church's teaching on sexuality and say, "The church has no right to come into my bedroom." The answer to that is "yes" and "no." The Catholic Church is the one true apostolic Church instituted by Jesus, the keys to the Kingdom being given to Peter, the first Pope. Jesus therefore entrusted to his Church the task of preserving and preaching his truth and he commands that we be obedient to the Holy father and the Magisterium, which is the teaching authority of the Church. This is the same thing as being obedient to Jesus himself.

We cannot dissent from the teaching Church and still call ourselves Catholic. The Church is not a self-serve salad bar, where one only eats what tastes good and ignores the rest. The Church has no option but to teach God's truth. Basically, the Church only asks three things from us in our intimate married lives:

1. We are to give ourselves to each other unselfishly and exclusively.
2. We must never abuse each other's minds or bodies.
3. Every sexual act must be open to the possibility of God's gift of a conception, and so if intercourse occurs, the husband's orgasm must not occur outside of the vagina.

Perhaps the best and most reliable rule for us to follow in leading a holy sexual life, is to ask ourselves this question. If Jesus came into our bedroom right now, would he approve of what we are doing or would we feel ashamed? The truth is that Jesus is present in your bedroom, not the Church. He loves you and he wants you to be happy with each other, and that can only happen if you are enjoying a truly holy sexual union as part of a truly holy marriage. Then when you laugh with your wife, you will know that God is laughing with you. Sexual love is playing in the Garden of the Lord. It is a profound ecstasy which God delights to give to us on this earth, but we must never forget that it is the Lord's Garden.

CHAPTER 8

Contraception: The Refusal of Blessing

"I am offering you life or death,
blessing or curse. Choose life
then, so that you and your
descendants may live in the love
of Yahweh, your God."
                    (Deut. 30:19)

If we are to properly articulate a set of objective moral standards concerning the problem of contraception, then our first duty is to consult the word of God, as revealed to us in Scripture. For this I am indebted to the marvellous work of Kimberly Hahn, a convert to the faith and a wonderful biblical scholar.

Right from the beginning, we discern that marriage was God's idea and that sex was God's idea. "God created man in the image of himself, in the image of God he created him, male and female he created them. God blessed them (i.e. God blessed their marriage union), and God said to them, 'Be fruitful and multiply and fill the earth'" (Gen. 1:27-28).

First of all, it was God himself who presided over the wedding of Adam and Eve. Therefore, for any other marriage to be valid, it too must be blessed by God. That is why marriage is a Sacrament. It is a sign of God's witness to our union with one another.

Secondly, it was not until God had blessed them, that Adam and Eve were commanded to multiply and fill the earth. Therefore, we can only legitimately enjoy the sexual act within the state of marriage. Sex outside of marriage is not, and never will be, blessed by God.

Thirdly, God insisted that marriage would have both a unitive and a procreative function, and that these functions were not to be frustrated. God's first decree was that we multiply and have children, and we are to take this command very seriously indeed. While God told Adam and Eve to multiply, he did not stop there, but commanded that the earth be filled. He did not say we should stop reproducing when there are four billion or five billion or six billion people on the planet. He gave no direction as to any end point whatsoever. He desired that the earth be filled, because he wanted countless souls, who would be given the awesome opportunity to join him forever in paradise. God never suggested that we would ever have a population crisis. That is a myth we have invented for ourselves.

In his infinite providence God said, "See I have given you every plant yielding seed that is upon the face of the earth and every tree with seed in its fruit: you shall have them for food" (Gen. 1:29). This was a promise from Yahweh that the earth would yield food in plenty, and in sufficiency for its population, even if we were ever to literally fill the earth. Contrary to today's alarmist secular experts, we are a long way from filling the planet. If there is a food problem now, it is due to our failure to share with underdeveloped countries, because we fear loss of profit on food prices. Since God intended the plants to be for all of his children, it is a grave sin for men to monopolise food and to engineer unfair profit by it. Food is not a man-made commodity. It is a universal *right* for all humanity, and thus we have a moral duty to feed one another and to see that no one in the world goes hungry.

"Yahweh God said, 'It is not right that man should be alone. I shall make him a helper'" (Gen. 2:18). "Yahweh God fashioned the rib he had taken from the man into a woman, and brought her to the man. And the man said, 'This one at last is bone of my bone and flesh of my flesh. She is to be called woman, because she was taken from man.' This is why a man leaves his father and mother and becomes attached to his wife and they become one flesh" (Gen. 2:22-24). It is God who blesses the sexual union of man and woman in marriage, and he wishes that union to be fruitful. "God blessed them and God said to them, 'Be fruitful and multiply and fill the earth and subdue it: And have dominion over the fish of the sea and over the birds of the air and over every living thing that moves upon the earth'" (Gen. 1:28). Therefore, while it is true that animals indulge in sexual intercourse, the sexual act for man was to have more significance than that of mere animals. Man was given dominion over the animals, and that includes man's sexual nature as well as his intellect. Animal intercourse is mere copulation. Human intercourse is holy union.

When Adam and Eve ate the apple and committed the Original Sin, God laid a curse on them, and the fullness of his blessing was taken away. "To the woman he said, 'I shall give you intense pain in childbearing, you will give birth to your children in pain. Your desire will be for your husband and he will dominate you'" (Gen. 3:16). Adam and Eve lost their innocent nature and were now condemned to a sin-nature. God prophesied the "battle of the sexes" as one of the consequences of their sin, which has pitted male and female against each other ever since.

After the flood, God again renews his covenant with humanity and commands Noah once more to be fruitful and multiply and fill the earth. So, no matter to what degree man has moved away from him, God still wants man to cooperate with his original plan and produce numerous offspring. Having children is therefore a visible sign of God's covenant with humanity. Most couples today make the serious mistake of believing that they somehow engineer their own children. That is not what Scripture tells us. In fact, it is God who opens and/or closes the womb. It is God who decides whether an act of love will be fruitful or not and we must not steal that privilege from him.

The book of Genesis (chapters 29 and 30) recounts the story of Jacob, who wanted to marry Rachel. Rachel's father cheated Jacob, and gave him Leah, Rachel's elder sister, instead. Years later, he allowed Jacob to marry Rachel also. Now Jacob loved Rachel and did not love Leah, so, "When Yahweh saw that Leah was unloved, *he opened her womb* while Rachel remained barren" (Gen. 29:31). "Rachel, seeing that she herself gave Jacob no children, became jealous of her sister. And she said to Jacob, 'Give me children or I shall die.' This made Jacob angry with Rachel and he retorted,

'Am I in the position of God, who has denied you motherhood?'" (Gen. 30:1-2). Therefore, it was not Jacob's fault that Rachel did not conceive. It was by God's decision and God's alone. God jealously guards this right, and when we indulge in intercourse and frustrate its purpose by the use of contraceptive devices, we are usurping God's prerogative to open or close the womb. We, the mere creature, have decided to close it by ourselves. This is a grave sin, which not only violates the very essence of our sexual nature, but also violates our covenant with God.

God tells us that children are much more than simply the fruit of our sexual union with one another. He says that if we obey his voice, "You will be blessed in the town and blessed in the countryside, blessed, the offspring of your body" (Deut. 28:3-4). Therefore children are a *blessing* from God and we are to consider ourselves blessed whenever we conceive a new child, even if that pregnancy is inconvenient according to our human way of thinking. "Sons are a birthright from Yahweh, children are a reward from him. Like arrows in a warrior's hand are the sons you father when young. How blessed is the man who has filled his quiver with them" (Ps. 127:3-5). "Your wife a fruitful vine in the inner places of your house. Your children round your table like shoots of an olive tree" (Ps. 128:3). Blessed indeed are the husband and wife who are open to God's creative wisdom and who welcome new life into their family as a product of their own love and the love of God.

At this junction, it would be helpful to dwell on the biblical account of the fate of Onan because it is so often misunderstood. In ancient Israel, there was a law called the Levirate Law. This law is fully explained in the Book of Deuteronomy as follows, "If brothers live together and one of them dies childless, the dead man's wife may not marry a stranger outside the family. Her husband's brother must come to her and exercising his duty as a brother, make her his wife, and the first son she bears must assume the dead brother's name: by this means his name will not be obliterated from Israel. But if the man refuses to take his brother's wife, she must go to the elders at the gate and say, 'I have no brother-in-law willing to perpetuate his brother's name in Israel. He declines to exercise his duty as brother in my favour.' The elders of the town must summon the man and talk to him. If on appearing before them, he says, 'I refuse to take her' then the woman to whom he owes duty as brother must go up to him and in the presence of the elders, take the sandal off his foot, spit in his face and pronounce the following words, 'This is what is done to the man who refuses to restore his brother's house' and his family must henceforth be known in Israel as House of the Unshod'" (Deut. 25:5-10).

Granted that the man would be publicly humiliated, but that is all that the Levirate Law demanded. It certainly was not a capital offence. But what happened to Onan? His brother died and so to Onan fell the duty of giving children to his dead brother's wife. "But Onan knew that the offspring would not count as his, so whenever he lay with his brother's wife, he spilled his seed on the ground so as not to raise up offspring for his brother" (Gen. 38:9). What punishment did God give to Onan? He killed him! But, if the only sin Onan was guilty of was to refuse to give children to his dead brother's wife, then by the Levirate Law, he only would have had his sandal removed and his sister-in-law would spit in his face. But he was *killed* by God. Why? It could not have been for breaking the Levirate Law, so it had to be for something else. That something was the action of *spilling his seed* upon the ground. In other words, Onan violated God's directive for our sexuality that a man must never spill his semen but rather, that every ejaculation must take place naturally within his wife's vagina. Onan practised *coitus interruptus*, withdrawing himself from the woman at the moment of ejaculation, so as to avoid giving her a child. This was so serious a violation of God's intention for our sexuality that he was killed on the spot.

The Catholic Church therefore, has no option but to teach that masturbation, coitus interruptus, and other practices which allow ejaculation outside of the vagina, are grave and mortal sins. The objection might be made that times have changed, and we have a different understanding of sex. But that won't do. "Jesus Christ, the same, yesterday, today and for ever more" (Heb. 13:8). God has not changed, and his moral design remains unchanged, regardless of culture and regardless of what we might think in the twentieth century or any other century.

Yahweh has made clear what he desires from married couples. In the Book of Malachi, he chastises Judah for being faithless to the wife of his youth. He says, "Did not the one God make her, both flesh and spirit? And what does the one God require but godly children?" (Mal. 2:15). So God expects all of us who are married by sacramental covenant with him to be *faithful* to one another, and to be open to having *godly* children. Not only are we to joyfully welcome children as a blessing, but we are to raise them to be godly. That is our solemn duty before God.

"The time came for Elizabeth to have her child, and she gave birth to a son, and when her neighbours and relations heard that the Lord had lavished on her his faithful love, they shared her joy" (Luke 1:57-58). Elizabeth was rightfully filled with joy at her pregnancy, and she knew that it happened only by God's faithful love. She rightly saw her child as a blessing, not as an inconvenience or an embarrassment. Today's society regards children as a burden, an economic liability, and a hindrance to the parent's pursuit of pleasure. If I have a large family, I won't be able to take expensive holidays. I won't be able to have a summer cottage or a boat or two cars. In contrast to this, Jesus says, "Let the little children come to me for it is to such as these that the kingdom of heaven belongs" (Matt. 19:14). Jesus extols children as God's possession and blessing, and even asks us to imitate them in their innocence. Children are therefore always a blessing because they are immortal beings who will live for ever. Nothing else can compare in value to the conception of children, certainly not a career.

It should be added here that, even in the case of a pregnancy resulting from rape, drunkenness, or violence, it is God who has opened the womb. *Even that baby is a blessing from God.* We may find this difficult to understand, but God's covenant applies in all cases, not just in pregnancies for married couples. God is always faithful to his side of the covenant, even if we are not. "If we are unfaithful, he will still remain faithful for he cannot deny himself" (2 Tim. 2:13).

Recently, at a pro-life conference, the presider asked the audience if anyone believed in abortion. No hands went up. He then asked if anyone believed in abortion where the mother's life was in danger. No hands went up. Then he asked if anyone believed in abortion in the case of rape. About twenty hands went up. At that point, a woman stood up and asked if she could make a comment. She said that these twenty people had just condemned her to death. She was a product of rape, but she blessed her mother everyday for having had the courage and the love to refuse an abortion and to have the baby. She asked the irrefutable question, "Why should an innocent little baby be punished for the horrible crime of its father?" So the presider asked the question again. This time no hands went up. Is it possible to have a child that God has not planned? All children are planned by God. "He chose us in Christ before the world was made" (Eph 1:4). Your parents may say you were an accident, but to God no child is an accident.

Many people today demand the freedom to do with their bodies whatever they please. Yet the Word of God tells us that our bodies are not strictly our own. Our bodies belong to God. "Do you not realize that your body is the temple of the Holy Spirit who is in you and whom you received from God? You are not your own property then; you have been bought at a price. So use your body for the glory of God" (1 Cor. 6:19-20). "I urge you then, brothers, remembering the mercies of God, to offer your bodies as a living sacrifice, dedicated and acceptable to God; that is the kind of worship for you as sensible people. Do not model your behaviour on the contemporary world but let the renewing of your minds transform you so that you may discern for yourselves what is the will of God, what is good and acceptable and mature" (Rom. 12:1-2). Therefore, we are to offer our bodies as a living sacrifice, and it is indeed sacrificial to let the Lord open your womb. Ask any young mother. She knows that she must give her time, her work, her energy, her teaching and her love to her little ones, even when she is tired and doesn't feel like it.

God has even linked chil bearing to a woman's salvation. "Nevertheless, she will be saved by chil bearing, provided she lives a sensible life and is constant in faith, and love and holiness" (1 Tim. 2:15). A woman, then, who receives new life is actually contributing to her own salvation. St. Paul even says, "I think it is best for young widows to marry again and have children and a household to look after" (1 Tim. 5:14). This should not surprise us, since God is simply reminding us that his prime directive to Adam and Eve and Noah to be fruitful is still in full effect in the New Testament.

Many of today's women express anger at St. Paul, accusing him of being a chauvinist. They excuse their own departure from scriptural teaching on sexuality by saying that he was only speaking to the culture of his time. The truth is, that he *was* speaking to the culture of his time, and also to *all* the cultures of *all* time, including *ours*. St. Paul's words were just as shocking and challenging to the Jews of his day as they are to modern man. Culture may change according to the fads of the age, but God never changes.

God takes our duty of having children very seriously. But do not misunderstand this teaching. Neither God nor the Church insists that you have babies until you die. We are not commanded to be baby factories. On the contrary, the Church blesses Natural Family Planning (N.F.P.) as a legitimate and holy practice for couples, provided it is done lovingly and responsibly. We are indeed to have children, provided we are not infertile. That is a directive from our God. But he gives us the holy right to limit their number according to our legitimate circumstances.

This does not mean that N.F.P. can be used indiscriminately. It is not merely a substitute for artificial contraception. Our motives in avoiding pregnancy must be pure and not tainted by a selfish desire for comfort or pleasure or unreasonable financial security. God expects married couples to be generous in answering his command to "go forth and multiply and fill the earth" (Gen. 1:28). N.F.P. should only be used after much prayerful consideration by the couple and only for grave reasons.

"You must not deprive each other (of marital rights), except by *mutual consent for a limited time,* to leave yourselves free for prayer, and to come together again afterwards: otherwise, Satan may take advantage of any lack of self-control to put you to the test. I am telling you this as a concession, not an order" (1 Cor. 7:5-6). In other words, abstinence is a good thing if both partners are agreed, but the Church refuses to order couples to abstain. It is their right and theirs alone to practice N.F.P. if they wish and if there are just reasons for doing so. The question might be asked, "What is the difference between artificial contraception and Natural Family Planning, since the intention not to conceive is the same for both?" The answer lies in the nature of the method used. Natural Family Planning uses abstinence from intercourse, while contraception allows illicit and selfish sex to thwart God's natural intention for our sexuality.

Some people subscribe to the naive argument that there is no substantial difference between eyeglasses and a contraceptive device. They hold that both are merely scientific inventions and are therefore morally neutral. This is illogical. The Catholic answer is that eyeglasses are intended to restore health and are therefore legitimate. Contraceptive devices, on the other hand, violate the natural order of the body, and as research has shown, also violate health. Therefore they are inherently immoral. Contraception transgresses the Natural Law implanted within every human person, that we should be open to God's gift of life.

If I insist that my wife and I use any form of contraceptive device, I am refusing to give of my total self to her. I am withholding my procreative self from her and am merely using her for my own orgasmic satisfaction. Likewise, she is withholding her life-receiving self from me, and both of us are cutting God out of our sexual act. We reduce our love making to a mere animal copulation, and it becomes a lie. "You keep your life-giving faculties to yourself, and I will keep mine." Another way of looking at it is to consider the man who wants a new car. He can buy it legitimately, or he can steal it. The end result is the same. He has a new car, but the means used are vastly different in either case. It is like that with N.F.P. and contraception. One is legitimate, the other never is.

It is interesting to note that up until 1931, not one single mainline Christian Church supported artificial contraception. Even the protestant reformers regarded contraception as an evil. John Calvin, John Knox, Zwingli, Martin Luther, all condemned any sexual act which frustrated God's design. But in 1931, the Anglican Church, at the Lambeth Conference, admitted contraception as an acceptable practice for married couples. Anyone who suggested that this sexual license would one day lead to abortion and ultimately to euthanasia was scoffed at. But the fact is, that abortion and euthanasia are the logical end points of a contraceptive policy, and this has been quickly shown to be true in the space of a mere sixty years. The Lambeth Conference decision was the beginning of the collapse of Christian sexual ethics in the modern world.

The Catechism of the Catholic Church says this, "Sacred Scripture and the Church's traditional practice see in large families a sign of God's blessing and the parents' generosity."

Some people, Catholics included, condemn couples with large families as being irresponsible. In doing so, they only draw condemnation down on their own heads. Large families are the product of a generous, sacrificial love by those couples who regard children as their greatest treasure. They deny themselves a luxurious house or fine furniture, or the vast array of worldly trinkets in order to raise children for the Lord.

When I was in Ethiopia during the famine of 1985, I saw a man squatting beside the road. With him were his wife and six children. They were all starving. I stopped the jeep and got out to speak to him. I wanted him to agree to come with us to our refugee camp, where we had the food and medicine he needed. Lying beside him was a small bundle tied with rope. I asked him if this was all that he had in the world. He looked up strangely at me, then pointed to his children and said, "These are my wealth." The man was a Moslem, and he had a profound truth to teach us Catholics. Our treasure in heaven is not money in an earthly bank. It is the raising of godly children for the kingdom of God. A poor couple with many children is poor in the eyes of the world, but is richer than Croesus, in the eyes of God.

The Catechism continues, "By safeguarding both these essential elements, the unitive and the procreative, the conjugal act preserves in its fullness the sense of true mutual love and its orientation toward man's exalted vocation to parenthood." Then the Church beautifully states, "A child is not something owed to one, but is a gift. The 'supreme gift of marriage' is a human person. A child may not be considered a piece of property, an idea to which an alleged, 'right to a child' would lead. In this area, only the child possesses genuine rights: the right 'to be the fruit of the specific act of the conjugal love of his parents' and 'the right to be respected as a person from the moment of his conception.'" Notice, the Church refers not only to Scripture, but also to its two thousand years of tradition.

Many today think that contraception is a twentieth-century invention. It is not. Contraception was widely practised, as was abortion, in pre-Christian pagan societies. The ancient Romans used condoms made from pig intestines. Revolting as that may seem, it is nonetheless true. But we as Christians *should* be revolted, not that they used pig intestines, but that they used contraception at all. It is a violation of the natural law implanted by God in the hearts of all human beings, and this natural law binds all people, whether they be Christian or not, and whether they believe it or not.

In 1962, leading Jesuit theologians met together for one month to consider the church's teaching against contraception. At the end of their deliberations, they issued a solemn statement that the church's teaching on contraception was *infallible*. That is to say, it is God's truth and therefore cannot and must not be rescinded. This was six years before the publication of *Humanae Vitae* by Pope Paul VI. Ironically, one of the signers of that declaration was Fr. Richard McCormick, S.J. Strangely enough, when *Humanae Vitae* was published, Fr. McCormick had done a complete about-face and was now supporting contraception as legitimate. He was not alone. Many so called Catholic theologians openly dissented from the infallible teaching of the Church on this and other issues. It is surely a strange thing, that the Vicar of Christ cannot teach the law of God, but disobedient theologians can!

Pope Pius XII stated that "any attempt by the spouses in the completion of the conjugal act, having the aim of depriving the act of the force inherent in it and of impeding the procreation of a new life, is immoral; no alleged indication or need can convert an intrinsically immoral act into a moral and lawful one."

Pope Paul VI in *Humanae Vitae* insisted that "each and every marriage act must remain open to the transmission of life." In his Creed of the People of God, Pope Paul VI emphasises two names of God: *Being* (i.e. Life; I Am Who Am) and *Love* (God is Love). Therefore, in God, life and love are inseparable. Since we are made in the image and likeness of God, then life and love are to be inseparable for us also. Vatican II echoed these words when it stated, "The integral meaning of marriage is a communion of life and love." The Church has given us an infallible statement concerning God's truth about marriage and God's prohibition of artificial contraception. We, as God's children, have no right to distort that design.

There are six ways to practice birth control.

1. *Contraceptive devices* such as, the intrauterine device (I.U.D.), condoms, the diaphragm and vaginal foam. The I.U.D. is not solely a contraceptive. It also can allow fertilisation of an egg, but the fertilised egg, which is now a distinct human person, cannot successfully implant itself in the womb, and so it dies. The I.U.D. therefore, is also an abortifacient and kills human embryos. As a doctor, I find it distressing to encounter the numerous Catholic women who have had I.U.D.'s implanted, and yet their doctor did not bother to inform them that it would cause silent abortions. I have had to treat many such Catholic wives, who felt betrayed by the doctors whom they trusted. Sadly, they had no conscience about using contraception, but were deeply offended at the thought of unwittingly aborting their babies. The stark truth, however, is that contraception and abortion are bed partners.

   The condom and the diaphragm are barrier methods, which prevent the sperm from moving into the womb and the fallopian tubes, where fertilisation can occur. With the condom, the sperm dies in the condom and it is discarded. With the diaphragm, the sperm is allowed to die in the vagina. The vaginal foam is a spermicidal agent, that is to say, it kills the sperm in the vagina. These methods are clearly contrary to natural law. The diaphragm has to be put in place and so signifies a deliberate intention on the part of the woman not to conceive. The condom has to be ignominiously put on the man before intercourse, while the woman has to squeeze the vaginal foam into the vagina, also immediately before intercourse. No one can perform these acts without knowing in their heart of hearts that they are unnatural and violate the beauty of their sexual union.

   Today, a blatant and deliberate lie is being told to our young people by the government, by our medical officers of health, by our doctors, by our media, by Planned Parenthood, by gay and lesbian activists and by misguided educators, even some in Catholic Schools. Teenagers are told that if they use condoms, then they will be safe from AIDS, and from other sexually transmitted diseases. The fact is, that the pores or holes in a condom are up to fifty microns in diameter, while the AIDS virus is only three microns in diameter. Where is the protection in that? In 1989, the Ottawa-Carleton Health Dept. issued an alert to health professionals stating, "Research on the sexual partners of H.I.V. infected people indicates that twenty per cent will eventually become infected *even when condoms are used*." Dr. John Seale, a member of the Royal Society of Medicine said in 1987, "The notion that condoms can have any significant effect on preventing the spread of Aids is utterly preposterous." Dr. Andre Lafrance says, "If this is the measure of protection condoms provide against AIDS, why should they be expected to provide better protection against the other STD's (sexually transmitted diseases)?"

The only *safe* sex is *abstinence* for young people. For married couples, the only safe sex is total faithfulness to one another.

2. *Chemical substances,* such as the birth control pill and RU 486.

It is very important to understand how the birth control pill works. Again, if a doctor wants to prescribe it for a woman, he will usually never give her the facts. There will, instead, be a conspiracy of silence. The pill is prescribed with no comment, and that, in my opinion is criminal, because it precludes informed consent by the patient. The pill is marketed only as a contraceptive, and is worth billions of dollars to the big pharmaceutical companies every year. But that is by no means the whole story. The Pill actually has three modes of action:

a. It prevents ovulation, but it does not do this all of the time. There are a significant number of cycles where a potentially fertilisable egg is released.

b. It creates a mucus plug at the cervix, (the neck of the womb) which helps prevent the sperm from moving up into the womb to reach the egg. Again, this is not effective all of the time, and many sperm escape intact through the plug.

c. It creates a chemically hostile environment in the womb whereby, if an egg was ever fertilised, the new human embryo would be unable to implant, and so it would be killed. This effect of the pill exists all of the time and for as long as the pill is being used.

Therefore, the birth control pill is not always a contraceptive. There is a scientifically proven probability of an abortifacient action. In the U.S. alone, it is estimated that there are 1.2 million silent abortions a year due to B.C.P. use, and sadly many of these are occurring in Catholic women on the pill. Even if it is argued that some of these abortions are "naturally occurring" this could never explain all of them. The pill is still a killer even if it only causes the death of one single fetus.

The RU486, or "morning after pill," is nothing more than a baby poison, deliberately swallowed by the baby's mother in order to kill her child.

3. **Sterilisation** is a surgical procedure designed to burn or excise sections of the fallopian tubes in women or to tie off and obstruct the vas deferens in men. The first prevents eggs from travelling to the womb. The second prevents sperm from being ejaculated. These procedures are permanent forms of contraception, and constitute an act of mutilation of the healthy body. Scripture tells us that our bodies are temples of the Holy Spirit, and that our bodies are not our property. Therefore, it is a grave sin to desecrate or mutilate any healthy tissue in our bodies. Surgery is only permissible for the correcting or cure of a disease. Healthy tubes are not diseased. Many people undergoing sterilisation believe that the procedure can be reversed down the road if they change their minds. This is not true. The success rate for sterilisation reversal is extremely low. Not only that, it is very, very expensive, and is not covered by most health insurance.

4. **Unnatural sexual practices,** such as coitus interruptus, masturbation and oral sex.

In these cases ejaculation is occurring outside of the vagina, and this is the old sin of Onan, who spilled his seed on the ground, and for which he was killed.

5. *Natural Family Planning,* which takes into account a woman's natural fertile and infertile phases.

This system recognises, along with St. Paul, that periodic abstinence is both desirable and good (1 Cor. 7:5-6). Those who practice contraception regard abstinence as a nuisance, or as inconvenient, or as impossible. They even claim that this abstinence is harmful to a marriage relationship. This is simply not true. The fact is that in the U.S., the general divorce rate is more than fifty per cent, while among practitioners of Natural Family Planning, it is only from three to five per cent. Natural Family Planning couples almost invariably report that periodic abstinence, instead of being divisive, actually heightens their love and respect for one another and strengthens their marriages. During the fertile period, husband and wife learn to show love for each other in non-sexual ways, and they give to each other the beautiful message, "I love you for yourself, not just for my sexual pleasure." What contraceptors seem to be blind to is the fact that even they have to abstain at times. They cannot indulge in lovemaking whenever they are aroused. When one partner is sick, or when they are separated for a time, or when the children are present, surely they must abstain.

6. *Total abstinence,* whereby a couple after having had their family, choose to take a vow of celibacy before God. They do this for the high ideal of evangelical chastity. This is the highest form of sacrificial marital love, second only to laying down one's life and is embraced solely for the love of God.

In today's society, we are so distorted in our thinking that a sterile body is deemed healthy, while a fertile body is considered to be sick. Sterile sex is extolled everywhere, and women who welcome more than 1.7 babies into their family are considered irresponsible and are regarded as contributing to the so-called population explosion. Willard Carter of the Centre of Disease Control in the United States once said, "Pregnancy is the second most common venereal disease." Is pregnancy now to be looked upon as a sexually transmitted disease? Have we degenerated this far? What do you think God would say if Mr. Carter told him that to his face? It doesn't bear thinking about.

Since so many couples, Catholics included, are practising sterile sex, can we be surprised if homosexuals ask the question, "If married couples can have sterile sex, then why can't we?" Should we be surprised if a teenager asks the question, "If my parents can have sterile sex then why can't I?" Contracepting parents and teachers are not competent to teach chastity to our youth. Maybe that is why so little is said about chastity today in our homes and in our schools. If parents know that it is good for their sons and daughters to abstain from sex before marriage, then surely it is also good for parents to abstain during fertile times, if they are regulating their family. Also, if parents have embraced artificial contraception, the children receive the message that their parents do not really like children. They know they are lucky to be alive. They can make the connection that the contraceptive mentality leads so easily to the acceptance of abortion, where contraception has failed. Robbed of brothers and sisters, they witnessed the materialism and the selfishness of their parents, who prefer money and pleasure to children.

So as always, if we mess around with one aspect of God's order, we end up interfering with the entire moral order. Simply put, virtue leads to life. Sin leads to death.

Another fact, which is blithely ignored, is that contraception is wiping out nations. For a nation to simply replace citizens who have died, it must have a fertility rate of 2.2 babies per couple. The U.S. and all of western Europe are reproducing at a lower rate, and so the indigenous population of these countries is dwindling. The only thing which is allowing these nations to survive at all is immigration.

Dr. Samuel Nigro has written, "*Humanae Vitae* said contraception was against the planet. And, as such, *Humanae Vitae* was the world's first ecological manifesto. It was first to object to the orgasm generation. *Humanae Vitae* warned against fraudulent freedom and was a beacon of unsettling truth, pointing out how dangerous it is to believe that feelings are the same as reality. It emphasised that one is never free from nature (the natural law). *Humanae Vitae* repudiated the 'me' generation."

It was only to be expected that the "me" generation took great offence at *Humanae Vitae* and did everything it could to dismantle its power. The media launched a vicious campaign of scorn on the Catholic Church, which was accused of being out of touch with modern society and culture. The fact that the Church is considered to be out of touch with so-called modern standards is probably a sure sign that it is fully in touch with the truth of God. Catholics themselves soon began to believe in the propaganda, and before long, they simply ignored the Church's teaching, or sought out a priest who would tell them it was up to their own conscience if they wished to use contraception. Should we be surprised that not only do many Catholics feel justified in using contraceptives, they now increasingly feel free to dissent from other unchangeable doctrines of the Church? Today, dissident theologians and lay people boldly demand that the church relax its laws on pre-marital sex, homosexual life style, and even abortion. This apostasy is in full swing, and unless we can reverse its momentum, it will inevitably end up with a major schism in the church. What a terrible tragedy for the kingdom of God.

It may come as a surprise to know that in 1931 an editorial of *The Washington Post* was written in response to the Anglican Church's about-face when it endorsed contraception. It is worth quoting here, and bear in mind, this was not written by a Catholic:

"It is impossible to reconcile the doctrine of the divine institution of marriage with any modernistic plan for the mechanical regulation of human birth. The church must either reject the plain teachings of the Bible or reject schemes for the 'scientific' production of human souls. Carried to its logical conclusion, the committee's report, if carried into effect would sound the death-knell of marriage as a holy institution, by establishing degrading practices which would encourage indiscriminate immorality. The suggestion that the use of legalised contraceptives would be 'careful and restrained' is preposterous. It is the misfortune of the churches that they are too often misused by visionaries for the promotion of 'reforms' in fields foreign to religion. The departures from Christian teachings are astounding in many cases, leaving the beholder aghast at the willingness of some churches to discard the ancient injunction to teach, 'Christ and him crucified.' If the churches are to become organisations for political and 'scientific' propaganda, they should be honest and reject the Bible, scoff at Christ as an obsolete and unscientific teacher, and strike out boldly as champions of politics and science as modern substitutes for the old-time religion."

It is hard to believe that such a solid Christian (dare I say thoroughly Catholic?) statement was written in a leading secular newspaper. It demonstrates that only sixty years ago contraception was an unthinkable abomination to any believing Christian. How times have changed.

Satan desires with all his unholy being to become God. But try as he might he is incapable of imitating any of God's works. He always ends up by doing the exact opposite. God creates life. Therefore, Satan is doomed either to destroy life (as in war, disease and abortion), or to prevent life from being conceived in the first place. Therefore, *Satan is the Spirit of "Contra-ception,"* which means he is the Spirit of Anti-life. When we deliberately contracept, we not only refuse God's blessing, but we worship the Spirit of Contraception, who is Satan himself. We are cooperating with the devil, and in fact we are worshipping him by taking part in a satanic liturgy, the ritual of sterile sex, where life is deliberately prevented and where God is ignored. Satan loves it and revels in it, and we give him the victory.

As Catholics, we must return to the truth of God and the teaching of the Church. We must give God his rightful place once more in our families and in our marriage covenant. He is life and love. Because we are created in his image, we too are life and love. Just as in the marriage sacrament, man must not divide what God has joined together, so man must not divide life and love. If we prevent life, we cannot love either ourselves, our children, or our God. Just as contraception is anti-life, it is also anti-love.

So let us worship, praise and glorify God in our marriages by always keeping our hearts open to God's perfect design for us. He wants to bless us. We should generously and joyfully welcome his blessing.

CHAPTER 9

Abortion: The Murder of the Innocents

"Thou shalt not kill."
                                    (Ex. 20:13)

As a prelude to this chapter, I would like to lay down one simple ground rule, which I believe is vital if we are to be followers of our gentle Jesus. It is the principle of civilised debate. There is no room for the strident voice in this discussion. There must be no rancour, no anger and no condemnation for those who hold opposing views. There is no ultimate usefulness in labelling pro-abortionists as murderers or stupid people or satanists. Such labels only serve to more deeply entrench their position. It is a well-known psychological fact that aggression merely increases resistance. It may win an occasional short-term victory, but in the long run it is self-defeating. If we call ourselves Christian, then we must put on the mind of Christ. Those who do not and who employ violence in the name of Christ are not Christians at all.

Therefore, the key question we should ask is, "How would Jesus relate to pro-abortionists?" He would not condemn. "For God did not send his Son into the world to condemn the world but that the world might be saved through him" (John 3:17). On the contrary, he would accord these people their dignity as children of God. *Then* he would gently call them to a higher level of goodness and understanding. But first and foremost, he would see to it that they would know they are loved. Therefore love, understanding, compassion and calm reason must prevail. We cannot begin to offer cogent reasons for our position unless we first imitate Christ, who was gentle and humble of heart, and so we must love those who have abortions and those who perform them. Jesus loves them. He ate and drank with prostitutes and tax collectors. He died for them and so he died for abortionists too. Can we do less and still be Christian? Jesus commanded us to "Love one another as I have loved you" (John 13:34). To compromise this imperative is to create God in our *own* image and likeness. Love and prayer will stop the abortionist far more effectively than an angry violent demonstration. Cardinal Cushing once said, "It is one thing to preach a positive message. It is another thing entirely — something we should *never* do — to condemn people even though they are guilty, because our mission is one of mercy." The beautiful proof of this principle is that it was the love of pro-lifers which embraced Jane Roe (of Roe and Wade infamy) and led to her marvellous conversion to the pro-life cause. Not only did love strike a blow at the pro-choice movement, but it saved a precious soul for God. Mercy and justice together are far superior than justice alone.

The contraceptive mentality inevitably leads to an abortion mentality. There is a direct, unmistakable link between contraception and abortion. If I contracept, I plan not to have a child. If my contraceptive strategy fails, then it becomes simple logic to assume that I can use abortion as a back-up strategy. Planned Parenthood not only admits this to be true, but actively promotes it. Abortion then, has become the fail-safe contraceptive. But that is illogical, because abortion cannot be a contraceptive since it destroys that which has already been conceived. Predictably, things have gone way beyond that. Abortion has now become much more than simply a failed contraception option. It has now also become a worldwide solution to problems of poverty, family size and low standard of living.

A Polish psychiatrist, Dr. Wanda Poltanska, stated, "On December 11th, 1967, representatives of thirty nations signed a declaration, an official sanction for contraception to eradicate abortions. This green light for contraception paradoxically multiplied, not reduced, abortions. With the latter's proliferation, a pressing demand for its legalisation — the green light for abortion — plus a sequential progression, that led to a quantum leap in abortions by the millions, ensued worldwide. Cognizant of this ironical phenomenon, the general meeting of Planning Familial in 1971 in Budapest conceded that abortion is the *best means of birth control,* and hence they pressed for more efficient abortive techniques. Undoubtedly a vicious pattern was firmly entrenched. Contraception is necessary to avoid abortion, which in turn is indispensable when contraception misfires."

Millions of women have fallen into the contraception trap. At its inception, the pill was thought to be the key to true sexual liberation for women at last. It has not proven to be so. In fact, it plunges women into a deeper sexual bondage. Men now expect women to be on the pill, and they feel justified in demanding sex whenever they want it, because the woman no longer has any legitimate excuse, such as fear of pregnancy. Now men expect women to have casual affairs and one-night stands. Where is the freedom in that? Numerous female patients of mine have complained that they cannot hope to have a steady boyfriend unless they give him sex. In fact, this sexual liberation goes against women's nature. Dr. William Senior, Professor of Sociology at the University of Houston, stated, "One of the characteristics of women that remained true throughout all this was their inability to become sexually aroused without becoming emotionally attracted." Anne Marie Cunningham, in a special report to the *Toronto Star* wrote, "Today, while we may retain some sexual frankness and freedom, the excesses of the 60's seem emotionally empty and downright dangerous. Others wonder if the pill was more for men who could enjoy increased sexual activity and expect women to take the responsibility for contraception." Women therefore do not have more freedom. They have merely embraced a more profound slavery to the often irresponsible and emotionally detached sexual demands of men.

Surely, the safest place in the world for a child ought to be his or her mother's womb. That was God's plan. But now it has become a very dangerous place, since there are nearly 60 million abortions taking place every year in our world. Today a child can consider himself or herself lucky indeed to get out of the womb alive.

Why is it that Catholics and the majority of Protestant religions consider abortion to be a moral wrong? Today's pagan society would have us believe that the unborn child is nothing more than a blob of tissue, a non-human collection of cells. Of course, this is nothing more than a pathetic attempt to justify its killing. Needless to say, the Word of God does not agree.

The Bible is replete with references to the validity and the sacredness of unborn human life in the eyes of God. While he allows man and woman to create the physical body of the child, he himself breathes an immortal soul into that little body. We are given the miraculous privilege of being co-creators with God in his divine condescension. God *cooperates* with us. Do we not therefore have a solemn obligation to cooperate with him?

"Let us make man in our own image, in the likeness of ourselves" (Gen. 1:26). Right from the beginning, God decreed that all human beings would lay claim to a built-in dignity, the dignity of having been created in the divine image. Therefore, to kill such a being is not only a crime against a human baby, it is also a direct attack on God himself.

"For no king has any different origin or birth, but the same is the entry into life for all" (Wis. 7:5). Note the distinction between origin and birth. The word of God is clear that life has its origin *before* birth. Entry into life is, and can only be, the moment of conception. No other scientifically identifiable point occurs in the life of the fetus where life can be said to have its origin. Birth is not a magic moment at which life begins where none had existed before. The moment of birth is an unpredictable variable which carries in itself only one significant property. It is merely the point at which a person becomes independent of the placenta for nourishment. This is no different from the later stage in life where a child becomes fully independent of his or her parents and moves out into the world. If dependency on the mother for nourishment is the justification for abortionists to abort, then the newborn infant who continues to be totally dependent on the mother for his nourishment could also be legitimately killed. To any biologist, it is astounding that the law can be so naive as to regard birth as the event which mysteriously accords a person the right of protection under the law. Earthly life is a continuum that begins with conception and ends with death. Death occurring at any point along that continuum constitutes the loss of a fully human life.

"Before I formed you in the womb, I knew you: before you came to birth, I consecrated you" (Jer. 1:5). A non-person cannot be consecrated. Only fully human persons can be consecrated to a godly purpose. Jeremiah was therefore a human person prior to his actual birth. God said so. At the Annunciation by the angel Gabriel to Mary, as soon as Mary said "yes" to God's request that she become the Mother of God, Jesus was immediately conceived in her womb. God had, at that very instant, become man in the form of an embryo. Was he any less God for being a fetus?

"Truly you have formed my inmost being. You knit me in my mother's womb. I give you thanks that I am fearfully and wonderfully made" (Ps. 139:13-14). Every human person is fearfully and wonderfully made, and this growth is orchestrated by God himself. When we stop this holy process by an act of abortion, we are snuffing out an act of God. We stand in defiance of his plan for that child's earthly life.

"Yahweh called me when I was in the womb. Before my birth he had pronounced my name" (Isa. 49:1). Note that God called me, a person, when I was in the womb. He didn't give a human name to a blob of jello or an inanimate embryo. He called *me* and I believe I am a fully human person with a right to life. God recognises our true identity in the womb. Why do we accuse him of being wrong about that? What do we know that he does not?

God, knowing that one day the abortion holocaust would be unleashed all over the earth, prophesied it and reassured us of his faithfulness. "Can a woman forget her baby at the breast, feel no pity for the child of her womb. But, *even if these forget*, I shall not forget you" (Isa. 49:15). God is asserting that it is against nature (the very nature which he himself designed) for a woman to kill the child in her womb. But even if that were to happen, and God knows that it is happening, he assures the child of his everlasting faithfulness and love. He has promised these innocent aborted babies that he will not forget them, because they are his children.

This truth of the personhood of the fetus was beautifully demonstrated when Mary went to visit her pregnant cousin Elizabeth. Elizabeth, filled with the Holy Spirit, exclaimed, "The moment your greeting reached my ears, the child in my womb leapt for joy" (Luke 1:44). Inanimate blobs of jello can neither leap nor feel joy. Only a conscious being can do this, and so it was an unborn six month old "fetus" (John the Baptist), who was first after Mary to recognize the reality of Jesus in the world, even though Jesus himself was as yet only an embryo of a few days old.

What have we lost as a result of a planet-wide abortion policy? We may have killed the very persons who would have solved our pollution problems, the conundrum of equitable food distribution, and even the cure for the epidemics of AIDS and cancer. God gives each person a purpose, and that purpose is also aborted when we abort him or her. Furthermore, abortion is not an isolated act, affecting only a single fetus. It is a *generational* act. That is to say it affects all the other beings who could have been his or her descendants. It wipes out a blood line. The laws of biology do not conform to the laws of physics. In physics, to every action there is an equal and opposite reaction. This is not so with the action of abortion. The biological law is better stated as, "To the action of abortion, there is an *amplified* and *multiple* reaction." If my mother had aborted me (and since her life was gravely endangered by the pregnancy, she would have had ample excuse, by modern standards, to do so), not only would I have died, but my children would never have been born, nor my beautiful grandchildren. A whole dynasty would have been annihilated.

The Lord said to Rececca, "Two *nations* are in your womb" (Gen. 25:23). If Rebecca had aborted her twins, Jacob and Esau, two *entire* nations would never have come into being.

So what precisely do we kill when we choose to abort? We know what God says about that, but what does science have to say? We live in a pagan society which extols science as the final arbiter of all things. So let us meet the debate at that level.

Cal Thomas, a syndicated newspaper columnist, once wrote, "The agreement over whether the unborn child is human or not has been bogus from the start. If it is not human, what is it? — a Buick?" The fetus is known to be a genetically unique being, distinct from his mother or father. The body of the fetus therefore is in no way a part of the equally unique body of his mother. A woman may claim the right to do with her own body whatever she pleases (and that is another moral debate altogether), but the unborn baby is not her body. He is a separate human person, who by the mother's argument also has the right to do with his body whatever he pleases. Neither the mother nor the law has any right to decide for the child his wish to live or to die. The fact that he has not yet developed language does not alter his claim to rights, especially to the most basic right of all, which is the right to life. Civilised societies have always protected the weak from the strong who would exploit them, and unborn children are the weakest members of our society.

The heart begins beating around the eighteenth day. The nervous system is structured by the twentieth day and nervous reflexes are present. At forty-two days all two hundred and six bones of the skeleton can be identified. By eight weeks the brain and all major body systems are developed. At nine weeks the fetus squints, swallows and moves his tongue. If you stroke his palm he will make a fist. At eleven weeks he sucks his thumb and breathes the amniotic fluid to develop the organs of respiration. Fingernails are present by the twelfth week and eyelashes by the sixteenth. He moves in the womb long before the mother can feel the movement. He has a blood supply separate from the mother's blood supply. Mothers' blood never crosses the placental barrier. By day thirty, the baby is ten thousand times larger than the fertilised egg. By day forty, brain waves can be recorded. By the ninth week, his fingerprints are present, and everyone knows that one's fingerprints are a unique identification mark for each human being. The baby's prints are not those of his mother. By week thirteen, the sex of the baby is apparent. By the end of the fourth month, he can hear the mother's voice and heartbeat, and can respond to outside noises such as music.

Dr. Frank Lake, an English psychiatrist, has also conclusively proven that we can recover memories of our pre-birth experiences while we were in the womb. It is difficult to imagine an amorphous mass of cells being capable of remembering anything. Newer scientific observation concludes that it is the fetus who controls the pregnancy, not the mother. The fetus is conscious, the fetus is alert and the fetus sees as well as hears.

One of the great contradictions in our health-care system today is that a surgeon can open up a pregnant womb, operate on a fetus and correct certain medical defects. The current medical insurance agencies will pay the surgeon a fee for the procedure. But fees are only paid for services to *bona fide* patients. The doctor has not treated the mother. Therefore, the fetus must be a patient. Therefore, the fetus is a human person, because only human persons are covered by medical insurance. So on one hand, the insurance plan pays for the killing of fetuses because they are not yet human, and on the other hand, it pays for treatment to fetuses because they are already human. Sin always contradicts itself.

We live in a violent society. Pope John Paul II calls it a culture of death. Our tax dollars are being used to support abortuaries whether we like it or not. Satan demands human sacrifice just like the ancient heathen god Moloch. In those days, parents sacrificed their infants to appease his terrible wrath. Moloch has been resurrected in our day, only now it is the unborn who are being offered to appease him. Nothing delights Satan more than the sacrifice of the innocent and nothing distresses the Most High God more than the sacrifice of the innocent. Satan murdered the innocents through Herod in Bethlehem after Jesus was born. The unspeakable numbers of deaths by abortion in our time must be beyond even his wildest evil dreams.

So how can we fight back? We fight back only with the weapons of the Christian. We fight with love and with prayer. There is no other way. If we use violence, we become like our adversaries. If we use love and prayer, we become like Jesus. Above all, let us say our Rosary for the unborn. The image of Our Lady of Guadalupe is miraculous, and it is the only such image in which Mary is pregnant. She, therefore, is the Mother of the Unborn. It is Mary who will put an end to the abortion holocaust. We cannot stop this bloodshed on our own, but she can. We should therefore, direct all of our prayers to Our Lady of Guadalupe that this diabolical human sacrifice will be brought to an end. We should also join our prayers to those of Mary of the Annunciation, beseeching her to protect our unborn babies, just as she protected the unborn Jesus in her womb. It is the duty of every Catholic to pray daily for an end to these crimes which are crying out to heaven for vengeance.

"When he broke the fifth seal, I saw underneath the altar, the souls of all the people who had been killed on account of the Word of God, for witnessing to it. They shouted in a loud voice, 'Holy, true Master, how much longer will you wait before you pass sentence and take vengeance for our death, on the inhabitants of the earth?'"(Rev. 6:9-11). Aborted innocents are martyred in their own blood and God will keep his promise never to abandon them. We should fervently pray that he will show mercy on those who commit these crimes for they cry out to heaven for judgement.

There is a terrible paradox in today's culture. If ever an animal has to be destroyed, the veterinarian is very careful to avoid inflicting unnecessary pain on that animal. An injection is given, which induces a merciful unconsciousness progressing to coma and death. This humane privilege is denied to our human unborn whenever the death sentence is pronounced by the parents and the doctor. Indeed, if a doctor were to give the baby a merciful injection to save it from suffering prior to the act of abortion, he would have to admit that the baby was indeed a human life. Since he must never allow himself to believe that, he denies the truth and submits the baby to a torture which would be unthinkable for the termination of a dog or a cat.

There are seven methods of termination of pregnancy, all of which ignore scientific fact and assume that the baby can feel no pain.

1. **DILATION AND CURETTAGE OR D. & C:**
   A surgical steel curette is inserted into the womb. With a scraping motion it strips the placenta off the wall of the uterus. Apart from the injury the baby suffers from the tearing action of the curette, which is inevitable since the surgery is performed blind, the baby dies from shut down of his or her circulation. This is not unlike a major heart attack in an adult.

2. **SUCTION:**
   This is the most widely-used technique. The baby is literally sucked into a vacuum cleaner. The baby's fragile body is distorted and often dismembered by the violence of the suction force and dies, if not by the trauma, then certainly from the shut down of his blood supply.

3. **SALINE SALT INJECTION:**
   This is performed into the baby's amniotic sac. The baby swallows the saline and is slowly poisoned. The saline burns

the skin, the lungs and the stomach. It takes forty-five minutes to one hour for the baby to die in agony.

4. DILATATION AND EVACUATION (D. & E.):

This method is used when the baby is too big to be suctioned. The cervix is dilated and the baby is dismembered without anaesthetic and removed in pieces. This is a cruel butchery performed on a baby capable of feeling the slightest pain.

5. HYSTEROTOMY:

This is, in effect, a Caesarean section performed, not to save the baby's life, but to terminate it. The baby must be killed while still in the womb, then extracted. If the baby is lifted outside the womb and then killed, the law regards that as murder! What significant difference could it possibly make to the baby if he or she is killed inside the mother's womb or a few seconds later outside of the womb? To the baby it is all the same. What a sad reflection on the legal minds of our day that such an illogical distinction could ever be made. What a sad reflection on the doctors and nurses who carry out this act without a flicker of conscience.

6. CHEMICAL ABORTION (RU486):

This is otherwise known as "the morning-after-pill." It is the deliberate use of a chemical device to kill a fertilised egg, either directly or by preventing implantation. It is simply a fetal poison, not substantially different from the use of strychnine or cyanide.

7. PARTIAL BIRTH ABORTION:

Partial birth abortion refers to the killing of a third trimester baby. With today's incubator technology, these babies could easily be kept alive and grow normally outside of the womb. The procedure is blatantly brutal. The cervix is dilated. The baby is turned and delivered feet first. When all but the head is outside of the womb, the surgeon uses scissors to stab the back of the baby's skull. The scissors are then pushed up into the brain. They are then opened and twisted back and forth in order to mash the brain. The now dead baby (remember, to stay within the law, the surgeon has to kill the baby while the head is still in the womb, not after the head has been delivered) is delivered whole or the baby is decapitated and the head delivered piecemeal. Are any of these interventions at least as humane as the gentle killing of a pet dog or cat? I think not.

Given such facts, is it too much to ask of those who support abortions to at least understand why we Christians are so repelled by what abortion is, what it does and how it does it? It attacks our weakest citizens, it violates all demands of motherhood, it violates a child in the very environment in which he or she ought to be most safe and it does so in a cruel and agonizing manner. Not only that, science, in spite of the best efforts of some, is incapable of denying the human nature of the fetus.

Dr. William J. Moneghan, M.D., has said, "We are choosing creatures. But this capacity tells only part of the human story. To choose rightly constitutes our ultimate task and dignity as human beings. Not just any choice will do." Therefore being pro-choice is not a virtue. It is the choice itself which is the virtue or the vice. Pregnancy is not an illness. Abortion therefore is not a medical procedure. It does not treat an illness, regardless of the uninformed opinion of Willard Carter, who once described pregnancy as a "venereal disease!" How many people today could comfort themselves with the thought that they had caused a venereal disease for their mothers when they were conceived? That is a thought light years away from the lofty notion that I am a conceived expression of the love of my mother and father and the love of my heavenly Father-God. Pope John Paul II put it very cogently when he said, "Their proponents (of contraception and abortion), claim a power that belongs only to God: man becomes the final arbiter as to when life should begin and when life should end."

The Post-Abortion Syndrome:

Every human action results in consequences, and so also does the action of abortion. The collective guilt of the medical profession ignores these consequences, and even has gone so far as to deny that there are any negative effects to abortion at all. While there are a number of psychologists and doctors working in isolation to treat the aftermath of abortion in their patients, little or no research money is being directed towards the study of the problem. The distributors of such funds are also the proponents of abortion, and so the topic of post-abortion syndrome is effectively closed to large scale investigation.

Today much is made of the principle of informed consent. It is a doctor's duty to fully inform his or her patient of the risks to herself of any proposed medical or surgical procedure. This simply is not being done in regards to the procedure of abortion. As such it constitutes a violation of the rights of the pregnant mother. Contrary to the mainstream of medical opinion there are serious consequences and they are both physical and psychological.

1. **Physical:**

Eating disorders are by far the most common consequence in mothers who opt for abortion. Post-abortion sterility is also very common. The subsequent incidence of ectopic pregnancies has risen by three hundred percent since abortion was legalised. The stillbirth rate is increased for later pregnancies. Immediate post-abortion bleeding and infections can occur, as do surgical shock, and perforated uterus, followed by surgically induced peritonitis. Apart from these major after-effects, how many doctors tell their young women that they might expect to experience intense pain immediately following the procedure? Worse still, how many are told that they might die? There is a mortality rate for abortion to the mother. While it is rare, is it not a terrible tragedy that the life of a healthy young woman should be lost for a procedure with no medical justification? The mortality rate for the fetus is of course one hundred percent.

Dr. Nadine Andriew, speaking at the eighth International Symposium on prevention and detection of cancer, reported her findings that for women with a family history of breast cancer, the more abortions they have, the greater their risk of breast cancer. Those who had undergone induced abortions were at greater risk than those who had spontaneous abortions. Why is this not being publicised by our media? All husbands, and for that matter boyfriends, should ask themselves, "If I were told of this risk, would I encourage the mother of my child to undergo an abortion?" The mothers might also ask, "If I had all these facts, would I be willing to take the risk?" I seriously doubt it.

2. **Psychological:**

Apart from the risks to the mother's body, abortion also puts her at serious risk to her psyche and her emotional health. Pope John Paul II said, "Psychiatry must proclaim the full truth about man, recognize the moral dimensions of treatment and have faith in the Divine Redeemer" who, I might be so bold as to add, created our psyche and understands it very well.

Dr. William Wilson, Emeritus Professor of Psychiatry at Duke University Medical Centre in North Carolina, stated that having an abortion can leave women with a life-threatening psychiatric illness. Not only the woman involved, but people less directly involved, the husband, boyfriend, friends and family. One of the main ill effects, he said, is the onset of eating disorders.

Doctors are ignoring the problem because it is an iatrogenic problem (i.e. caused by the doctor), and so doctors who perform abortions often feel guilty. They have been trained to preserve life and have to make a major effort to deny the significance of killing an unborn baby. This is called denial or repression, and any psychiatrist will agree that such emotions are very powerful, and must re-surface later as guilt, anger or sadness.

Dr. M. Ekblad, M.D. in 1955 reported that two percent of abortion patients had severe psychiatric sequelae in the form of actual psychosis. Drs. Sim and Neisser reported, "that abortion is bad treatment for mental illness and for its prevention. Doctors who refuse to use abortion for such purposes are acting in their patient's best interest." In other words, the old contention that abortion could be done to prevent mental illness in a prospective mother can no longer be supported. Moore-Carver, reporting to the International Institute for the Study of Human Reproduction, Columbia University, stated in 1974 that, "severe guilt is found in anything from two to twenty-three percent depending on the type of study." Dr. Kent, in the British Columbia Medical Journal 1978, was even more pessimistic when he reported that, *"without exception,* there are feelings of guilt and profound regret." Drs. Liebman and Zimmer, working from the pregnancy aftermath help line in Milwaukee, Wisconsin, reported the following psychological after-effects of abortion:

a. Guilt:

Invariably the women felt they had done something very wrong. Those who mentioned God expressed two ideas. Some believed that God forgave them, but they could not forgive themselves. Others thought God was punishing them through the emotional trauma they were experiencing or through subsequent miscarriages.

b. Anxiety:

This could be anything from a pervasive uneasiness to outright fear and panic attacks. Often it is similar to a post-traumatic anxiety state and can even escalate to a full-blown panic disorder.

c. Depression:

This is very common and is associated with feelings of guilt. It is often accompanied by a morbid preoccupation with death. In my own experience, such women require anti-depressant medication, and a long course of psychotherapy to help them grieve in a healthy way, and of course to help them believe in God's forgiveness, in forgiveness from their aborted baby and to forgive themselves.

d. A sense of loss:

This applies not just to the loss of the baby, but a loss of the values they once had that were obliterated by the abortion. Most women admit that it had never entered their heads in their younger years that they would ever have considered abortion. It was just too horrible to contemplate. Having succumbed to pressure from family and from their spouse or boyfriend, they feel a deep sense of having betrayed their most cherished beliefs.

e. Anger:

A significant number of women express anger at the abortion clinic counsellors, who failed to give the other side of the picture, and who did not warn them of the emotional consequences. Many are horrified at their physician, who could perform such a brutal act. They feel betrayed and they express that betrayal with anger. Many are angry that the clinic did not offer them an alternative to abortion.

Other complaints include a change for the worse in their relationship with the husband or boyfriend, deterioration in self-image, regret and remorse, worries over subsequent infertility, nightmares, loneliness and alienation, marital problems, phantom child (in which the mother is disturbed by images of the child as old as he would have been if he had lived), flashbacks and a deep sense of helplessness, which takes the form of feeling victimised by the doctors and counsellors. I have seen almost all of the above reactions in my medical and psychotherapy practice.

How can these unhappy women be treated? The first and foremost therapeutic tool is acceptance of, and love for, the woman. The therapist must not judge her but rather listen with a compassionate heart and accept her painful feelings as valid. All cases must be explored for clinical depression and evaluated for suicide risk. Medication may be essential to lift the depression so that therapy can proceed, and even to save the woman's life. The therapist should ask how she feels about herself as a person and as a mother. Even if she denies any religious beliefs, she should be asked her thoughts on what God thinks of her. Often she will express horror at killing, or elaborate on ideas around sin, remorse and repentance and atonement, which is her need to make up for what she has done. At this point, it is helpful to explain the grieving process and to show her that she is experiencing a genuine grief reaction. I always affirm her own unique grieving pattern.

The next stage is to suggest to her that her baby is in fact alive in another place, and that one day the mother will also go to that place where she can hold her baby. I then ask her what she thinks her baby is doing now, and then suggest that the baby is happy and has forgiven his or her parents. In fact, the baby is praying constantly to God for his parents' well-being.

Now I try to get the mother to name her baby. It does not matter if she knows the sex of her aborted baby, the name in her heart is valid and powerful. Naming the baby gives flesh, substance, and meaning to a new relationship between mother and child. I then use imaging to help the mother visualize her baby, to tell him or her she is sorry, to tell him that she loves him, to see herself holding him, to ask him for forgiveness and to see her baby forgiving her. If the patient will accept prayer, I always pray over her, bringing the love of Christ and his forgiveness and mercy into her heart. If she is Catholic, I always try to lead her to the healing power of the Sacrament of Confession and Holy Eucharist. I draw her attention to the wonderful forgiveness of God. "Come, let us talk this over, says Yahweh. Though your sins are like scarlet, they shall be white as snow" (Isa. 1:18).

I try to bring her to the realization that she is forgiven both by God and by her baby, but that she also needs to forgive herself. Finally, we plan a funeral rite for the baby, inviting the mother to say her farewell. I encourage her to write the prayers for the service and it is amazing how powerful such a liturgy and ritual can be in bringing the past to closure.

We would do well to meditate on the words of that wonderful mother of the Old Testament, who watched her seven sons being tortured to death for their faith in God. "I do not know how you appeared in my womb. It was not I who endowed you with breath and life. I had not the shaping of your every part. And hence, the Creator of the world, who made everyone and ordained the origin of all things, will in his mercy give you back breath and life ... my son, have pity on me. I carried you nine months in my womb and suckled you three years, fed you and reared you to the age you are now and provided for you. I implore you, my child, look at the earth and sky and everything in them, and consider how God made them out of what did not exist and that human beings come into being the same way" (2 Macc. 7:22-23 and 27-28).

CHAPTER 10

Suffering: Torment and Triumph

> *"And if we are children, then we*
> *are heirs, heirs of God and*
> *joint-heirs with Christ, provided*
> *that we share his suffering, so*
> *as to share his glory."*
>
> (Rom. 8:17)

Throughout the two thousand years of Church history, Catholics have regarded suffering as not only inevitable but as a badge of our faith to be worn and borne with dignity and courage. In these days, however, a dramatic change has occurred with respect to this long accepted doctrine. The modern world is enjoying such technological sophistication that most people believe science can ultimately relieve *all* of our suffering. Medicine is taking great strides in the alleviation and cure of many previously hopeless diseases, while psychologists offer relief from our psychological and emotional ailments. Industry tantalises us with devices to provide more leisure time and ever-increasing comfort. The result is that modern man finds suffering repulsive. He believes he can and should avoid it at all costs and he becomes angry and petulant when he cannot. He feels cheated by the extravagant promises of medicine and psychology and when these let him down, he rushes off to avail himself of dubious alternative medical practices such as the enneagram, therapeutic touch, flower remedies and magical cures.

This neurotic drive to avoid suffering forces many to seek frantic pleasures in a never ending sequence of videos, sports, parties, toys, drugs and alcohol. Any diversion will do as long as it prevents us from having to face reality. Yet reality never stops being real. It will force itself upon us no matter how much we play at "ostrich" and hide our heads in the sand.

We must avoid pain at all cost, we must never become sick, we must never accept any kind of inconvenience in our comfortable lives and it is sheer madness to ever think of sacrificing ourselves for the good of another. Naturally, we prefer not to dwell on death at all. Death is always too far in the future for it to disturb our present complacency.

Such aversion to pain is so pervasive that even many Christians distort the Word of God to assuage their own fears. In spite of numerous references in Scripture to the inevitability and the value of suffering, they prefer to ignore these passages. Instead they naively assume that their prayers will be answered exactly as they want and the Divine Benevolence will instantly cure all their ills. Of course, Jesus did tell us to pray for healing and we should do so in faith and expectancy, but the Word of God still has much to say about the importance of the Cross in our lives. In fact, the Cross is the *centrepiece* of our faith.

We are Christians and Jesus makes no apology for what that truly means. "If anyone wants to be a follower of mine, let him renounce himself and take up his cross and follow me" (Matt. 16:24). To be a true disciple then, imposes three obligations upon us. Firstly, we must renounce ourselves. That means we must overcome the body's demands for constant gratification. We must bring the appetites under the control of the spirit. Secondly, we must take up our cross. A cross is a heavy, cumbersome and painful object which we would rather not carry at all. Yet it is an indispensable burden in our journey through life. Sometimes in the midst of pain it is hard for us to really believe Jesus when he said, "My yoke is easy and my burden is light" (Matt. 11:30). Thirdly, we must follow Jesus and that means to walk in his blood-stained footsteps. At the end of the journey our own Calvary awaits us. The beauty of it all is that beyond this cross there is the eternal joy of our own personal resurrection. "But we believe that if we died with Christ, then we shall also live with him" (Rom 6:8).

The truth is that suffering is inevitable. No one can escape from it. Not even the wealthiest billionaire can buy freedom from pain of one kind or another. Suffering is not a respecter of persons. It afflicts the rich and the poor, the powerful and the weak, the righteous and the evil-doer, and this is a fact of our human condition. In the Garden of Eden there was no suffering. Adam and Eve lived a blissful pain-free life, having been born without Original Sin. They enjoyed the perpetual blessing of God and it would have continued for ever had they not listened to Satan and consumed the forbidden fruit. This sin was so devastating that it resulted in consequences for the entire human race and these consequences are sin, sickness, sadness and death. From that day forward, all of mankind would be so easily tempted to sin. Sin can be both personal sin such as anger, lust, envy, pride, gluttony, avarice and sloth and also sin committed against others, such as gossip, violence, theft, lies and murder. "Yahweh asked Cain, 'Where is your brother Abel?' 'I do not know,' he replied. 'Am I my brother's keeper?'" (Gen. 4:9).

From the moment of the Original Sin our bodies would no longer be healthy and obedient to the demands of holiness but would succumb to sickness and disease. From that day forward, our minds would be given to sadness, that is to say to all kinds of mental and emotional disorders. From that day forward, we would all have to die, either suddenly by accident or violence, or by the degenerative processes of old age. We can rage all we want against these awful tragedies but our rage will not make them go away. "Well then, it was through one man that sin came into the world and through sin death, and thus death has spread through the whole human race because everyone has sinned" (Rom. 5:12).

One of the regrettable consequences of the fallen human condition is that many people who are experiencing pain of one kind or another become angry with God. They rave against him, accusing him of not caring, of not loving, and they may even scoff at him for not being powerful enough to take away their hurt. This is unjust. It was not God who tempted Adam and Eve to sin. It was

Satan who enticed them and our anger ought to be placed where it truly belongs. We should attack, hate, revile and renounce Satan, who is the ultimate cause of our sufferings. God is innocent and God suffers when we suffer. Satan rejoices when we suffer and tempts us to blame God for it.

Children die of hunger, unborn babies are never allowed to see the light of day because of abortion, people of conscience are imprisoned and tortured, innocent people are massacred over a miserable piece of land or for greed, six million Jews are gassed and cremated by the evil of Nazism, and the powerful control the little people with guns and with the even more sinister weapon of poverty. Not only is man inhumane towards other men, but man is also inhumane towards God. We commit personal sins without ever thinking that by so doing we are nailing Jesus to the cross again and again. Was it not for these very sins that Jesus was cruelly crucified?

We fail to make the obvious connection between sin and misery, both the misery we cause for ourselves and the misery our sin inflicts upon others. If I choose to turn my back on God's law and live a life of sin, I will engineer my own misery and bring pain to my neighbour. In my psychotherapy practice I see a lot of pain. Naturally, many of my patients are suffering from specific diseases such as depression, post-traumatic stress disorder, obsessive-compulsive disorder and so on, but the remainder are either inflicting their own pain on themselves by leading a life of sin or they are being sinned against by others. Either way, sin is a major cause of pain in our society.

Yet there has to be some purpose to suffering, otherwise life is indeed an unbearable valley of tears. There has to be some hope in the midst of the tragedies which surround us. Even if all people were converted and gave up sinning against God, against themselves and others, we would still have to face the pain of illness and death. There would still be children dying of leukaemia. In the end, everyone asks the questions, "Why?" and "How can God allow it?"

There are seven building blocks which can help us to arrive at a proper understanding of the profound mystery of suffering. The first of these is to remember that suffering was not God's invention. It was the dreadful consequence of the Original Sin of Adam and Eve. The world has no idea just how terrible that first offence was to an all perfect God. It was a *monstrous* act and in all justice, deserved the annihilation of the human race. And it was precisely because of this sin that suffering entered into our lives. It was the *mercy* of God which prompted him to predict the coming of Jesus by which we would be redeemed and by which our suffering would no longer be meaningless. God's love gave our pain a whole new purpose in the scheme of things.

It is important to understand that when Lucifer, the brightest and most intelligent of all the angels, decided that he wanted to oppose God, he was cast into Hell for all eternity. Why was that same punishment not meted out to Adam and Eve, since they too decided to oppose God? The reason that God chose to be merciful to us and not to Satan is that Satan tempted himself and therefore deserved Hell, while we were tempted by Satan and weakened by his lies. It was not a self-generated act by Adam and Eve. Lucifer, being so close to God, made an *eternal* choice by his act of rebellion. There could be no hope of redemption for the angel who had seen God and yet defied him, but there was hope for us. Therefore, although we might rail against God for permitting sickness and death, God's allowing the human race to continue, even in pain, was a wondrous act of divine mercy. He considered us to be salvageable. The consequences of our sin could have been much worse.

The second building block in our understanding of suffering is that the second person of the Holy Trinity, Jesus Christ the Son of God, came to earth as a little baby, lived in this valley of tears with us, suffered hunger, thirst, fatigue, grief, heat and cold, just as we do, then died a horrible death upon the cross. Whatever we might think about suffering, however much we might protest that it is unfair, we cannot ignore the fact that *our God suffered.* He accepted terrible torture in humility, silence and love, "led like a lamb to the slaughter" (Isa. 53:7). We who are mere creatures are in no position to criticize the God who suffered and died that we might live. He identified himself with the pain that we suffer from the sin in the world and from the on-going evil work of the Devil.

Stephen Lawhead, in his novel *Byzantium,* describes the conversion of a Viking barbarian called Gunnar. Gunnar has finally understood the differences between his former god of war, Odin, who inflicted pain, and his new true God, Jesus, who accepted pain.

He finds himself explaining this mystery to a former priest called Aidan, who has lost his faith because of having been tortured in prison. "Did you really think that Christ would blunt the spear points, deflect the lash, cause the chains to melt away when they touched your skin? Did you expect to walk in sunlight and not feel the heat, or to go without water and not grow thirsty? Did you think that all the hatred would turn to brotherly love the moment you strode into view? Did you think both storms and tempers would calm because of the tonsure on your head? Did you believe that God would shield you forever from the hurt and pain of this sin-riven world? That you would be spared the injustice and strife others were forced to endure? That disease would no longer afflict you, that you would live forever untouched by the tribulations of common humanity? Fool! All these things Christ suffered and more."

Earlier Gunnar almost cries out, "Sure, this is the heart of the great mystery: that God became man, shouldering the weight of suffering so that on the final day none could say, 'Who are you to judge the world? What do you know of injustice? What do you know of torture, sickness, poverty? How dare you call yourself a righteous God! What do you know of death?' *He knows, Aidan, He knows!*" God does not know simply because he is God. He knows because he became a man. Gunnar *found* the Faith because of suffering. Aidan *lost* the Faith because of suffering. We too have the same choice when we are asked to suffer.

The third stone in the building of our understanding is that suffering is *redemptive.* So often our pain seems useless and pointless, yet it never is. It has a redemptive action, which is to say that our suffering mitigates against our own time in Purgatory, and it is honoured by God in the conversion of sinners who are otherwise bound for Hell. Suffering saves souls. Some may ask then, if the crucifixion of Christ was not sufficient. It is a good question. Christ's redemptive act was much more than sufficient. One solitary drop of his Precious Blood would have been enough to redeem the world, but we are told by St. Paul, "Now I rejoice in my sufferings for your sake, and in my flesh I am filling up what is lacking in the afflictions of Christ on behalf of his body which is the Church" (Col. 1:24). St. Paul recognised that, while Jesus had mightily redeemed the entire world, the Mystical Body of Christ, which is you and me, still has to suffer "to fill up what is lacking." In spite of the crucifixion, we must as a body, atone for our collective sins against God's justice and his justice must be appeased. It is said that no man is an island, and indeed it is true. Everything I do affects all of my brothers and sisters. If I sin, I give Satan the power to work more evil in the world. If I perform a loving act, I give God the opportunity to show more mercy to the world. "If one part is hurt all the parts share its pain. And if one part is honoured, all the parts share its joy" (1 Cor. 12:26).

As a result of that connectedness of every human person to all other human persons, the sins of the world will afflict me, even though I may be innocent. Therefore a good woman may be violated by a drunken husband, an innocent unborn may be ripped from his mother's womb, a beautiful child may die of cancer, a man may commit a murder in a remote part of the world and by all of these, I am somehow weakened. In a word, our suffering does not come from God. It comes from the unbearable load of sin in the world and the innocent are often caught up in its evil net. The Mystical Body of Christ still has to take up its cross, follow Jesus along the Via Dolorosa to its own Calvary, and beyond that to the joy of resurrection.

Yet God is a merciful God. The suffering of the innocent, while it is in and of itself an evil thing, is transformed by God into a powerful act of his on-going redemptive work in the lives of men and women. Evil is evil and human beings cannot bring good out of it, yet God can. "Nothing is impossible to God" (Luke 1:37). God is able to somehow bring good fruit out of what appears to be dark and crushing. He allows Satan to do his evil and that is the mystery of evil which we can not fathom, but he turns Satan's evil work against him. When the innocent suffer, God responds by saving souls, while Satan, who at first rejoices in this suffering of the innocent, ends up gnashing his teeth in frustration. When all is said and done, his worst efforts only give glory to God.

The fourth building block is that through suffering we learn *obedience,* a virtue greatly valued by God. "Son, though he was, Christ learned obedience from what he suffered" (Heb. 5:8). Jesus was God, yet in his human state he had to learn total obedience to his Father in Heaven, and that was accomplished by means of suffering. Therefore we too can learn to be docile before our God when we suffer well. Suffering tempers the will, brings us to a recognition of our own helplessness and leads us to rely completely on the Providence of God. Suffering humbles us, for by it we realize that our own power is never enough. "I shall pass this third through the fire, refine them as silver is refined, test them as gold is tested. He will call on my name and I shall answer him" (Zech. 13:9). God therefore allows our suffering to refine us and to test us. Just as gold is purified in a crucible so we become purified by pain and our faith is put to the test. The evil of our suffering is graciously turned around by a good God to our spiritual benefit. "My dear friends, do not be taken aback at the testing by fire which is taking place among you, as though something strange were happening to you; but in so far as you share in the sufferings of Christ, be glad, so that you may enjoy a much greater gladness when his glory is revealed" (1 Pet. 4:12-13).

It is part of the mystery of God's plan that, aside from the beneficial effects of suffering for me personally, my suffering also benefits others. When a man sins against me, my suffering can be used by God to redeem that same man. For example, a wife who is being abused by a violent husband and who decides to stay in her marriage is obviously destined to continue suffering at the hands of her husband. If she generously offers up her pain to God for her husband's soul, then the pain he is inflicting will rebound from Heaven upon his head and may save his soul from damnation. The wife's willingness to sacrifice herself becomes a redemptive grace for the perpetrator. "If we have died with him we shall also live with him. If we endure, we shall also reign with him" (2 Tim. 2:11-12).

The fifth stone in our building is that suffering unites us to the passion of Jesus. St. Rita of Cascia was a wonderful example of this kind of heroic suffering and its marvellous results. She married Ferdinand, a man of violent temper who was impulsive and often cruel. He associated constantly with a criminal element in the town. Rita decided to bear it all for love of Jesus, and she did this for many years. Miraculously, her forbearance resulted in a beautiful conversion for Ferdinand, who became a devout Catholic and a devoted husband before his violent death. He was murdered one evening on his way home from Cascia by his former criminal associates.

Rita's two sons seemed to have developed many of their father's violent traits and they repaid Rita's love with coldness and ingratitude. She simply increased her prayers for their salvation. Indeed she begged the Lord to take her two sons to himself before they would commit any rash acts which would endanger their souls. God answered her prayers. They both fell into a prolonged illness and the suffering they experienced brought them to reflect on their lives of sin, with the result that they repented and died peacefully less than a year after their father. St. Rita then embarked upon a long life as a religious and suffered terribly with the stigmata of the Crown of Thorns. The sacrificial suffering in her marriage was the powerful force which saved the immortal souls of her husband and her sons. The sacrificial suffering in her religious life was the powerful force which saved the immortal souls of many sinners. Our suffering carries with it the same privilege.

The sixth building block for our understanding is that when we suffer on earth, we reduce or even eliminate the punishment due to us in Purgatory. Purgatory is the place of purification, a wonderful sign of God's mercy. We pray that no one dies in mortal sin, for that can only be rewarded by eternal fire. But many of us will die in venial sin, which although it is not deadly, leaves the soul defiled and as Scripture says, "Nothing defiled shall enter it" (Rev. 21:27). That is to say, we must be purified of all sin before we can be allowed to enter heaven. Therefore, while God's justice must be appeased, it is by his mercy that we may have to undergo that final purification. "It all shows that God's judgement is just, so that you may be found worthy of the kingdom of God; it is for the sake of this that you are suffering now" (2 Thess. 1:5).

This is not a cause for despondency. It is a cause for joy and gratitude to our loving God. The wonderful fact is that God has stacked the deck in our favour. There is only one thing that works against our salvation and that is sin, but there are numerous things which counteract the effects of sin and which can reduce and even eliminate the time due to us in Purgatory. These consist of our own personal suffering, the Masses we attend during life, the Masses offered up for us by others, the Sacraments and the graces they bestow upon our souls, especially our contrition in the Sacrament of Reconciliation, our own prayers, the prayers of others for us, the prayers of the holy souls in Purgatory for us, the prayers of the saints, our staunch faith, our own good works, the sufferings of Christians all over the world of which we are beneficiaries, and especially the generous suffering of victim souls. All of these wondrous things are balanced against our sins and the atonement due for them. Indeed, God is infinitely generous. It is a well-known fact in Catholic theology that it is far better to suffer here on earth, even for a long time, than to spend one day in Purgatory. Our earthly suffering, then, is by far preferable to any experience of Purgatory. This may be difficult for us here on earth to understand but the holy souls in Purgatory surely do understand it.

When we die we go before Jesus and we see him in all his splendid glory. We see the Beatific Vision. If we must then go to Purgatory, we lose that heavenly vision and the greatest pain of all is to have seen him and now not to see him for a time. Ask any holy contemplative who has been given the grace of beholding Jesus and then has to enter the "dark night of the soul." It is a very dark night indeed, and is in fact, an experience of Purgatory on earth. Purgatory, apart from any suffering (as we think of suffering), is really an all consuming *longing* for Jesus which cannot be relieved "until we have paid the last penny" (Luke 12:59). Therefore our suffering on earth is a grace. It hurts but it will hurt a lot less than having beheld Jesus in his glory only to lose him for a time.

How beautiful it is for us to suffer generously and offer it up for the souls in Purgatory that their time may be shortened. They, in their turn, will constantly pray for us that we might never have to experience the torment of Purgatory but rather will go directly to heaven on our death.

In addition to the inevitable suffering which all of us experience, the sicknesses, the emotional pain, and the death of loved ones, as well as our own death, it is also a good and holy thing to take on additional suffering for the sake of the kingdom. There are heroic souls called "victim souls" who are personally asked by Jesus to suffer for a holy purpose. They agree to take on a particular pain whereby a special act of redemption dear to the Sacred Heart of Jesus can take place.

St. Francis of Assisi, who suffered so much, was able to write, "My Good Shepherd, who have shown your very gentle mercy to us unworthy sinners in various physical pains and sufferings, give grace and strength to me, your little lamb, that in no tribulation or anguish or pain may I turn away from you." Blessed Henry Suso said, "Suffering is a short pain and a long joy." Blessed Sebastian Valfre wrote, "When it is all over you will not regret having suffered; rather you will regret having suffered so little and suffered that little so badly." These holy people knew the real merits of suffering and continuously offered up their suffering for the good of souls. Undoubtedly, because of the work of victim souls, countless people have been converted, brought to repentance and have returned to their Father's house. "You will only have to suffer for a little while: the God of all grace who called you to eternal glory in Christ will restore you, he will confirm, strengthen and support you" (1 Pet. 5:10).

The most visible sufferings of the elect occur in those souls who have been given the privilege of living the passion of Jesus Christ through the stigmata. They bear on their bodies the marks of the nails, the spear wound in the side and sometimes the crown of thorns. St. Paul himself was the first to suffer the stigmata. "I carry branded on my body the marks of Jesus" (Gal. 6:17). Many saints have lived with the stigmata, perhaps the most famous being St. Francis, and there are many in our own day. The most famous of all the modern stigmatists was Padre Pio, now Blessed, whose wounds bled at the Consecration of the Mass. He had an insatiable hunger for souls, and countless souls must have been saved by his sharing in the sufferings of Christ.

Everyone is familiar with the gospel account of doubting Thomas, the Apostle who refused to believe that Jesus had risen from the dead unless he was able to touch the wounds in Jesus' hands and side. Jesus, in his mercy and love for Thomas, did appear to him and allowed him to do precisely that. But Jesus did not do this simply to prove to Thomas what he ought to have already believed. Pope Gregory the Great wrote, "The disbelief of Thomas has done more for our faith than the faith of the other disciples. As he touches Christ and is won over to belief, every doubt is cast aside and our faith is strengthened. So the disciple who doubted, then felt Christ's wounds, becomes a witness to the reality of the resurrection." Therefore Jesus was also giving us absolute proof that he had died and was now risen when he displayed his wounds. In our own day, by means of his stigmatists, he continues to give us that very same proof. When we see the wounds of Christ on a saintly person we are being confirmed in the death and resurrection of our Lord and our faith is strengthened.

One of the guaranteed signs of being a Christian is that he or she will be persecuted. We are a sign of contradiction to the non-Christian world and therefore become targets for the hatred of a world which rejects Jesus. "In truth I tell you, there is no one who has left house, brothers, sisters, mother, father, children or land for my sake and for the sake of the gospel who will not receive a hundred times as much houses, brothers, sisters, mothers, children and land — *and persecutions too* — now in this present time and, in the world to come, eternal life" (Mark 10:29-30). Jesus promises persecution for being his disciples, but he also promises eternal life. "Blessed are those who are persecuted for righteousness' sake for theirs is the kingdom of Heaven" (Matt. 5:10). Jesus takes it even further and tells us "Blessed are you when people abuse you and persecute you and speak all kinds of calumny against you falsely on my account. Rejoice for your reward will be great in heaven" (Matt. 5:11). It is hard to rejoice in the midst of persecution yet Jesus tells us that by it we have great cause for rejoicing. The pain will come to an end. Our heavenly reward never will.

Many souls embrace self-inflicted suffering, which is called penance or mortification. Indeed, the Church commends this practice as a way of bringing the body and its appetites into submission and as a way of growing in virtue. That is why we voluntarily deny ourselves during the season of Lent as a preparation for the remembrance of the passion of Jesus at the Passover. However, the Church does not ask us to confine ourselves to Lent only. We are required to mortify ourselves every Friday either by not eating meat or by some other chosen sacrifice. These kinds of suffering are very powerful and are to be encouraged throughout the year since we grow thereby in self-control and in holiness. Jesus greatly values these little acts of mortification for the sake of his kingdom.

The greatest and ultimate of all sufferings is of course martyrdom. "No greater love has any man than to lay down his life for his friends" (John 15:13). Jesus is our very best friend and to be given the grace of martyrdom is the most wondrous of all privileges. All is forgiven and atoned for and so such a soul is admitted straight to heaven. The supreme sacrifice merits the supreme reward. It is a grace not given to all, but those who receive it are also given the grace to endure it. Many cowards have died heroically for the Lord and they could not have done it without the special grace of courage given by the Holy Spirit.

Martyrdom, however, need not always be the red martyrdom of violent death. It can be, and more often is, the white martyrdom of prolonged suffering on earth. Our Blessed Mother suffered such a martyrdom as she witnessed the terrible death of her Son. She was not asked to die for the kingdom but she was asked to undergo a living death with her Son. The history of the Church is filled with unsung heroes and heroines who lived out a life of relentless suffering, offering it up to God. As Fr. John Hardon, S.J. said, "Not all of us are called to a martyr's death, but all of us are called to a martyr's life."

None of this is intended to mean that we are to become masochists who enjoy having pain. Certainly, many saints have often expressed a superhuman joy in suffering for Christ, but for most of us, pain is pain. Suffering is torment and we can often hardly bear it. Perhaps it will help a little to know that suffering for a Christian is a very high form of prayer. We tend to think of prayer as talking with God, and indeed it is, but it is better described as communication with God. Suffering is a powerful way of communicating with the God who also suffered. One who is suffering is automatically praying because he or she is sharing in the cross of Jesus. When the good thief hung on his cross beside Jesus and asked for mercy, Jesus said, "Truly I tell you, this day you will be with me in Paradise" (Luke 23:43). The suffering of the good thief became united with the agony of Jesus and that was enough to guarantee his entry into heaven *that very day.*

When we suffer well, and offer it up to God for his holy purpose, we too are united with the agony of Jesus and our salvation is as secure as that of the good thief. God will never be outdone in generosity. His reward for us is "a full measure, pressed down, shaken together and overflowing" (Luke 6:38).

It is very helpful, when in the midst of pain or suffering of any kind, to ask the question, "Which part of the cross of Jesus am I being asked to carry?" For example, if I am depressed, I am identified with Jesus in the Garden of Gethsemane whose "heart was sorrowful even unto death" (Matt. 26:38). If I am betrayed, I experience the treacherous kiss of Judas. If my body is sick or racked by pain, I carry the physical agony of Jesus in his scourging, the crowning with thorns and the crucifixion. If I am ridiculed, I experience the taunting of Jesus as he hung upon the cross. Even in poverty I live the poverty of Jesus, who was born in a stable had no place to lay his head and was buried in a borrowed tomb. No matter what suffering I am being asked to endure I can connect it to the passion of Jesus. This insight makes it easier to see the privilege of our own pain, to shoulder our cross with courage and to know that Jesus "knows" because he experienced the self-same pain. As a result, I am empowered to embrace the cross instead of trying to flee from it and I am prompted to offer it up for the world. In our suffering we are not alone. Jesus walks beside us sharing the pain with us. Just as Simon of Cyrene helped carry Jesus' cross, so Jesus is there, helping us to carry ours.

The seventh and last building block is that suffering is a kind of spiritual boot-camp. It is valuable in that it trains our spiritual muscles, thereby rendering us more fit for the great battle between the forces of good and the forces of evil. Oftentimes, we balk at a pain which is inflicted upon us and we cry out that it is unfair. We insist that we could bear it a lot better if only this would happen or that would happen. While this is a very understandable human reaction, it really does not help much. Its effect is only to entrench within us an attitude of resentment and even self-pity which blocks our ability to cope. St. Francis de Sales said, "Many people would be ready to accept suffering so long as they were not inconvenienced by it. 'I wouldn't be bothered by poverty' says one, 'if it didn't keep me from helping my friends, educating my children, and living respectably.' 'It wouldn't bother me' says another, 'so long as people didn't think it was my own fault.' Or another would be willing to suffer evil lies told about him as long as no one believed his detractors."

The point is that we are not in a position to bargain with God about the exact dimensions of our cross. The fact that it is always so hard to bear is what makes it a cross. All we can do is ask the Lord for the grace to bear it. Naturally, it is a good and holy thing to pray that it will be lifted, but while we wait on God's answer, it is still easier on us if we embrace it.

When we are given a heavy cross to bear, it is all too easy to give in to bitterness. This is a trap. Fr. James Sullivan writes, "Dear Lord, how do I act when I am faced with a cross? When people misunderstand me, when they are sarcastic and cruel, when my fears are ridiculed or my plans rejected, how do I feel? Or when someone else is preferred before me, or when I am fired and have no recourse, when I am told that I have cancer and nothing can be done, am I not tempted to let these things make me bitter and resentful? Teach me to be like you instead. For me, as for you, acceptance of his will can put meaning into every cross, can turn Calvary into an act of redeeming love. I do accept your will for me, my Father."

Jesus, at the Last Supper offered his body and blood for us, "This is my Body which will be given up for you" (Luke 22:19), "This cup in the new covenant is my blood poured out for you" (Luke 22:20). We too can offer our own body and blood back to God, that is to say our suffering, which God will graciously accept. In doing so, we reject useless bitterness and in embracing the pain, we transcend it. Bitterness merely makes our suffering much worse. Acceptance transforms it into rejoicing.

Another strategy which we often use is to bargain with God by suggesting how he should work things out. We think we know the best solution and we plead with God to do it our way. For example, a man may be abandoned by his wife, who has left her family to live with a lover. The distraught man then begins to ask God to immediately bring his wayward wife to her senses. This is a good thing to pray for and it is right that he should do so. But when it seems to take forever to see a change of heart, the man begins to get angry with God. "Are you God or are you not? Why do you not bring my wife back?" The answer is that God agrees with this poor man and dearly longs for his wife to come to her senses but even God is bound by the gift of free will which he gave to the woman.

God will definitely hear the husband's prayers and answer them to the extent that he will show her how wrong her actions are, but he can never *force* her to choose the right path. He cannot, and will not, violate her free will. We must pray for those who sin against us but it is foolish to blame God when they refuse to change.

We in turn cannot impose our solution upon God. God being God has the complete picture. The past, the present and the future are all "present" to him and so he can see what we cannot. The result is that while we are desperately praying for what we want, God may desire to give us something much more precious. Suffering is still a mystery but we can be sure of one thing. When one person is hurt and another person is responsible for that hurt, God will set about trying to ensure the salvation of both parties. He loves the one sinned against and he loves the sinner equally. God has no favourites. He wants the injured party to find relief but he also wants the sinner to come to repentance. Therefore he may seem to be slow in responding to our pleas as he waits for the best moment in which to try and reach the heart of the perpetrator. As St. Peter wrote "But there is one thing, my dear friends, that you must never forget: that with the Lord, a day is like a thousand years and a thousand years are like a day. The Lord is not being slow in answering his promises, as some people think he is; rather he is being patient with you, wanting nobody to be lost and everybody to be brought to repentance" (2 Pet. 3:8-9).

Catherine Doherty of Madonna House once said, "Pain is the kiss of Christ." Scott Hahn, in his book *A Father Who Keeps His Promises,* writes, "Let's face it, we humans really don't want God to love us *that* much. It's simply too demanding. Obedience is one thing but this sort of love clearly calls for more than keeping commandments. It calls for nothing less than total self-donation. That might not be a difficult job for the three infinite Persons of the Trinity, but for creatures like us, such love is a summons to martyrdom. This invitation requires much more suffering and self-denial than giving up chocolate for Lent. It demands nothing less than a constant dying to self." Yet we should take courage. "We are afflicted in every way but not crushed; perplexed but not driven to despair; persecuted but not forsaken; struck down but not destroyed; always carrying in the body the death of Jesus, so that the life of Jesus may also be manifested in our bodies" (2 Cor. 4:8-10). Therefore we might as well face the fact that as Catholics we will not be able to avoid suffering, but our cross will also never break us. It will be tailor-made for our shoulders by the same Jesus who died for us. If we choose to be disciples of the Lord, he will grant us the grace to be able to persevere in our pain. If pain is truly the kiss of Christ, then should we not also return the kiss by accepting our cross with love?

There is an amusing story about a man who was feeling overburdened by the weight of his cross. So he decided to call in at the Cross-distribution Centre in town. On arriving there he asked if he could swap his cross for another. The attendant told him to go ahead. The man laid down his cross and proceeded to try the others on for size. The first cross was too long, the second was too short and he carried on until he found the perfect one. Delighted, he asked if he could keep that one. "Sure!" said the attendant "No problem." As the greatly relieved man was going out the door the attendant called out "By the way, that is the cross you came in with!" The moral of the story is simply that our own particular cross is fashioned by the Lord and no one else can carry it.

As Catholic families we experience all kinds of suffering. We face the challenge of constantly dying to self in order to love as we should. We all have to cope with the irritating habits and even the sins of our spouse. We have to sacrifice our time and energy for our children and live with their pains in growing up. Sometimes we wonder how we can ever cope with the needs and demands of the others. Added to the daily grind of self-sacrifice we must also face illnesses, accidents, bereavements and the malice of others towards us.

We cannot be expected to welcome all this with joy but we can *endure* it. We can persevere and never break since we have the firm assurance of Jesus that he will be by our side. He will also take our pain and make it into a powerful weapon against Satan and a mighty force for the fullness of the kingdom. Moreover, it is suffering that can unite our family as never before. In sharing adversity, we learn to love one another more deeply. "For just as the sufferings of Christ overflow into our lives, so too does the encouragement we receive through Christ. So if we have hardships to undergo, this will contribute to your encouragement and your salvation" (2 Cor. 1:5-6). Therefore take heart. We all have to suffer but it is never without meaning or purpose. The torment can be turned into triumph. "The sufferings of the present are as nothing compared with the glory to be revealed in us" (Rom. 8:18).

CHAPTER 11

Depression: From Darkness to Light

> *"All night long she is*
> *weeping, tears running*
> *down her cheeks."*
>
> (Lam. 1:2)

It is reasonable to ask why there should be a chapter on depression in a book about the Catholic family. The answer is two-fold. Firstly, one out of five people in the general population suffer from the illness, so it is likely that one or more persons in any family are afflicted. Unfortunately, healthy members of a family often do not recognize the disease in a loved one until it becomes dangerously severe and the sufferer's behaviour is dismissed as being due to bad moods, sinful tendencies or personality. It is alarming that the condition is frequently missed or mis-diagnosed by medical doctors who ought to know better. Secondly, depression is seriously misunderstood by Christians in particular, with the result that major damage can be inflicted upon depressed people by well-meaning would-be healers. This will be addressed in detail later on in this chapter.

If a person has never been depressed then he or she should never presume to judge someone who is. There is no way for a non-depressive to appreciate the darkness and pain within a depressive's mind, heart and soul. Depression is a living hell.

It can become so hopeless within that the patient is completely unable to visualize any other way to find relief than to commit suicide. A person in this extreme is mentally sick and is no longer capable of tapping into his former notions of right and wrong. As such, his moral judgement and his moral responsibility are greatly impaired and may even be totally inoperative. Therefore, even if such a person does take his own life, we have the right to expect that God's love and mercy will be given in full measure. God's commandment "Thou shalt not kill" (Ex. 20:13) was given to people in their *right mind,* people who could freely choose between good and evil. When the freedom to choose has been annihilated by disease, will God not judge a man differently from one whose free will is intact? This is the teaching of the Church. Surely this is very good news for the countless Catholic families who have had to live through the suicide of a loved one. How many family members have come to me over the years, in bitter despondency, believing that their brother or sister, son or daughter, must be in hell because they took their own life? Our God is a God of mercy and justice. Neither of these divine attributes would permit God to condemn one of his children who no longer had control over his decisions and actions.

Naturally, this is not a defence of suicide as a legitimate option for someone in full possession of his or her faculties. Suicide is never legitimate. It is an act of killing and as such violates the prerogative of God and God alone to take human life. No true Catholic could ever excuse self-annihilation by someone in his or her right mind. By the same token we can never admire a doctor who collaborates in a so-called "assisted suicide." This is nothing more than murder with the patient's full consent. It is the ultimate perversion of the virtue of mercy and condemns both the doctor and the patient.

Depression is a disease not a choice. It may surprise some to know that depression is not so much a mental disorder as a real physical and chemical pathology. Certainly, it has mental symptoms but these are secondary to an underlying chemical dysfunction in the brain. Many other "physical" diseases also exhibit mental symptoms. To take only one example, a person with hardening of the arteries (arteriosclerosis) may exhibit loss of short term memory, delusions, confusion, anger and thought disorder, all of which are mental manifestations, but these arise out of the physical changes in the blood vessels of the brain. Likewise depression and its attendant symptoms arise out of chemical changes in the brain.

Current research indicates that depression occurs when certain chemicals called serotonins become depleted. The brain requires an adequate level of serotonins for it to function normally. As the serotonins drop below a critical threshold then the symptoms of depression will become manifest. But like all things human, nothing is that simple. Research has also shown that depression is a *genetic* disorder. People who develop depression have inherited a gene for depression from one of their parents. In fact, if one parent suffers from depression then all of the children in that family have a one-in-three chance of carrying the defective gene. This does not mean that such a person is born depressed. However, it does mean that he or she is at risk for developing the disease somewhere down the line. At some point in his or her life, an event will occur which triggers the gene and the depression is activated. Such an event may be a bereavement, a failure, a financial crisis, a rejection or any other occurrence perceived by the person as overwhelming. It can also occur in apparent response to a trivial event. This is the "last straw" phenomenon, whereby a genetically pre-disposed person is exposed to many minor stresses to the point where he loses his resilience and simply folds with the next stress which comes along, no matter how insignificant it may seem. With some people, it may be much less dramatic and unrelated to an identifiable occurrence. These patients just slowly and imperceptibly sink into a deeper and deeper depression and are usually not diagnosed until they are in severe straits.

Research in this field is growing at a rapid rate and all kinds of new information is surfacing regarding complex enzymes in the cells of the brain. There is no need here to elaborate on that work. For the purposes of this chapter, it is enough to understand that depression is an inherited tendency, that once the gene is triggered there is a dramatic fall in the level of serotonins in the brain and that all of its symptoms arise out of this chemical imbalance.

The symptoms of depression are very characteristic and when one is looking for them, they are relatively easy to recognize. A sufferer will complain of at least five of the following symptoms over a period of time not less than two weeks:

1. Difficulty falling or staying asleep. Waking several times during the night or waking up early in the morning and cannot get back to sleep.
2. Sleeping too much even during the day.
3. Feeling tired during the day.
4. Low energy. A loss of former drive.
5. Poor appetite or overeating.
6. Little interest or pleasure in doing things, that is to say, poor motivation.
7. Feeling sad, down, hopeless or guilty.
8. Crying a lot or wanting to cry but cannot.
9. Feeling bad about oneself, thinking of oneself as worthless or a failure.
10. Inability to concentrate on such things as reading the newspaper or watching television.
11. Feeling fidgety, restless and moving around a lot more than usual.
12. Recent and recurring thoughts of death.
13. Suicidal or self-mutilating thoughts.
14. Irritability and anger.
15. Anxiety for hours at a time with no discernible cause.
16. Many depressed Christians find it very difficult or even impossible to pray.

Depressed people will often be heard to make such statements as:

"I feel tense all the time."
"My heart pounds and races."
"I feel nervous and shaky inside."
"I have trouble falling asleep."
"I wake up early in the morning and can't get back to sleep."
"I often wake up in the middle of the night."
"I feel that everything I do is an effort."
"I can't stop crying. I feel so sad and hopeless."

"I have no interest in my daily activities."

"I always feel tired."

"I wish I were dead. It would stop the pain."

"I cannot pray. I do not love God anymore. Therefore I must be dammed."

If ever anyone experiences such symptoms or perceives them in another, then a doctor should be consulted without delay. The longer nothing is done, the greater the risk that the depression will be intensified, perhaps to the point of suicide. It is wrong to assume that "it will pass." Indeed it might pass but that could take up to two years. Meanwhile the sufferer may deteriorate and his or her life will be in danger. Waiting merely prolongs unnecessary pain since depression is now a treatable disease and medical science can guarantee a seventy-five to eighty percent cure rate with the simplest of medications and effective psychotherapy.

There are a variety of types of depression, each with its own distinctive features:

1. Unipolar depression, now also called major affective disorder. This occurs in a previously healthy person and can have a sudden or gradual onset. It can be mild, moderate or severe and when severe can result in a suicide attempt. The term unipolar refers to the fact that the patient's mood does not fluctuate. The mood simply goes down and stays down unless treatment is initiated. The disease therefore has only one pole, namely depressed mood, hence the term "unipolar."

2. Bipolar depression. As the name implies, this disorder is characterised by having two poles rather than only one. As a result the mood tends to swing up and down, from very low to abnormally high. When in the low pole, the patient exhibits some or all of the symptoms of depression as previously listed. When high however, the person displays a persistently elevated, expansive or irritable mood. He or she may have inflated self-esteem, grandiose ideas, decreased need for sleep, talkativeness, racing thoughts, and very short attention span. The person may also indulge excessively in foolish activities such as unrestrained buying sprees, sexual indiscretions or

outrageous business investments. Such patients are at grave risk for suicide when they are in the down pole. When high they are at risk for hurting themselves through unrestrained behaviour and hurting others by their actions.

3. Dysthymia. This is a very large group within the general population. It is very easy to miss this condition since it is not as severe and obvious as a major affective disorder. Once the gene is triggered, these people will now be dysthymic *for life* and if it is recognized and treated, they will have to remain on therapy for the rest of their lives. Stopping treatment will simply result in recurrence of the disorder. Once dysthymia is activated, a person's mood hovers below the normal almost all of the time. There may be insomnia or hypersomnia, poor appetite or overeating, low energy or fatigue, low self-esteem, difficulty making decisions, poor concentration or feelings of hopelessness. Often there is irritability. If something good or pleasant occurs, the dysthymic may instantly become cheerful, sociable and happy. But as soon as the pleasant stimulus is over, he plunges back into his chronic low mood. As a result, dysthymic persons often seek out ways to help themselves "feel alive again" and so they are at risk for alcoholism or they indulge in compulsive masturbation, sexual indiscretions or use street drugs, especially marijuana. Some dysthymics are at risk for bouts of severe unipolar depression and in such cases the term "double depression" is used. That is to say they now have dysthymia plus major depression.

It is very, very difficult for a spouse to live with a dysthymic. His or her moods are unpredictable and there is often a dramatic response out of all proportion to a negative event. When he is in such a mood, there is simply no reasoning with him and all attempts to cheer him up will likely fail. He, himself, is not likely to have any insight into his own thought distortions and irritable behaviour and will tend to blame everyone or everything else for his misery. The good news is that most cases can be effectively treated.

4. Seasonal affective disorder or S.A.D. This is a variety of unipolar depression which is directly related to lack of

sunlight. Therefore, it occurs in the winter months, usually from November to March. The patient is perfectly well for the remainder of the year. Treatment consists of using an ultraviolet light device for about half an hour every morning during the winter. For those who work indoors, there is a light-screen which can be located on a desk or in the work place which provides low intensity ultraviolet light as a constant background.

Some children do get depressed and they are unique in the way it is expressed. Irritability, anger and consistent disobedient behaviour in my experience are often the signs of an underlying depressive disorder in a child. Certainly it is easier when one is faced with a chronically sad child. In such a case depression comes immediately to mind, but so often, the child does not display sadness. He or she is more likely to be irritable, complaining, negative and given to angry outbursts for trivial reasons.

Depressed teenagers will tend to be angry, disobedient and unreasonable, often getting into foolish activities, with painful consequences for themselves and their families. In other words, they exhibit similar features to the depressed child but the havoc they create is much more intensified and destructive. Teenagers are generally noted for their impulsiveness and this puts them at grave risk for unpredictably deciding, then and there, to commit suicide. As soon as they feel sufficiently hopeless, they may well take their own lives. If only they would wait a little longer, the severity of their depression would lift enough to give them some interest in living again and they would reject the suicidal impulse. Male teenagers will tend to use firearms if these are available. Females will prefer to overdose on pills. That is why I advise all parents never to have guns or drugs in the house while they have teenagers at home. To do so is to ask for trouble. If these means are not readily available to a depressed teenager, then by the time they find some other way, the depression may well have been alleviated enough to save their lives.

There are many other sub-classifications of depression but the major groups have been described and this is sufficient for the needs of this chapter.

Treatment of depression has come a long way in the past twenty years. There are six ways of approaching the problem and often it takes a combination of two or more of these to be effective.

1. Psychotherapy. The most effective form of psychotherapy is called *Cognitive Therapy.* The theory behind this work is that a person *feels* according to what he *thinks.* Therefore if someone is feeling sad then he or she must be thinking sad thoughts. Treatment is directed towards changing the thought pattern of the patient, to contradict illogical thinking and to redirect the mind into more normal patterns. This can be very effective but it requires dedication on the part of the therapist, who has to work hard to motivate the patient to persevere with the exercises.

2. Physical exercise. A good workout, which consists of thirty minutes of maximum effort three times a week, will release *endorphins* into the brain. These endorphins are the body's natural morphine and they counteract the chemical disorder of depression. However this is only effective for mild to moderate depression. It will not work for severe depression. There is also the problem of motivating a person to go out and exercise when he or she is suffering from fatigue and loss of energy.

3. Serotonin-enhancing foods. There are foods which are known to boost the levels of serotonin in the brain and which therefore have the potential to counteract depression, albeit mildly. These foods are melons, bananas, raspberries, strawberries, peanuts, cashews and almonds. It is interesting that dysthymic patients often express a craving for one or all of these. The body seems to "know" what it needs.

4. Herbal Preparations. There are many herbs which are being sold as antidepressants. They do not work. There is only one effective herbal preparation known thus far and that is *St. John's Wort.* The active ingredient is called *hypericum* and is excellent in the management of mild to moderate depression. It is not effective for the severe form. Its only draw back is that it can take a long time for it to show any beneficial results. Some people see no response for up to six months. In Germany,

medical doctors have found St. John's Wort to be so effective that it is now the "drug of choice" in the management of mild to moderate depression.

5. Modern Drugs. Many people today, and especially Christians, seem to have a strong prejudice against drugs because they are "unnatural." Likewise, they are willing to take all kinds of herbal preparations because they are "natural." This needs to be put into perspective. In any herbal medicine there is, of course, an effective ingredient but it is inevitably mixed with scores of other plant chemicals which are not therapeutic and may even be harmful. Herbal preparations are never pure in the therapeutic sense. Also there is good reason to believe that the dosage of the effective chemical is not consistent from one bottle to the next. For example, it was found in the nineteenth century that an extract of the foxglove could help patients with heart failure. But no guarantee of standardised dose could be given and so, at times, the patient received too little, which allowed the heart failure to get worse. At other times, the patient received too much and began to have nausea and vomiting. The chemists of the day simply extracted the effective ingredient, called *digitalis*, then discovered how to make it in the laboratory, and so the drug *digoxin* is now available, which guarantees a uniform dosage of the medication in every pill. The "unnatural" drug is by far preferable to and more effective than the natural extract.

The Bible clarifies this aspect of medicine very well. "He endows men with the knowledge to glory in his mighty works, through which the doctor eases pain and the druggist prepares his medicines; thus God's creative work continues without cease in its efficacy on the surface of the earth" (Sir. 38:6-8).

Therefore, medical discoveries are part of God's on-going creative work and he intends that we should take advantage of them. In displaying prejudice against these remedies, and that includes drugs, we are showing ingratitude to a loving God who has revealed them to medical science. This is absolutely not to say that all drugs are pristine pure and good. The fact is that God has only seen fit in his wisdom to reveal to us what we know to date. No doubt, if we were a truly holy people, which we are not, then God would have given us treatment tools much more effective than those we now have. Drugs do have undesirable side effects and that is simply what we deserve, given our continued sinfulness. Nevertheless, when I graduated from medical school in 1963 there was not one single drug effective for depression. Many patients died by suicide. Today I praise our benevolent Creator for giving us the as yet impure but effective drugs which we do have today, by which lives are saved. I continue to pray however that in his infinite mercy, he will show us even more perfect ways to cure this disease without side effects. "God's creative work continues without cease in its efficacy on the surface of the earth" (Sir. 38:8). Praise his holy name.

It is a good and holy thing to pray over any medication prescribed by a doctor. I have written a short prayer which I use on all prescriptions issued by me. "Heavenly Father, you know that all medicines are impure. I humbly ask that the Holy Spirit will breathe on this preparation so that its side effects will be eliminated, to the dismay of the Evil One, and its curative properties enhanced, to the glory of God. I thank you Father for you are a faithful and healing God. Amen." I would encourage every Catholic to pray this prayer when they or a loved one is given medication of any kind.

The new generation of antidepressants are remarkably effective and low in potential side effects. As with all drugs, some people do experience undesirable effects but very few have to discontinue the medication. These new drugs are absolutely non-addictive. They can be taken over very long periods of time (even for life) without any dependency whatsoever. There do not seem to be any unexpected long-term reactions but to be fair they have not yet been available long enough for this to be determined with absolute confidence. There is little risk of being able to commit suicide by overdosing on these drugs, and this makes them a good deal safer in the management of severely depressed persons. The dosage is always very simple, usually only once a day or, at most, twice a day, which makes it easy to remember, and improves patient compliance with the medication. As previously stated these medications will be successful in seventy-five to eighty percent of patients. Unfortunately, there are people who seem to be hypersensitive to even small doses of drugs and they need to be managed differently, often with poorer results.

6. Prayer. All diseases are amenable to prayer. "Paul went to see him and after a prayer he laid hands on the man and healed him" (Acts 28:8). "Any of you who is ill should send for the elders of the church, and they must anoint the sick person with oil in the name of the Lord and pray over him. The prayer of faith will save the sick person and the Lord will raise him up again and if he has committed any sins he will be forgiven. So confess your sins to one another and pray for one another to be cured" (James 5:14-16).

Note here that God does not *guarantee* a cure. James says to "pray for one another to be cured." God will decide whether a cure is appropriate or not for that person. God, in his infinite wisdom, knows what is best and it may be best for that person's immortal soul that he or she continue to suffer for his or her own sake and for the sake of sinners. God does promise that "the prayer of faith will *save* the sick person and the Lord will raise him up." This is a guarantee of *spiritual* healing, whereby a soul will be saved from sin, which is a far more deadly disease than any bodily ailment. Notice that James tells Christians first of all to confess their sins before praying for a cure. This is a vital prerequisite for healing prayer. So many Christians launch expectantly into prayer for cure and miss out the indispensable step of confession and cleansing. It would seem that before we can hope for God's healing, we must take our sins to the Lord and seek his forgiveness. Soul sickness must first be healed as a preparation for the healing of the body.

One day in my office, a slightly retarded young man was complaining of a problem with anger. After appropriate psychotherapy I asked if I could pray over him. He was a good Catholic and readily agreed. After the prayer for healing was over he astounded me by saying, "Your prayer won't have started to work yet because I need to go to confession." He was absolutely right and in spite of his low I.Q. he instinctively knew what many bright scholars do not. The soul must be cleansed before healing prayer can take effect. I still bow before that young man's wisdom, which did not come from himself but was infused in him by the Holy Spirit.

Many Christians labour under the misapprehension that all they have to do is to pray, lay on hands, and God will always cure the malady. This is a serious error and reduces God to a mere "sugar-daddy" who indulgently gives us everything we ask for. He is *God* and his holy will is much better for us than our own will, even when we pray for something which is good. God is not content with the merely good. He wants the very best for us and healing may or may not be the very best to his divine way of thinking.

This kind of misinterpretation of God's will leads to other distortions when it comes to praying for healing, and nowhere is this more potentially dangerous than in the area of depressive illness. A major problem that many Christians have with depression is that they believe it to be sinful. But the Bible makes no reference to depression at all. So how can Christians come to hold this opinion? They reach this conclusion because Scripture insists that Christians should have hope in the Lord and depressed people often feel hopeless. Also, the church teaches that it is a mortal sin to fall into despair, which is the conscious abandonment of all hope. But despair and depression are two very different things. Despair is a deliberate decision, made by a *mentally healthy* person, that God will never forgive him for his sins. He rejects the loving mercy of God and that is a sin against the Holy Spirit. Scripture tells us that such a sin is unforgivable. It is unforgivable because the man in despair will never ask for forgiveness and so God cannot give it. God offers it but it is rejected.

A depressed person on the other hand is sick. It is true that a severely depressed person may come to believe he is dammed but that is not despair. That is an uncontrollable chemical action in the brain whereby the part of the brain responsible for hope, joy, and laughter is overwhelmed and no longer able to function. God does not punish the sick. He has compassion on them.

Another cause for scandal amongst Christians who do not understand depression is that depressed people cannot pray.

Depressed people who formerly were faithful to the Mass, the rosary, morning and evening prayer, and the sacraments, become mentally paralysed. Because depression causes a loss of the ability to concentrate, the patient cannot pray. He cannot focus his attention on the prayer long enough to finish it. The mind keeps on wandering into a million distractions.

It helps to point out to someone who is trapped in the living hell of depression that while he cannot seem to pray in the usual sense of the word, he is actually praying the most valuable and powerful prayer of all. He is, as it were, hanging on the cross and so is sharing in the passion of Jesus Christ. The most powerful prayer Jesus ever prayed was to hang in awful pain upon the cross. It was the cross which redeemed us. The depressive hangs on his own cross of pain and so his pain is also redemptive. If he can think to offer up his agony to Jesus for the kingdom of God, many souls will be saved who might otherwise have been lost. Prayer need not be restricted to words. Suffering is also a prayer, highly regarded by Almighty God. If God valued the suffering of his Son Jesus, does he not also value the suffering of all his sons and daughters?

Jesus our Lord knew what depression was. In the Garden of Gethsemane he cried out, "My soul is sorrowful even unto death" (Matt. 26:38). Would we ever dream of condemning Jesus for his sorrow?

Some well-meaning Christians criticise depressed brothers or sisters, telling them that they must really be sinful if they no longer pray. This merely adds guilt on top of the guilt the patient is already feeling and could deepen his illness to the point of "being sorrowful even unto death." No right-minded Christian would ever wish to do such a thing. A depressed person needs affirmation, not criticism.

Many wonderful Christians are willing and eager to generously give of their time to pray over their sick brethren. This is a powerful ministry and is to be encouraged. But again, great care must be taken with depressed persons. There are pitfalls which must be avoided when ministering to the depressed.

Firstly, after perhaps several prayer sessions when the person is not any better, he may be told that he is not being cured because he does not have enough faith. This is a grave mistake since the man or woman will take on even more guilt. He or she will feel even more unworthy because depression stimulates unrealistic feelings of guilt and unworthiness. Such well-meant but thoughtless comments from the elders whom he trusts will only deepen the depression, and he will come to believe that God is displeased with him.

The second pitfall is that if the depression is not being alleviated by intense prayer, then the ministers conclude that the patient must have some major sin in his past of which he has not repented. This is a serious error. When we go to confession we are completely cleansed by the Lord. All sins of the past are forgiven *even those which we have forgotten.* Therefore, to imply that a person is still in need of repentance for some long forgotten sin is to deny God's complete forgiveness in the Sacrament of Reconciliation. Again this only adds to the guilt load of the patient and makes him worse instead of better. Job's comforters were very poor comforters indeed. Christians must beware of imitating them.

The third error, made by well-meaning Christians, is to pray over a depressed person and then announce that they have now been healed, when there is no evidence whatsoever that a healing has occurred. They then command the patient to "claim his healing" by discarding his medication. This is extremely dangerous advice. I have seen patients who were suicidal as a result of stopping their life-saving medication because they were told to do so. They believed in those who prayed over them and so plummeted into a life-threatening level of their illness.

The fourth and most serious of all mistakes is to conclude that a person who is not being healed is suffering from possession by a demon of depression. The prayer team then sets about exorcising the imaginary demon. If anything is designed to make a depressive dangerously worse, this is it. Certainly there is such an entity as a Spirit of Depression but it requires someone with a powerful gift of knowledge and discernment of spirits to recognize that a demon is truly present. Without such a gift in the prayer team, only terrible harm can be done. And if, God forbid, the patient were to commit suicide, the misguided ministers might then conclude that the demon had made him do it when there was no demon present at all. In fact, it is more likely that the patient could have been treated medically and been saved. Even if there is demonic possession, the patient is still depressed and needs treatment to lift the illness so that he can have the strength of will to cooperate with the deliverance prayer.

The fifth pitfall occurs in patients who have bipolar disorder. These persons suffer from alternating bouts of deep depression and manic highs. When such a person is being prayed over, he can feel the love and attention from the prayer team very powerfully. It is possible for him then, in response to these strong emotions, to bounce out of depression and into a manic state. This will look like a miraculous answer to prayer when it is not, and so a false miracle is claimed. It takes experience to know the difference between a healing and a regrettable rebound.

To claim a healing from God is meant to be an act of faith in God but if it is not accompanied by the charismatic gift of discernment that a healing has truly taken place, then it is nothing short of presumption. As mere creatures, we must not presume on God's will. God is not a Coke machine into which we put a coin and out pops a Coke every time. God cannot be restrained by a human formula. We petition. He decides. He is Lord and he knows best what is good for us. Perhaps in his estimation we need to suffer for a time longer, in order to save us from just punishment due to us in Purgatory for our personal sins. Perhaps God wants us to suffer generously for the sake of another soul who is heading for hell unless he can be converted. Perhaps the time is not yet right for a powerful healing, for reasons only God knows. Perhaps God is asking us to be content with our medical treatment even though it is not perfect, and to be grateful to him for giving these medicines to us. Perhaps he simply wants us to suffer cheerfully in order to be an example to others. We cannot second-guess God. We must, as subjects of the King, respect his right to decide what his perfect will is for us. Even Jesus the Son of God said in the Garden of Gethsemane, "Not my will but thine be done" (Matt. 26:39). Jesus, who was fully God, submitted himself to the will of his Father in heaven. We are to imitate him. Indeed, it is a good and holy thing to pray for healing but it is a better and far holier thing to pray, "not my will but thine be done." This is called trust in God, by which we abandon ourselves to his perfect plan. It means giving up asking for what I want, even though it is a good thing. Instead I rely confidently on God to decide for me. This is true poverty of spirit and Jesus said, "Blessed are the poor in spirit: the kingdom of God is theirs" (Matt. 5:3). No matter what I may want, I can never want anything more beautiful or exalted than the very kingdom of God.

Nevertheless, Scripture is very clear that we ought to pray for healing for our sick brothers and sisters, but it should be done by putting on "the mind of Christ" (1 Cor. 2:16). And it should be done in the spirit of acceptance of the perfect will of the Father. "For God did not send his Son into the world to condemn the world but that the world might be saved through him" (John 3:17). Therefore we too should never condemn a depressed person who is not being healed by our prayer. Rather, like Jesus, we should lift him up, encourage him, persevere with him and advise him to seek medical help where appropriate. We should be patient with him, always treating him with great compassion for his suffering.

It is vital to know that being depressed is not the same thing as being in a sad mood. A mood is a temporary feeling which may last from a few minutes to several hours but it always goes away. In the natural course of things our moods are always moving up and down and a low mood does not require treatment. Depression does. Jesus does not condemn the sick person but he does expect those who are healthy to rise above their low moods. So many people allow their feelings to dictate their actions and this is un-Christian. We are called to ensure that our *will* dominates our *feelings,* not the other way around. Someone in a low mood often justifies his refusal to perform a loving act because "I don't feel like it." Yet it is clear that even if I am feeling sad or hurt, I am still able to set aside that feeling and to go and help my neighbour. Jesus did exactly that. When he received the news that his cousin John the Baptist had been executed, he felt grief for him. He decided to cross the Sea of Galilee and go to a deserted place to rest and pray. He needed time to be alone and cope with his grief. But when he reached the far shore there were hundreds of people waiting on him begging for him to speak his Word to them and to heal them. Jesus could have explained to them that he was grieving and in need of solitude, and they would have no doubt understood and let him go. Instead, Scripture tells us, "He took pity on them because they were like sheep without a shepherd and he set himself to teach them at some length" (Mark 6:34). Jesus set aside his own feelings and his own needs in order to minister to his people. He rose above his feelings by a loving act of will. This lesson applies equally to us. We too can rise above our moods and refuse to allow our feelings to tell us what to do. The miracle is that when we do this and answer the call to love our neighbour, we usually find that the negative feelings simply disappear. We find joy in dying to self. But it is of great importance to remind ourselves that a depressed brother or sister simply cannot do this. The chemical disorder controls one's feelings and even one's decisions.

In conclusion, it would help countless families if they could be alert to the symptoms of depressive disorder in their loved ones. By early recognition, and seeking out the right help, much needless suffering could be avoided, including tragic loss of life. By all means, pray over those who are depressed but remember, "Then let the doctor take over; the Lord created him too; do not let him leave you, for you need him. There are times when good health depends on doctors. For they in their turn will pray the Lord to grant them the grace to relieve and to heal and so prolong your life" (Sir. 38:12-14).

CHAPTER 12

Euthanasia: Murder by Mercy

*"He who sheds the blood of
man, by man shall his blood
be shed."*

(Gen. 9:6)

To come to a knowledge of God and his design for human life, we must learn what God has spoken with regard to life and suffering. Then, and only then, can we hope to articulate the laws by which we must live and die. Our society was once Christian, but now it has largely rejected Jesus and his truth in order to embrace either paganism, agnosticism, atheism or other non-Christian religions. This has resulted in the current devaluation of human life which stands in opposition to the truth of God. It is taking the form of *murder by mercy.* Once we depart from Jesus, who says, "I am the way, the truth and the life" (John 14:6), then we lose the *way,* falling deeper into our own darkness, we lose the *truth,* becoming convinced of false doctrines, and we lose our *life,* which is the life of God, because it is no longer valued. We kill others and we kill ourselves since we have lost the vision of who we are and who God is.

We are an avaricious, consumer society and when consuming becomes a god, we end up consuming ourselves. The god of disordered consumption is Satan himself, who tempted Adam and

Eve into the original sin by persuading them to consume the forbidden fruit. He has been tempting us with forbidden fruit ever since and in our world today, we cannot get enough of it.

The end point of all sin is death. "For the wages of sin is death" (Rom 6:23). The sin of anger leads to murder. The sin of lust demands more and more sexual stimulation which ultimately culminates in the ultimate perversion by which sexual gratification can only be experienced in the death of the victim. Refusal to love leads to the death of those who could have been given life by our love. Refusal to forgive leads to vengeance by the hard of heart and that may progress to a death-wish for one's enemy. Likewise slavery to consumption leads to a death-dealing society. Sin not only leads to the deaths of our brothers and sisters in war, torture chambers, slavery, famine and plague, but it also and always leads to death of our own souls, and that is a double death: "Let anyone hear who can hear, listen to what the spirit is saying to the churches: for those who prove victorious will come to no harm from the second death" (Rev. 2:11). If we kill our own souls then not only will we experience the first death, which all of us must face, but we will suffer the second death in hell for ever. Death is the inevitable end-point of all sin. We should diligently flee even from venial sin, for venial sin more easily leads to mortal sin and mortal sin is death itself.

"Of man, as regards his fellow-man, I shall demand account for human life. He who sheds the blood of man, by man shall his blood be shed" (Gen. 9:5-6).

"Yahweh asked Cain, 'Where is your brother Abel?' 'I do not know' he replied. 'Am I my brother's keeper?' 'What have you done?' Yahweh asked. 'Listen! Your brother's blood is crying out to me from the ground. Now be cursed and banned from the ground that has opened its mouth to receive your brother's blood at your hands'" (Gen. 4:9-11). God therefore not only regards the taking of life as a grave offence, but expects us to be our brother's keeper, to come to the aid of our defenceless or sick brothers and sisters, to respect their lives and do all to preserve them.

The book of Genesis states that we are made in the image and likeness of God. Therefore we have the gift of life, not death. It was not God who brought death into the world. It was Satan and his evil intention for mankind. God is love, as St. John tells us, and love does not seek the death of the beloved. We are commanded by Jesus to love our neighbour as ourselves. Therefore we may not kill our neighbour, nor may we kill ourselves. Love forbids it.

"In your love you gave me life, and in your care watched over my every breath" (Job 10:12). Not only does our God generously give life to us, he watches over our every breath right up to the very last breath that we take. Each breath is precious in the eyes of the Lord and so we must glorify him and his rights throughout our entire lives. We must bless his name with our every breath whether it be painful or not.

"The Lord gives. The Lord takes away. Blessed be the name of the Lord" (Job 1:21). Therefore no matter how much we are suffering, no matter how much our loved ones are suffering, we should bless the name of the Lord. It is God's right *alone* to give life and to take it away, with one beautiful exception: "No greater love has any man than to lay down his life for his friends" (John 15:13). We are permitted by God to imitate his Son Jesus by sacrificing our own life so that another may live. Notice again, that it is supreme love which prompts such a selfless act. It is only when we imitate God with perfect love that we can imitate God by forfeiting our life. There is a vast difference between perfect love and the mushy misguided notion of mercy which doctors and families use today to justify the killing of people who are ill.

Again Job echoes this principle when in grief he cries out to Yahweh, "Why give light to a man of grief? Why give life to those bitter of heart, who long for a death that never comes?" (Job 3:20-21). Job was at the end of his rope, yet he never doubted God's right to take his life. In spite of dreadful torment, he never dreamed of committing suicide. While he had the right to ask God the question, he still chose life even when it was filled with pain and sorrow.

"I am offering you life or death, blessing or curse. Choose life then, so that you and your descendants may live in the love of Yahweh your God, obeying his voice, holding fast to him" (Deut 30:19-20). God gave us the free will with which to choose life or death, but only in choosing life can we live in his wonderful love, and in choosing life, even in the midst of suffering, we can endure it by obeying his voice and holding fast to him. If we cling to him, our suffering will be bearable. Certainly, we are "free" to choose death, but in so doing, we rob God of his rights and we are freely choosing eternal damnation.

The New Testament reinforces the Old Testament call to life as opposed to death and also the prerogative of God over both.

"Nor is he (God) in need of anything, that he should be served by human hands: on the contrary, it is he who gives everything including life and breath to everyone. From one single principle he not only created the whole human race so that they could occupy the whole earth, but he decreed the times and limits of their habitation" (Acts 17:25-26).

"For no one lives as his own master and no one dies as his own master: while we are alive we are living for the Lord and when we die, we die for the Lord: and so alive or dead we belong to the Lord" (Rom. 14:7-8). Therefore, as long as we are alive and drawing breath, we are to live for the Lord. Scripture does not say that we are to live only if we are not suffering. No matter what the conditions, we are commanded to choose life. Jesus says we must take up our cross and follow him and him alone.

St. Paul understood this call to life. "All in accordance with my most confident hope and trust that I shall never have to admit defeat, but with complete fearlessness, I shall go on, so that now, as always, Christ will be glorified in my body, whether by my life or by my death" (Phil. 1:20). We too are called to glorify Christ, not only in life, but also in death. Nor are we to fear death. "Since all the children share the same human nature, he too shared equally in it, so that by his death he could set aside him who held the power of death, namely the devil, and set free all those who had been held in slavery all their lives by the fear of death" (Heb. 2:14-15). This one "who held the power of death" is Satan, our adversary, who still seeks the death of God's people, and he is having the evil time of his life in our day. Fifty million babies a year are being sacrificed to him in their mothers' wombs, offering to him the blood of the most innocent of our race. War is fomented by him and so hundreds of thousands die in wars all over the earth. Since Satan can never get enough blood, he is now lusting after the lives of our elderly, our chronically sick and our terminally ill. Being the Prince of Lies, he achieves it by more lies, persuading us that euthanasia is an act of mercy. He tells us that a loving God would never condemn us for killing out of love. He would have us believe that it is our infirm that are an economic drain on society, and so killing them legitimately frees us up to care for the healthy with a better standard of living. No wonder Jesus said, "You cannot serve both God and money" (Matt. 6:24). Economics and our own selfish comfort have become the moral absolutes of our time, not God and his commandments. Therefore in the name of profit, any human act, no matter how evil, can be justified and that includes murder.

For a Christian, death is no longer to be feared. We are free: "And after this perishable nature has put on imperishability and this mortal nature has put on immortality, then will the words of Scripture come true: 'Death is swallowed up in victory. Death, where is your victory? Death, where is your sting?'" (1 Cor. 15:54-55). Therefore death is actually nothing at all. At the moment of conception, we were given an immortal nature which means we will live for ever. Therefore our souls can never die. Bodily death is nothing more than an instant in time, a marvellous moment when the soul leaves the body to go to its reward. It is merely a change of address, an instant transition from earthly existence to eternal existence. Death is not the problem. As previously mentioned, it is the dying which is the problem and that forces Christians to grapple with the difficult question of suffering as discussed in chapter 10. Some further points need to be made in this regard.

The people of the Old Testament did not understand the concept of redemptive suffering but there is a hint of it in Isaiah. "By his stripes we are healed" (Isa. 53:5). The full meaning of this prophesy could not be fully appreciated by the Jews since it had yet to be fulfilled in Jesus Christ. As people of the New Testament, we are privileged to know that the Son of God had to suffer for our redemption. As a result, our own human suffering can also be imbued with redemptive power. All we have to do is offer up our pain for our Lord's Kingdom. Our suffering is never pointless. "It all shows that God's judgement is just, so that you may be found worthy of the Kingdom of God: It is for the sake of this that you are suffering now" (2 Thess. 1:5). We therefore suffer in order to become worthy of the Kingdom of God. Euthanasia robs the victim of this profound benefit from his suffering.

The good news is that we never suffer alone. We are intimately bound up with one another. We share our pain with others and they share their pain with us. "If one part suffers, all the parts suffer with it: If one part is honoured, all the parts share its joy" (1 Cor. 12:26). We benefit from the sufferings of our courageous brothers and sisters and we, in turn, benefit them by our own suffering. Therefore, euthanasia not only violates the victim, but it also harms everyone else who stood to benefit from his redemptive suffering for the Kingdom. In addition, we are personally rewarded in our own suffering. Jesus himself tells us in the Beatitudes, "Blessed are you when people abuse you and persecute you and speak all kinds of calumny against you falsely on My account. Rejoice and be glad, for your reward will be great in heaven" (Matt. 5:11-12). Therefore a Christian does not focus on his pain as though that were everything. He focuses on heaven and life after death, because that *is* everything. This does not mean that we should avoid relief for our suffering. On the contrary, God has, in his great generosity, revealed to the medical profession numerous remedies to alleviate pain and distress. "The Lord has brought forth medicinal herbs from the ground and no one sensible will despise them. Did not a piece of wood once sweeten the water, thus giving proof of its power? He has also given some people knowledge so that they may draw credit from his mighty works. He uses these for healing and relieving pain. The druggist makes up a mixture from them. Thus there is no end to his activities: Thanks to him, well-being exists throughout the world" (Sir. 38:4-8). The science of medicine is blessed by God and he expects us to take advantage of it. It will be pointed out later on that we, nevertheless, have the moral right to refuse treatment if it proves to be too burdensome.

All of the foregoing is relevant when it comes to understanding the teaching of the Church with respect to euthanasia. It begins with the fact that all human persons are created in the image and likeness of God and as such are created good. "God saw everything that he had made and behold it was very good" (Gen. 1:31). Therefore all human life is a fundamental good. As images of God we are a created good, in spite of our inheritance of the original sin of Adam and Eve. More than that, by dint of Baptism and the redemptive action of Jesus, we are family of God, sons and daughters of the Father and heirs and heiresses to the Kingdom. An act of violence against one of these offspring of the Father is an act of violence against the Father also. In purely human terms, if you murder my son, you do grave violence to him, but also to me his father, and of course you do grave violence to yourself as murderer. God expects us to be our brother's keeper, to guard his life as precious and God regards killing as a violation of himself, the victim, the killer and the family of man.

The word "Euthanasia" comes from two Greek words, "Eu" and "Thanatos" and means "Good death." Few people would argue with the notion of a good death as opposed to a bad death but, unfortunately, in modern usage, the term euthanasia has come to mean five very different things:

1. *Death with dignity.* Promoters of death with dignity regard dignity as the supreme good, not life itself. Therefore where "dignity" no longer is seen to be present, it would be permissible to terminate that patient's life. A doctor holding this view would allow a patient to die a natural death only so long as dignity was deemed to continue. There are two problems with this viewpoint.

   a) The concept of dignity is very elusive and difficult to define. Dignity for one person may mean something very different to another.
   b) Even if dignity could be defined, whose definition should take precedence; the patient's, the family's or the doctor's? If the patient's ideas are to dominate the decision, the patient may be suffering a great deal or may be afraid of future suffering or may be severely depressed and so make a disordered subjective moral decision. If the family's decision is to be taken, the family may be prejudiced by a false compassion for the suffering of their loved one, or be desirous of saving themselves the bother of having to care for him. They may even have a death wish for the patient, for such reasons as hatred or greed for their inheritance. If the doctor's definition is to prevail, that too may be biased by his own moral or immoral views on life, his own

dedication or lack of it to the healing art, and perhaps whether he likes to play at being god or not. Death with dignity is too vague a notion and when people are challenged to define dignity there is no clear objective logic brought to bear.

2. *Mercy killing.* This simply means the use of medical technology for the deliberate purpose of inducing death. It is an act of killing and can be done in one of two ways: a) actively by lethal injection, or b) passively by withholding life-sustaining fluids and food, or by refusing to give simple ordinary medical care such as antibiotics for a pneumonia. The defenders of mercy killing cite pity as their motive and they claim to respect a patient's suicidal wish. Mercy killers are dominated by their feelings, not their thinking. They elevate feelings to the highest good and relegate thought to a lower level. But feelings belong to the realm of our animal nature, while thinking is what distinguishes us from the lower animals. As Christians we must rise above our animal nature, and become more and more human as we become subject to and motivated by our higher nature. Jesus expects us to control our feelings and never allow them to dominate our spiritual selves. He told us not to be angry, not to be afraid, and not to be anxious. God does not want our feelings. He wants our will and he wants our will to conform to his Divine Will. Pity tries to justify killing. Enlightened thinking rejects it.

3. *Death selection.* This is the ultimate end point of any euthanasia policy. By the process of gradualism, what is at first a procedure restricted to the very worst of cases soon degenerates into the inclusion of more and more sick persons. Eventually it becomes easy to step over the final line and justify killing for any political or economic or eugenic reason whatsoever. This poses an obvious threat to the habitual criminal, the aged, the mentally and physically handicapped and the psychotic.

In 1935, Nazi Germany launched a program of involuntary sterilisation in order to prevent the weakest members of German society from reproducing. This was quickly followed by involuntary euthanasia or death-selection for institutionalised, severely mentally handicapped persons, and was then extended to institutionalised psychotic and psychopathic patients. The silence of most German doctors about this crime soon led to the passing of the Nuremberg Laws for the purification of German blood. The way was then paved for a total eugenics program and for the subsequent Holocaust. Could it ever happen in our country? All we have to do is let down our guard, become silent and the ungodly of our society will gleefully offer their services for a death-selection policy.

4. *Vitalism.* This is the disordered opposite of euthanasia. Vitalists such as Dr. David Kornofsky elevate human life to the highest good, (the summum bonum) and speak of the medical imperative to use every stratagem known to medical science to ward off death, "until the issue is taken out of the physician's hands." This approach applauds the indefinite use of extraordinary medical procedures even when all that is being achieved is the cruel prolongation of the dying process. To the vitalists, prolongation of suffering is merely an acceptable side effect. The Catholic Church does not subscribe to this view.

5. *Agathanasia or Benemortasia.* This position holds that life, in and of itself, is not the absolute good or summum bonum. While it cherishes and values all human goods such as life, freedom, integrity and dignity, it regards God and God alone as the supreme good. Man, therefore, is called to love God above all created goods including even human life. Life, while it is a good, need not be clung to at all costs. To use medical technology merely to prolong the dying process would be immoral. As stated earlier, although death is not a good, and therefore, not worthy of human choice (except in the saintly case of laying down one's life for one's friend as a supreme act of love), a person has the right to refuse medical treatment which causes unacceptable suffering. The principle of Agathanasia also holds that, while a doctor may not kill a patient, he can allow his or her patient to die. This is a very important point. If I kill a sick person by a fatal injection or by withholding the food and water he needs, then I have

chosen to kill and I stand in violation of the moral law. If however, I know that a patient is dying and I honestly recognize that the disease is not reversible, I will humbly accept the natural progression of the disease, concentrate on relieving suffering at all times, and accompany the patient to his or her death with compassion and without extraordinary heroic measures.

Agathanasia is in accord with the teachings of the Catholic Church on death and dying. The church holds that the morality of death is rooted in the Natural Law (by which we all possess an innate instinct and respect for life), which has to be deliberately paved over if we are to become takers of life. This teaching is founded upon the words of Jesus Christ in Scripture and the two-thousand-year Tradition of the Church.

One does not have to be a Catholic to know that life is sacred. One does not have to be a Catholic to know that taking a human life is a grave moral disorder. Every human being is born with this built-in moral code. Respect for life is based upon this Natural Law and it should not surprise us that 2400 years ago, before ever Jesus was born on earth, the Greek pagan physician Hippocrates respected life. He stated, "I will neither give a deadly drug to anybody that asked for it nor will I make a suggestion to this effect, in pureness and holiness I will guard life and my art." Unhappily, the Hippocratic Oath is no longer a requirement for graduating doctors in the majority of our Western Universities and this is a tragedy for our sick brothers and sisters, many of whom can no longer trust their physician to respect their right to life.

Pope Pius XII at the International Congress of Anesthesiologists in 1957 stated, "Natural reason and Christian morals say that man has the right and duty in the case of serious illness to take the necessary treatment for the preservation of life and health. This duty that one has toward himself, toward God, toward the human community and in most cases toward certain determined persons, derives from well-ordered charity, from submission to the Creator, from social justice and even from strict justice as well as from devotion to one's family. But normally one is held to use only ordinary means, according to circumstances of persons, places, times and culture, that is to say, means that do not involve any grave burden to oneself or another." Pope Pius XII is reiterating a very important principle of the care of the dying. The patient does have the right to refuse treatment but does not have the right to choose death. The first option is the refusal of an unacceptable burden of treatment, thereby allowing the disease to progress naturally, while the latter would be a specific request for a lethal act.

In recent years, great medical advances have been made in the area of relief of suffering for dying patients. This is called palliative care. In the course of administering pain relievers such as morphine or heroin, the doctor may know that as the dosages have to increase, so the patient's life is being shortened by the undesirable side-effects of the drugs. This is morally acceptable because it falls under the law of "double-effect." That is to say, the primary aim of giving the drug is to relieve pain. The secondary effect is to shorten life. In this case we accept an undesirable evil to promote a greater good. This is in direct opposition to giving a lethal injection. In such a case, the primary aim is to kill and this violates all moral law.

There is a problem, however, with Pope Pius XII's principle of ordinary versus extraordinary medical procedures. What constituted extraordinary technology thirty years ago may well be quite ordinary in today's medical environment. No one would deny that it is ordinary to provide food and fluids to any sick person. It would also be quite ordinary to prescribe antibiotics for a pneumonia even in a terminally ill patient. Consider, however, the use of cardiac life support for a comatose person whose brain tracing confirms brain death. Technologically speaking, cardiac life support is quite ordinary nowadays, but humanly and morally speaking, is it or is it not violating a basic human good? The perfect arguments have not yet been formulated, but the ordinary/extraordinary debate does not help us, partly because it raises the danger of becoming too mechanistic. Good might better be served if we consider whether we are merely prolonging the dying process with our technology and therefore extending the patient's suffering unnecessarily. If a doctor can see that the patient is dying, that his illness is irreversible and that the machines are only holding the person in suspended animation, then it would be morally permissible to abandon life-support. For example, where a person is brain dead (that is to say, his brain-tracing is recording no activity), then a life-support machine is simply keeping the heart and lungs alive. In this case, it is no longer possible to believe that life is recoverable. The patient is merely being trapped and maintained in the last stages of the dying process. As such it is a cruel and unnecessary suffering. In such circumstances, it would be supported by moral law to switch off the artificial technology. This would not be a death decision because the patient is *in extremis* (clearly dying), and it is known that many patients live on for a considerable time after life support has been discontinued. Therefore, it is not a deliberate act of killing but is a humble recognition of the fact that God is calling his son or daughter into eternity, and that medicine has done all it can do. It is only fair to say that this dilemma is still open to a fuller understanding and it definitely has very serious legal implications.

The Christian Medical and Dental Society of Canada upholds the following six beliefs:

1. We are all created by God and are not to be understood as the products of random processes.
2. We are therefore responsible to God for our actions.
3. The time of the giving of life and the termination of life should be God's prerogative and not ours.
4. Death is not the end because we have immortal souls.
5. Suffering should always evoke compassionate care, and euthanasia should not be used as a way out.
6. Those who suffer are important members of society who should be affirmed. We believe that the courageous bearing of suffering has the utmost moral and social benefit to society, and the recognition by society of that contribution affirms the individual.

The College of Family Physicians of Canada has, as of 1990, adopted a pro-life stance with respect to euthanasia. It stands behind the following statements:

1. All human lives demand an identical level of respect regardless of health status, social usefulness or mental function.

2. Physicians have a duty to provide continuing, compassionate and professional support to dying patients and their families.
3. Physicians are bound to provide, where possible, relief from suffering in its broadest sense, be it physical, emotional, social or spiritual.
4. All patients at all times are entitled to basic and ordinary means of sustenance and medical care.
5. A patient has the freedom to refuse non-curative, death-preventing interventions where these are too burdensome.
6. A physician shall not knowingly terminate life.
7. A physician is not obligated to prolong the dying process by extraordinary means.

In January 1997, two hundred physicians from Manitoba, Canada, placed an advertisement in the *Winnipeg Free Press*. It stated that these physicians believe that when doctors help to kill, they sacrifice patient trust, disparage the ill and infirm, and encourage the ill and the elderly to seek death. As well, there exists the possibility of killing patients where it is not wanted, consented to or appropriate. It can even lead to the choice of death over cure. These doctors affirm that suicide is ethically wrong, that any choice driven by a depressed state of mind is not rational, and that palliative care can improve the condition and state of mind of patients who might otherwise choose to die.

One might be tempted to conclude that human life is protected in Canada by the medical profession and by the Criminal Code of Canada, which regards euthanasia, whether passive or active, as culpable homicide or murder. At present, euthanasia carries a fixed, minimum penalty of ten years in prison. However, much of this is smoke and mirrors. Many doctors secretly harbour a personal conviction that euthanasia is acceptable in the so-called "right" cases. Also Canadian judges are now watering down the law by handing out paltry sentences or even none at all, to those who have performed acts of mercy killing or who have taken part in assisted suicide. The pro-death movement is relentless and will never give up trying to force it's agenda onto the nation.

In the United States assisted suicide is receiving a lot of publicity these days and is already legalised in the State of Oregon.

In the Netherlands, elderly people are afraid to be admitted to hospital for fear that they will be terminated by their own doctor. Dr. Karel Gunning, a Dutch physician stated, "The lesson we (The Netherlands) can pass on to the world is that when you start to admit killing as a solution to one problem, you will have many more problems tomorrow for which killing may also be used as a solution." The killers talk about the right to die, but that is an oxymoron. Dying is not a right, it is a given. Everybody has to die one day. In societies such as The Netherlands, the *right* to die has now evolved into the *duty* to die and puts a cruel burden of guilt onto those who are already suffering because of serious illness. Dr. Linda Emmanual, Vice-President of the American Medical Association and Director of its Institute for Ethics, said this, "If doctors are allowed to kill patients, the doctor-patient relationship will never be the same again. If killing you is an option, how can I expect you to trust me to do all I can to heal you?"

It is very interesting and sad that our society and our politicians seem to think that doctors should be the ones to do their killing for them. Yet doctors are trained to preserve life, not to eliminate it. As Dr. Donald Jansen wrote recently, "Why not take all this killing out of the hands of doctors? The philosophers, Members of Parliament and journalists can do the killing of the old and terminally ill. I think for reasons of compassion, that would be a nice touch." He is not being entirely facetious. Killing can be nice and clean and sterile if you are not the one doing it, but if you are, it is ugly, dirty and bereft of respect for the temple of the Holy Spirit.

"When this happens, people will long for death and not find it anywhere: They will want to die and death will evade them" (Rev. 9:6). In the end times, people will be powerless to hasten their own death, even though they earnestly wish it. They will not be able to commit suicide. God will fully enforce his divine prerogative and will decide when they are to die. All choice will have been taken away, so that they come to know who is the true Lord over life and death.

Dietrich Bonhoeffer wrote, "In the sight of God, there is no life that is not valued, that is not worth living; for life itself is valued by God. The beggar, Lazarus a leper, lay by the rich man's gate and the dogs licked his sores; he was devoid of any social usefulness; yet God held him to be worthy of eternal life. And where, if not in God, should lie the criterion for the ultimate value of a life? We cannot ignore the fact that the supposedly worthless life of the incurable evokes from the healthy the very highest measure of self sacrifice and even genuine heroism; this devoted service which is rendered by sound life to sick life has given rise to real values which are of the highest utility to the community."

The Sacred Congregation for the Doctrine of the Faith issued a Declaration on Euthanasia May 5, 1980 and it stated, "It is necessary to state firmly once more that nothing and no one can in any way permit the killing of an innocent human being, whether a fetus or an embryo, an infant or an adult, an old person or one suffering from an incurable disease, or a person who is dying. Furthermore, no one is permitted to ask for this act of killing, either for himself or herself nor for another person entrusted to his or her care, nor can he or she consent to it, either explicitly or implicitly. Nor can any authority legitimately recommend or permit such an action. For it is a question of the violation of the divine law, an offense against the dignity of the human person, a crime against life and an attack on humanity."

Dave Hinsberger, a therapist for people with disabilities, was invited to speak at the "Not Dead Yet Rally" held outside the U.S. Supreme Court. Inside the court were the young and healthy debating the issue of assisted suicide, while outside were the disabled, many in wheelchairs chanting, for their right to stay alive. Dave spoke with some of the disabled, four of whom had Down's Syndrome. Suddenly he realised that this may be the last generation of Down's Syndrome people who love and laugh, and who experience pain and hope. They are genetic undesirables. These are the very people a German dictator once denounced as "useless eaters." These would be gone soon by means of a so-called medical victory saving them from the pain of existence. He finished by saying, "Hiding bigotry behind compassion is a wonderful trick."

We are Christians. We belong to God. Let us render unto Caesar what is Caesar's and unto God what is God's. To God goes our life, love, adoration, praise and our self-sacrifice. Caesar only gets our taxes. He cannot take our taxes with him anyway, when it is his turn to die. We live for ever in the heart of God. We have life, so let us resolve to love the life we have.

CHAPTER 13

The Holy Family of Nazareth: The Earthly Model

*"The Angel of the Lord
appeared to him in a dream
and said, 'Joseph son of
David, do not be afraid to
take Mary home as your wife,
because she has conceived
what is in her by the Holy
Spirit. She will give birth to a
Son and you must name him
Jesus because he is the one
who is to save his people
from their sins.'"*

(Matt. 1:20-21)

A truer understanding of what it means to be a Catholic family is only possible by learning to appreciate the mystery of the Holy Family of Nazareth, the perfect earthly model of family life. Like the "little church," it consisted of father, mother and child, but it reached the very pinnacle of perfection consisting as it did of a woman, conceived without Original Sin, a man, who was a great saint, and a child, who was the only Son of God. Naturally, a Catholic family cannot ever hope to achieve such sublime sanctity, but be that as it may, we are all still called to a personal sanctity. It is only by keeping the vision of Nazareth before our eyes, that we can know our true possibilities. Without an ideal to strive for, the family will merely stagnate, but with our feeble human efforts and God's grace, it becomes possible to scale the heights. "Nothing is impossible with God" (Luke 1:37).

It is a rewarding education for men, women and children to study the Holy Family, to admire its virtues and to aim at some imitation of its sanctity, taking each of its members as a role model according to one's state in life.

Scripture states that Joseph was a "just man" (Matt. 1:19). It is appropriate, at this point, to explore this concept in greater depth. To any Jew familiar with the Old Testament, the appellation of "just man" had a profound meaning. The Psalms extol the virtues of such a man and he had three principal attributes.

Firstly, he is noted for his *generosity*, giving especially to the poor and lending money liberally without interest (Psalms 112 and 37). Joseph then, though poor, was willing to share what little he had with those who were poorer than himself. He understood the generous heart of Yahweh, who commanded his people to care for the poor, the widow and the orphan. Joseph was dedicated not just to the care of his own family, but also to the care of others.

Secondly, the just man is known for his *prudence* when he speaks. Not only does he avoid sins of the tongue, such as slander and gossip (Psalm 15:3), but he also utters wisdom and justice (Psalm 37:30). This is the virtue of custody of the tongue. By that is meant that Joseph would never call down anyone, but rather speak well of others, looking only for the good in them. He left the judging up to God and God alone. He also enjoyed the charismatic gift of wisdom, whereby he could give fatherly instruction to Jesus in Scripture and in the ways of Jesus' heavenly Father. He would be gentle, yet firm in his fathering, humbly accepting his vocation as guardian to the divine child. In this he imitated Jesus, who was later to say, "Learn from me for I am gentle and humble of heart" (Matt. 11:29).

Thirdly, the just man is known for his *steady heart.* He is described as steadfast and firm (Psalm 112:8). This is the great virtue of purity of heart. Purity is often confused with chastity. While it indeed includes chastity, it is much more than that. It means to be single-minded in the pursuit of the things of God. A pure heart never deviates from the pathway of holiness and is never content, in that it is constantly aiming for higher and higher levels of holiness. It is a kind of holy stubbornness. Such a person derives joy only in God and finds little pleasure in the fleeting distractions of the world. His favourite topic of conversation is God and he is not offended by being scorned as overly-religious or a religious fanatic but delights in worshipping God and God alone. Joseph, therefore, was a lover of God's truth and was willing to defend it under any circumstances. The Psalms clearly state that the just man stands on the foundation of the law of God in his heart and it is in the law that he takes his delight (Psalm 1).

As a good Jew, Joseph observed and loved the law of Moses and the festivals and traditions of the Old Covenant. At the Passover, as head of the family, he would explain to the boy Jesus, that the feast recalls what God had done for his people when he brought them out of slavery in the land of Egypt. "And you shall tell your son on that day, 'it is because of what the Lord did for me when I came out of Egypt'" (Ex. 13:8). Jesus, divine though he was, must have marvelled in his little human heart at the astounding power and love of his mighty heavenly Father as he listened to the words of his earthly stepfather.

Joseph carefully observed the religious practices of everyday Jewish home life, prayers, teaching, reading the Torah, purifications, dietary laws and fasts, and attendance at the Synagogue, as well as the annual pilgrimage to the Temple of Jerusalem. He knew very well the promise made by God to the virtuous man, "Your wife shall be like a fruitful vine within your house. Your children will be like olive-shoots around your table. Lo, thus shall the man be blessed who fears the Lord" (Psalm 128:3-4). Fear of the Lord is also "the beginning of wisdom" (Prov. 9:10), and so Joseph was indeed wise in his raising of Jesus and in his protection of Mary.

In first century Jewish society, marriage would not take place without consent on the part of the young bride-to-be. She, not the responsible male relative, accepted the token which stood for the dowry. Therefore, for Mary to have agreed to her marriage with Joseph, she must have freely given her active consent. Since she was "full of grace" (Luke 1:28), and therefore totally immersed in love of God, there must have been a very profound spiritual affinity between herself and Joseph. She had to be attracted by his powerful love of God and his holiness. Mary, the sublime perfection of womanhood, could never have been attracted to anything less.

Catholics have always believed that Joseph was a virgin before his marriage and certainly after his marriage. Some writers in the past speculated that Joseph was married before, that his first wife died and that Mary was therefore his second wife. This is not held to be true by the Church today. In fact, knowing the sublime value God places on virginity, and that he insisted on virginity as a pre-requisite for Mary to be the mother of Jesus, it is reasonable that he would also desire virginity from the man who was to be the guardian of Jesus. Surely God had to choose a great saint for so holy a purpose. It is generally held that Joseph was a Nazirite, that is to say, an unmarried man, who offered his sexuality as a spotless gift to God through a lifelong vow of virginity. This quality of committed chastity for Yahweh had to be a major factor in attracting the spotless virgin Mary to Joseph.

Mary and Joseph then, came together in mutual virginity and in mutual love for God, and they determined to keep it that way, even after their marriage. "There are eunuchs born so from their mother's womb, there are eunuchs made so by human agency and there are eunuchs who have made themselves so for the sake of the kingdom of Heaven. Let anyone accept this who can" (Matt. 19:12). Jesus is teaching that God values holy virginity as a very great virtue. Since thousands of lesser saints have lived out this virtue, offering their sexuality to God as a holy sacrifice, would not Mary and Joseph also have been committed virgins, they who were the greatest saints of the entire Church?

Imagine then, the consternation of Joseph when he discovered that Mary was with child. He must have felt devastated and bewildered. He, in his human way of thinking, could not reconcile her pregnancy with what he knew of Mary, who had so carefully preserved her virginity for God. He knew she could never have been unfaithful since she was betrothed, nor could she have been unfaithful to God by committing a sexual sin. He was in an agony of turmoil and the just man was challenged to the very core of his being.

A woman's honour was the responsibility of her husband and scripture relates, "Joseph, unwilling to put her to shame, resolved to send her away quietly" (Matt. 1:19). The great loving heart of Joseph could not bring itself to condemn her, so he made the most merciful decision possible. He decided to divorce her, which was quite acceptable under Jewish law. In this way, he could save Mary from the terrible retribution of a society which would condemn her to death by stoning. Adultery was a capital offence. By not denouncing her and by divorcing her, he was taking public condemnation upon himself for Mary's sake. The people of Nazareth would likely assume that Mary was carrying Joseph's child and would lose respect for a man who had betrothed her, and then abandoned her in her pregnancy. Joseph was prepared to face this loss of reputation rather than see the woman he loved being killed. God had tested Joseph's love and his willingness to sacrifice himself for that love and he withstood the test.

Having now proven the worthiness of the chosen stepfather for Jesus, God sent an angel, who appeared to him in a dream and said, "Joseph, son of David, do not be afraid to take Mary home as your wife, because she has conceived what is in her by the Holy Spirit" (Matt. 1:20). At last, Joseph's understanding was opened and his agony was over. Now he knew that he was called by the Most High God and that his mission in life was to love and care for both Mary and this miraculous child. He was being asked by God to empty himself of any natural desire for parenthood. He would not be the child's natural father, nor was he to be any child's father. Instead he was to become the shadow of God the Father and he was to support Mary's vocation, by means of their mutual virginity.

According to Jewish custom, it was the father's prerogative to name his child. But Joseph was not the father and so God the Father jealously reserved that right to himself when the angel said to Joseph, "She will give birth to a Son and you must name him Jesus for he will save his people from their sins" (Matt. 1:21). Joseph, therefore, was to assume the public and legal role of fatherhood by giving the name, but the name was not Joseph's choice. It was God's. The name Jesus means "He who saves," and so the angel was clearly revealing to Joseph the future redemptive mission of this Divine Child. Some modern scholars assert that Joseph had no idea who Jesus was, asserting that he was nothing more than an ignorant carpenter, but this is an error. He *knew* because the angel told him. How he must have marvelled at the ways of the Almighty. "My thoughts are not your thoughts and your ways are not my ways, declares Yahweh" (Isa. 55:8).

Joseph then was to take Mary as his wife, not in the carnal sense, but in a relationship founded totally on the mysterious plan of God. It was to be the perfect union of two hearts, two minds and two spirits, but not of two bodies. Many Christians believe that Joseph and Mary had normal sexual relations after Jesus was born, but Scripture disagrees. "Behold, an angel of the Lord appeared in sleep to Joseph saying, 'Arise and take **the child and his mother** and fly into Egypt'" (Matt. 2:13). Any Jew reading this passage would know that this was extraordinary language. If Joseph was living married life with Mary in the usual way, then the passage would read, "Arise and take **your** child and your **wife** and fly into Egypt." The language used here distances Joseph from Mary and Jesus in a very special way. It makes it clear that Jesus was not the son of his own body and that Mary was not living with Joseph in the natural conjugal manner of man and wife. Both Mary and Joseph were virgins **before, during and after** the birth of Jesus.

Joseph is the model for all good Catholic husbands and fathers. No one was permitted to intrude upon his sacred sacramental bond with Mary. He placed himself in total and joyful service of God and of his family. He exercised his role as head of the household, but he did it in a spirit of humble service. His own royal Davidic line came to an end with himself, but his great sacrifice was rewarded by raising the very Son of God, who would, in turn, raise millions of sons and daughters for the kingdom of God. Joseph, then, became the spiritual father of countless Christians down through the ages.

Catholics believe that Joseph died in the arms of Jesus and Mary. He enjoyed the happiest of deaths which is why he is honoured as the Patron Saint of the Dying. Who better to turn to at the hour of our death than the one who closed his eyes in the presence of his Saviour and the Mother of his Saviour? It is a good and holy thing to ask Joseph to intercede for us, that we, too, might enjoy the happiest of deaths, by dying like him in the arms of Jesus and Mary.

Not one single word from Joseph is recorded in scripture. This is a silent witness to Joseph's great humility. His hiddenness displays his holy joy as he renounced any personal glory, in order that only the Most High God should be glorified. All men would do well to imitate this virtue and give God the glory for everything.

When it comes to Mary, it is so easy for the flawed human mind to discount her as merely an uneducated Jewish girl who was merely "used" by God for his grand purpose of redeeming the world. This is a dreadful error. First of all, how could anyone accuse the thrice-holy God of using one of his beloved creatures? He is forever faithful and he never forgets that he gave all human beings the right to choose. It is a source of wonder that God sent his angel messenger to *ask* this young girl Mary if she would condescend to become the Mother of his son. God did not impose his will upon her but honoured her freedom to refuse. This is a sublime testimony to the humility of God.

Secondly, the holy Tradition of the Church has it that Mary was raised in the Temple of Jerusalem, and so she was very well educated in the Scriptures of the Old Testament and in the Torah. In those days, young virgins were often dedicated to the Temple by holy and generous parents, who knew, as all of Israel knew, that the Messiah would be born of a virgin. It was their sincerest hope that the Most High God would condescend to select their daughter to carry the Saviour of Israel.

Thirdly, Mary had been conceived without Original Sin. Her soul was therefore *pre-redeemed* by the future death of Jesus on the cross. This is not an easy idea to grasp, but since past, present and future are all present to God (he lives in eternity and not in time), then, it was no problem for Jesus, *before* his actual birth in human history, to prepare his mother to receive him into her womb. It was unthinkable that God could take up residence in an unholy place. Since all of us have inherited Original Sin, we all labour under the burden of a sin-nature. As a result, we are under the power of Satan, and by our very nature, we cannot avoid sin, at least not without grace. The Holy One can only live in a holy place and that is why Jesus prepared his mother Mary before hand, his new Ark of the Covenant, by freeing her from any stain of sin. It simply had to be that way. This does not mean that Mary did not need a Redeemer. She did, but she was simply redeemed ahead of the rest of humanity.

The Angel Gabriel confirmed this truth when he hailed Mary as "full of grace" (Luke 1:28). When a vessel is full, it cannot receive more and therefore Mary was without the slightest stain of sin. It is easy to surmise that, being full of grace, she had dedicated her whole life and her entire being to the perfect will of God. She was the perfect contemplative, in that she must have spent countless hours in prayer of union with God, and she was perfect in her love of neighbour. Sin to her was unthinkable.

This perfect holiness was manifested immediately at the Annunciation. As soon as her fiat was uttered, the promise of Yahweh was fulfilled. "The Holy Spirit will come upon you, and the power of the Most High will come upon you" (Luke 1:35). At that very moment the Holy Spirit fulfilled his promise to come upon her, he "overshadowed" her and Jesus entered her womb. Immediately Mary entered into ecstatic union with the Divine Son who had taken up residence in his "living monstrance." Who could have blamed her if she had simply remained in holy contemplation with her God, who was now also her son? Yet, she did not. She remembered that the angel told her of her elderly cousin's pregnancy and so she wasted no time in preparing for a three-day journey into the hill country in order to be of help. Mary abandoned her own ecstasy for the higher demands of her cousin's needs. What a marvellous lesson this is for all of us. Loving our neighbour is the greatest of prayers to God, greater than any other and Mary understood that.

Again, the silence of scripture about much of Mary's life speaks volumes about her humility and her joy in giving her son all the glory. Everything she did in those days and everything she does today from heaven points us to Jesus. She requires no glory for herself and like a good mother, she only wishes to lead us to her Son.

Yet, at the same time, it is clear from Scripture that God wishes to *glorify her*. Jesus said, "Do not think that I have come to abolish the law or the prophets; I have come not to abolish, but to fulfil" (Matt. 5:17). In other words, Jesus, by his practical example, showed us how to obey the Ten Commandments perfectly. The fourth law of the Decalogue is "Honour thy father and thy mother" (Ex. 20:12). The Hebrew word for "honour" is much better translated as "glorify." It is therefore certain that Jesus would perfectly glorify his own mother and this was intended to be a model for all of us. Since Jesus also gave Mary to us at the foot of the cross, as our mother, then we too are required to glorify her. This is not the same thing as worship, as Catholics are so often accused of doing. We do not give Mary the status of God, but we "glorify" her by acknowledging that she is truly the Mother of God (Jesus was indeed God), and that, since Jesus can refuse her nothing, we are well-advised to ask her to go to Jesus on our behalf. We have no difficulty in asking a friend to pray for us, so why not ask Jesus' mother to pray for us?

As a result of this desire of God to glorify the lowly virgin, the Holy Spirit inspired her to sing out the great canticle, which is called the Magnificat. When Mary met Elizabeth, she was filled with the power of the Holy Spirit and she said, "From this day, all generations will call me blessed" (Luke 1:48). Mary was not extolling herself with these words. *It was the Holy Spirit who was extolling her.* In her own spotless heart she was rejoicing in God's wondrous generosity. She would have preferred to remain hidden, but if God wanted her to speak such words, then so be it. It is therefore our holy duty to call her "blessed."

Returning to the great day of the Annunciation, it is edifying to ponder on that sublime moment after the Angel had conveyed God's request to Mary. I like to imagine that all of the angels in heaven, all of the created universe and yes, even God, held their breath, waiting in anxious excitement for her answer. Mary, knowing that she had consecrated herself as a virgin to God and knowing that he would never reject her consecration, humbly asked how he was going to bring this pregnancy about. When the answer was given, she did not hold Heaven in suspense any longer. She joyfully cried out, "I am the handmaid of the Lord. Let it be done unto me according to thy word" (Luke 1:38). Then there must have been a mighty shout of jubilation throughout the entire creation. Angels sang and God smiled. The great redemption could now proceed, thanks to the "fiat" of a little Jewish virgin. That fiat changed the world forever and it is fitting that we should do great and solemn honour to the woman who uttered it. In glorifying Mary, we are only imitating Jesus who, in all righteousness, glorified her.

The Catholic Church has always extolled Mary as a virgin before, during and after the birth of Jesus. Her virginity up to the moment of the conception of Jesus in her womb, is not in question.

Scripture confirms that she remained a virgin during her pregnancy. "When Joseph awoke from sleep, he did as the angel of the Lord commanded him; he took her as his wife, but had no marital relations with her until she had borne a son; and he named him Jesus" (Matt. 1:24-25). The problem arises in what happened after the birth of Jesus. At first glance, in reading these words, it might seem as though Mary and Joseph had marital relations subsequently. First of all, this is a misunderstanding of the Jewish figure of speech used in this passage. The phrase "until she had borne a son" strictly applies *only to the time of the pregnancy*. It is never used to imply what went on afterwards. For example, we read "Sit at my right hand *until* I make your enemies a footstool for your feet" (Heb. 1:13). Does this mean that once God has made the enemies of Jesus a footstool for his feet that Jesus will no longer be allowed to sit at the right hand of the Father? Surely not. Likewise the phrase "until she had borne a son" cannot be used to predict Mary's subsequent married life with Joseph.

Secondly, at the Annunciation, Mary conceived Jesus by the power of the Holy Spirit. The Holy Spirit was therefore her true spouse. Joseph was her *legal* spouse in the eyes of men, but Mary's *actual* spouse was the Holy Spirit. Mary was now irrevocably and forever married to the Holy Spirit, so how could she have ever been unfaithful to her Divine husband? How could she ever revoke her most holy vow of virginity, she who was totally fulfilled by her union with the Holy Spirit in a divine marriage, and by the fruit of their pure love, which was her son Jesus? Such infidelity would have been unthinkable for the spotless Mary.

It can be concluded then, that Mary was the perfect wife, a woman of foresight, strength, dignity and wisdom. How else could she be able to raise the Son of God? All Jewish girls were trained by their mothers to one day assume the demanding roles of wife and mother. To her fell the duties of drawing water from the well, preparing food and baking bread, of spinning and weaving. The order and cleanliness of the home were her responsibility and these were not regarded as in any way menial. On the contrary, order and cleanliness were regarded as virtues and therefore pleasing to God. Most importantly, the education and nurturing of children was the mother's primary role as the heart of the home. The father, of course, had the duty of teaching his own trade to his son and adopted the priestly role in the household, especially at the Feast of the Passover. In the Jewish culture, nothing took precedence over the raising of children to become holy worshippers of Yahweh, and Mary attended most assuredly to that task.

She also enjoyed another great womanly ability. She "pondered these things in her heart" (Luke 2:51). She, of all women, was able to gaze upon the mystery of her Son and to treasure that mystery, savour it and marvel at it. Men can do that too, but women do it more easily. Only in Mary however, did this pondering find its perfection.

Another of Mary's virtues was that of obedience. While her purity and humility rendered her a fitting vessel in which the Son of God could be conceived, it was her obedience which made it a reality. Her "yes" to God brought the Incarnate Word into the world. She and Joseph also made a powerful act of obedience when they went to the Temple after Jesus was born. There, Mary had to undergo ritual purification, she who was the purest of all earthly creatures. Jesus was at the same time presented to the Lord, he who was the Lord himself. In a sense, Jesus was presenting himself to himself! What a mystery this is. It is a thing of great wonder to consider the sublime obedience of the Holy Family as they submitted themselves to the demands of the Mosaic law.

It can be concluded, that for God, obedience is a highly valued virtue. In today's culture, obedience is rejected. The "me-generation" extols the disorder of self-determination and personal opinion and is incapable of understanding the need for obedience. "Nobody tells *me* what to do" is in direct opposition to the humble submission of the true Catholic to the precepts of God. Mary was greater than Joseph, yet she obeyed him. Jesus was greater than both Mary and Joseph, yet he obeyed them. This is the manner in which God turns man's wisdom upside down. In God's Kingdom, the greatest are the least, and the greater one is, the more one is called to serve. As one holy priest once said to me, "I am a priest and therefore I am your servant. Please instruct me as to your needs." The greatest crisis in the Church today is the crisis of obedience. It is being discarded in the name of following one's own conscience (usually an ignorant, disordered conscience) and "doing one's own thing." But, reliance on human reason alone is a dangerous road, so often paved with pride, and always ending in error. Reason, if it is to be properly utilised, must be placed at the service of God, not arrogantly used to examine him. "Do not put the Lord your God to the test" (Deut. 6:16). If God himself can be obedient, is it not reasonable for him to ask the same from us, even when our reason does not fully understand? Mary was perfectly obedient. "Blessed is she who trusted that the Lord's words to her would be fulfilled" (Luke 1:45). She was obedient to the awful extent of having to relinquish Jesus to his terrible death on the cross. Like Jesus, she had not only to forgive his murderers, but even to love them. For that alone, she deserves to be glorified by the Church.

We know a great deal about Jesus as an adult, but at first glance, we seem to know very little of him as a child. It was the holy will of God the Father that the little family of Nazareth live in hiddenness and obscurity until the public life of Jesus should begin. Much of what we know of the child Jesus has to be inferred from the few words given to us in Scripture.

We know that he valued poverty. He was God before his incarnation, he remained God after his incarnation, and yet he purposely chose to be born on a cold winter's night in a stable, which was really only a cave where animals were housed. "And this will be a sign for you; you will find a babe wrapped in swaddling clothes and laid in a manger" (Luke 2:12). The crib of the Most High God was a humble feeding trough and Jesus had to borrow it from the cattle. This was a wondrous sign of the poverty of God. He owned nothing except the love of his mother and stepfather. His first visitors were not the three kings, but the most despised and poverty-stricken members of Israel, mere shepherds. They had no princely birthday gifts to bring, apart from the most cherished gifts of all, namely their joy at the music of the angels and their faith that this baby was indeed the Messiah. This love of poverty was to continue throughout Jesus' life, in the humble house of Nazareth and later as he trudged all over the country, seeking the lost sheep of Israel. "Foxes have holes, and birds of the air have nests; but the Son of Man has nowhere to lay his head" (Matt. 8:20). Later, when the Pharisees tried to trap him by asking if it was lawful to pay taxes to Caesar, Jesus had to ask them to show him the coin of tribute. He did not possess one of his own. He did not escape poverty even in death. Just as in infancy he was laid in a borrowed manger, so at the end, he was laid in a borrowed tomb.

In spite of being divine, Jesus emptied himself (this is called *kenosis*) and submitted his will to his earthly parents. In his perfect obedience, he cheerfully and eagerly served his mother and his stepfather in whatever way he could. No doubt, he gently took on the heavier chores from his mother and willingly allowed Joseph to teach him carpentry. How many people in Nazareth came to own a table or a chair made by divine hands, and did not even know it? It was Joseph, a simple Jewish carpenter, who made the wooden table at which Jesus ate his bread. It would later be a gentile Roman carpenter who made the wooden cross on which would hang Jesus, the bread of life for the world.

By the time he was twelve years old, he was impatient to be about the redemptive plan of his Heavenly Father, hence his seemingly thoughtless act of staying behind in Jerusalem and conversing with the doctors in the Temple. But this act was not thoughtless at all. It was, in fact, his newly conferred legal right as a grown man. Like all twelve-year-old Jewish boys, he had been admitted to the Jewish initiation rite called the Bar Mitzvah, which recognised him as a man, with full privileges to comment on Scripture in the Synagogues. Jesus now could rightfully make his own decisions and pursue his chosen vocation. He was quite simply eager to take up his true mission, which was not the carpentry of his earthly father, but the redemptive work of his Heavenly Father.

Yet, out of love for his parents, he quickly submitted his own urgency to their authority. He went back to Nazareth with them and spent the next eighteen years in hiddenness, and in obedience. "Although he was a son, he learned obedience through what he suffered; and having been made perfect, he became the source of eternal salvation for all who obey him" (Heb. 5:8-9). This reminds us that the humanity of Jesus still needed to grow towards perfection and he achieved it by means of obedience. His divinity was perfect, but his human-nature had still to learn it.

As a result of his decision, made in the Temple, Jesus, "went down with them and came to Nazareth and lived under their *authority*. His mother stored up all these things in her heart. And

221

Jesus increased in wisdom, in stature, and in favour with God and with people" (Luke 2:51-52). This short passage could be expanded into a whole encyclopaedia of the spiritual life. Jesus chose to live under the authority of his parents. After all, he came to perfect the law and it can be assumed that he thoroughly fulfilled the fourth commandment. Unlike many young teenagers, he would never have questioned his parents' rights to tell him what to do. He would never have defied or disobeyed them in anything. He would never have given his parents the slightest grief. More than that, his obedience would always have been cheerful and eager, never surly or performed with a grudge. His parents never heard him complain that a command was unfair.

Because Jesus adopted this holy attitude, he was able to grow in wisdom. He cherished every word of Scripture and took it to heart, not only in the sense of believing it, but also, in its practical application to all whom he met. He was not just a knower of the word, he was a doer of the word. His wisdom had already impressed the great doctors of the Temple, but now it was becoming even greater, as he grew in years. His divinity was, of course, infinitely wise, but his humanity still had to grow in wisdom, and this was accomplished by living "under their authority." The people of Nazareth must have secretly marvelled at the quiet wisdom of one so young and coming as it did from the son of a mere carpenter.

Jesus also grew "in favour (that is to say grace) with God and with people." This is a very important observation. In his personal holiness, he was perfect, which deepened his favour in the eyes of God. But he also grew in favour with people and this attests to the love of Jesus for his neighbours and his fellow citizens. Like Mary his mother, he was willing to set aside his own needs for personal communion with God, if there was a more urgent need to care for a neighbour. We are not allowed to pry into the exact ways in which Jesus won the favour of the citizens of Nazareth, but we can assume that they recognised and received his perfect love and concern. It could not have been otherwise, for to grow in grace means to be filled with the Holy spirit, to enjoy his manifold gifts, to exhibit the fruits of the spirit and to grow in virtue. Such was Jesus the child, then Jesus the young man and finally, Jesus the mature adult who freely laid down his life for all of us.

A clearer picture now emerges of the holy family of Nazareth and therein it is possible to discern God's beautiful plan for the millions of holy Catholic families of today.

As far as the external lives of Jesus, Mary and Joseph are concerned, there are few extraordinary features, at least Holy Scripture does not record any. In fact, all was very simple and very ordinary. They experienced much the same things as countless other families in the world: birth, building a home, making a living, delighting in Jesus' first baby steps, household chores and the death of Joseph. This is a wonderful truth. By its very ordinariness, the holy family can indeed be taken as our perfect model.

In another sense, however, the holy family was extraordinary. It was bathed in a divine light, the actual presence of God himself, in the incarnate Jesus. God was performing great, but hidden works in Nazareth and these were revealed in what is called *the sacrament of the present moment.* We too should treat the present moment as an encounter with God's will. God reveals himself to the poor in spirit in the humblest of things, while the so-called great do not discover him even in great events. Mary, Jesus and Joseph understood the gift of the present moment. It was in performing ordinary things extraordinarily well that they lived out the real presence of God in their daily routine. This was achieved by a profound inner silence. As Catherine Doherty of Madonna House once said, "A silence that is warm, loving: that is filled with a charity beyond words: that stops harsh ones, before they are uttered: kills little irritations before they become gaping wounds that may break up the bonds of love: silence that understands, upholds, heals."

Silence is living in the presence of God. Silence is in knowing that Jesus is within your heart, but he is also in front of us, behind us, to our right and to our left, above us and below us. In this way, he forms a protective cross within which we reside. When we are in silence, we become aware of his loving cruciform presence, and we can hear the promptings from his holy heart. From time to time, our own hearts respond with exultation and break out in praise of his divine condescension. We can rejoice in carrying our cross because we know that the cross is Jesus himself.

Thus silence is vital to today's families. How can we know the presence of Jesus if we plunge ourselves into a world of noise?

Noise is Satan's hammer striking upon the anvil of our souls, which can no longer hear the voice of Yahweh because the "gentle breeze" of his voice has been drowned out. For the first time in history, a person can journey from womb to tomb with non-stop noise, twenty-four hours a day, from radio, stereo and television. As a result, our brains are never at rest and there is no quiet time within which to ask ourselves one single important question such as, "Why was I created? Is there life after death?" We can simply and easily live in the living death of a relentless cacophony.

At a retreat a few years ago, a priest gave a beautiful talk on the holy family and held it up as the model for all Catholics. After the talk, a man came up to him and said, "That is ridiculous, father. Joseph was a saint and I am not a saint. Mary was spotless and my wife is far from spotless. Jesus was the Son of God and my son is certainly not the son of God." That man was wrong on all three counts. He is in fact, called to be a saint, his wife is called to be pure and spotless, and his son is a baptised Son of God. Today's families often suffer from a poverty-stricken view of their possibilities. They forget that, by grace, they can accomplish marvellous things. But they have to believe in the dream. They must once again claim their birthright as Catholics and set out on the journey of heroic sanctity. God wants nothing less for us. On our own, we can accomplish nothing, but, "with God all things are possible" (Luke 1:37).

Jesus, Mary and Joseph have lived out the perfect example of what it means to be a holy family. Naturally, we will fall short of the ideal, but everything depends upon how close to it we come. The first letters of the word "family" spell out a beautiful motto for all Catholic families to live by.

Forget About Me I Love You.

Stick it up on the door of the refrigerator. It is a lovely reminder of what we are all called to be.

CHAPTER 14

Trinity, Divinity and Humanity:
The Heavenly Model

*"What good is it to be able to
explain the doctrine of the
Blessed Trinity if you displease
the Blessed Trinity by your lack
of humility? It is a good life that
makes you pleasing to God, not
high sounding words and clever
expressions."*

(Thomas A Kempis)

It should be admitted at once that this is the most difficult chapter in the entire book. By the same token, it is actually the most important one, in as much as the Trinity lies at the very foundation of who we are by nature. We cannot hope to understand marriage and family, or even ourselves as individuals, unless we try to grasp something of who God is. I apologize for my feeble and inadequate efforts to write about the greatest Mystery of Mysteries, but it was quite necessary for me to make the attempt. I believe that, if the reader will take the time to read this chapter, to ponder it and take it to heart, he or she will have a deeper appreciation for all that has gone before.

It might come as a surprise to many Catholics to learn that the perfect model for the Christian family is not the Holy Family of Nazareth but rather the Divine Trinity in Heaven. The Nazareth family of Jesus, Mary, and Joseph was indeed the wonderful model of a holy family in action in our fallen world, but while we can and must look to it for inspiration, nevertheless it was a reflection of a much greater perfection. That perfection is the sublime Family of Families, the Trinitarian relationship of God the Father, God the Son and God the Holy Spirit. The heavenly Trinity is totally divine, while the Holy Family is a blend of the human and the divine. Mary and Joseph were human beings, creatures of God, while Jesus enjoyed a dual nature, being both God and man.

God is one. "Hear O Israel the Lord Our God is One Lord" (Deut. 6:4). God is therefore a unity, but a unity of what? He is a unity of Divine Persons, and these are three Persons truly distinct from and equal to each other, Father, Son and Holy Spirit. The Father begets the Son in an eternal begetting, and the Holy Spirit eternally proceeds from the Father and the Son. Each of these persons is God. There is therefore a Divine Family which has no beginning and no end, and as such is Perfection itself. The Trinity is our perfect model of family.

Catholics and other Christians know that there is a Trinity, and of course they only know it because Jesus said so. No unaided human mind could ever have postulated a trinitarian God simply because it is beyond our human reason and experience. This truth could only have been given to us by a divine revelation. As human beings we can only conceive of single and solitary personhood, for that is what *we* are. Therefore, the idea of three persons comprised in one being is beyond our limited understanding. As a result many Christians know of the Trinity but do not really appreciate the doctrine of the Trinity at all. We hear the word of God on the subject, after which we drop the idea as though it were some superfluous comment by Jesus which we have to accept, and then we leave it at that. The doctrine seems too far above our reality for it to have any practical meaning. Yet we cannot ignore the fact that Jesus went to great trouble to reveal to us the Divine Family from which he came. For this reason, we need to acknowledge that this doctrine has powerful implications for us, if we are to understand ourselves and our relationship with God more fully. As Peguy wrote, "Jesus did not come down to earth to tell us fairy tales." Rather, he came to bring us the Word of God, which is himself, and to give us life through his death on the cross.

Therefore we must re-examine for our own sakes, not for God's, our appreciation of the Threeness of God. If the doctrine of the Trinity is an entirely esoteric truth, which tells us nothing about who we are, then why did Jesus bother to emphasize it? Are we to suppose that it could only be of importance to God himself and of no value to us in our striving for salvation? Many of our brothers and sisters feel that struggling with their own sinfulness is task enough, without also struggling with a divine conundrum. Nevertheless, we must struggle, because the very essence of ourselves and our relationships is to be discovered in the Trinity itself.

Jesus, who is the Holy Perfect Word of God and who is incapable of distorting the Word (for that would be distorting himself) has expressed the divine reality in our own human language. Thus, he reveals the First Person to us as a Father. God the Father is Paternity itself. As Father he begets and he begets all of life, but his first begetting is of his Son, who receives everything from his Father. Theologians describe this as God's "knowing" of himself. He knows himself with infinite clarity, and so the Son is the one who is known. Because this knowing is infinite and perfect, just as the Father is, then the Son possesses all of the attributes of his Father and so is equal to the Father. "I and the Father are one" (John 10:30), "The Father is in me and I am in the Father" (John 10:38). Jesus, the Son, is therefore also God.

As a consequence of this knowing by the Father of the Son, there springs forth an infinite and perfect love, one for the other. This love is freely given and freely received; the Father pours out his entire being and the Son does likewise. This outpouring is called the Holy Spirit, and so the Nicene Creed states that the Holy Spirit "proceeds from the Father and the Son." The Holy Spirit is therefore also God and he is the "out-breath" of Father and Son. As St. Bonaventure wrote, "For the love which is the Holy Spirit does not proceed from the love which the Father has for himself, nor from the love which the Son has for himself, but from the love by which the one loves the other."

In his book *The Trinity: Mystery of Love,* Gaston Salet, S.J. writes, "It is impossible for human love to be perfect and completely reciprocal between two hearts, for neither of these two hearts can fathom the depths of this exchange of love itself. But in God the intimacy and the perfection of the mutual love between the Father and the Son is so great that this love expresses itself in a living Third Person, who is the Spirit of the Father and the Spirit of the Son, the encounter of their charity, the mutual exchange of their love.

"For God is love" (1 John 4:8). This is the golden key that allows us to make a feeble attempt to understand the Trinity. God is love and, unlike us, his love is perfect. Perfect love is a complete mutual giving, holding nothing back. It is also a perfect capacity to receive the love that is perfectly given. In his book *Theology and Sanity,* Frank Sheed states: "What is an adequate object for a love that is infinite? Not men, nor angels. If God has only these to love then his love never has an object worthy of it, for they cannot conceive infinite love and they cannot return it. If that is all, God is forever loving his inferiors, as he is doomed to the companionship of his inferiors. The only and adequate object of infinite love is an infinite being, God himself."

Therefore, with the doctrine of the Trinity, God's isolation vanishes. There is an "otherness" within the Godhead, an infinite love among three which is infinitely given, infinitely received, and infinitely returned. The pagans had a cold concept of an isolated lonely deity far removed and aloof from the affairs of mankind. This idea became so impossible and hopeless to sustain that they had to invent a multiplicity of gods to alleviate the divine loneliness. Jesus, the Word, swept away these pagan inventions and revealed the Triune God who can never be alone. *Our God is a family.*

In the light of Jesus' instruction on the nature of God, we can no longer think of God as a gigantic ego, living in eternal loneliness and loving only himself. God is not a monolith, but a family, whose persons give and receive perfect familial love. As a sublime out-pouring of this divine love, God creates in his own image and likeness and so the Trinity becomes the sublime template from which all human beings and their relationships are forged. It is as though God delights in reflecting himself in creation. "God created man in his own image, in the image of God he created them" (Gen. 1:27).

Like God, we are not meant to be one huge, ever-swelling ego, as many modern psychologists would have us believe. On the contrary, we are called to destroy our self-absorbed ego, to die to self, in order to give and receive love and thereby be fit for relationship with both God and other persons. John the Baptist said, "He must increase but I must decrease" (John 3:30). He understood that shrinking the ego does not mean self-annihilation, but the exact opposite. It is in dying to self that we find our true identity, for then Christ lives within us and we become a living icon of him on earth. It is in allowing Jesus to live fully within the tabernacle of our hearts that we find our true selves. John the Baptist fully understood, and it bears repeating, that *the size of my ego is the exact measure of the distance between me and God*. The bigger my ego, the farther I am removed from his Life.

Therefore, if we are to know who we are, both as individuals and as a community, we must try to understand the Divine template and to conform ourselves to it with all of our ability. Fr. Bernard Haring, C.S.S.R. explains that "God speaks to us because he wishes to be in one society with us and this desire is rooted ultimately in the mystery of the Trinitarian Society."

God, then, in his Triune nature, is the origin and the model for all of humanity. There is a "threeness" to us as individuals and to us as families. He reflects himself in the sense of creating in his own image and likeness. The love of God for himself is so compelling that he loves to reproduce and to disseminate his own likeness by means of that same love. We are created by Love, out of love, and for love. This creative begetting force of God's love also compels us, since divine love demands a return of love from what has been created. Thus, imitating God's love becomes our true vocation, and we can only do this if we love through God and with the heart of God. "We love him because he first loved us" (1 John 4:19). The Trinity is our dwelling place, our home, our Father's house, and it is only therein that we can be fully human. It is only therein that we can be "divinised." For us to be divinised means that we become all that God intends for us to become. Ultimately, it means that we should become "perfect as your Father in heaven is perfect" (Matt 5:48). In this way, we will be glorified in Heaven in a way that we cannot yet understand. As it says in the prayer of the Mass, "We shall become like you and see you as you are."

The three divine persons act in us. At Baptism we truly become children of the Father, brothers and sisters of the Son, and we are continually acted upon, inspired by, and loved by the Holy Spirit. As Bossuet wrote: "United as we are to God, let us form the Blessed Trinity in our hearts, by knowing God and by loving God. And since our knowledge, which at present is imperfect and obscure will soon pass away, and since love is the only thing that will never pass away and be lost, let us love, love, love. Let us do ceaselessly now what we shall do eternally."

The Divine Trinity is represented in the diagram at the end of this chapter, by the large purple triangle within which all other trinitarian creations are contained. The colour purple indicates the Royalty of God, and his Supreme Sovereignty over all Creation.

The ground is now prepared for us to take a closer look at God's splendid creation in the light of our awareness of the Trinity.

It is appropriate to begin with ourselves as individual creatures. "God created man in the image of himself, in the image of God he created him" (Gen. 1:27). Therefore, we cannot begin to understand what we are until we comprehend in what manner we are in the image of God. If God is a trinity, then we too must possess a trinitarian essence. That Godly essence is reflected in our three-fold or tripartite nature which is spirit, body and soul. These correspond in a figurative sense to the persons of the Divine Trinity, Father, Son and Holy Spirit. Our spirit is our highest faculty and it is, as it were, a small part of the Divinity himself. God designed it to be the Ruler, the King of our nature. While it is not eternal, having had a beginning, it is immortal in that it will have no end. The human spirit is our connection to God and our claim to kinship with him. It is the spirit which gives right alignment to the body and the soul and which makes us yearn in our deepest being for that perfection which is God and which reminds us of God. Atheism is the denial of our spirit and so it is the denial of our supreme faculty, thereby condemning us to a mere dual nature of body and soul, and that places us no higher than the animal kingdom.

The human spirit, being like a part of God, is akin to God the Father. The body is our humblest part and as such is akin to Jesus the Son, who also took on a human body. Our body is intended to be obedient to our spirit just as Jesus was obedient to his Father. "I seek to do not my own will but the will of him who sent me" (John 5:30). When we allow our bodies to rebel and to dominate our higher faculty, we become slaves of the flesh and we sink into the darkness of sin. Jesus subdued his body and made it serve his own spirit, thereby giving us the perfect example of how we also can live in our own bodies. Indeed, one bright day, the day of resurrection, our ponderous earthbound bodies will become new and glorified bodies for the eternal life hereafter. God intends us to keep our trinitarian essence for ever and so our mortal flesh will be magnified by him, becoming like the glorified body of Jesus, who also lives in his body for all of eternity. Meanwhile, God asks us to be in the world but not of the world.

The human soul consists of the intellect, the emotions and the will or, in other words, the mind. This is the choosing faculty and as such it is like the Holy Spirit, for through it we choose God and not the world. It is by means of the soul that we are able to love. It is the soul which is the seat of the gifts of wisdom, understanding, counsel, strength, knowledge, piety and fear of the Lord, which all come from the Holy Spirit himself. It is the soul which manifests our own unique personality, and just as the body will one day be glorified, so too our soul will become perfected in order to be worthy of heaven.

In our three-fold existence, each part is intricately bound up with the other two. The spirit rules the soul and the body. The soul loves the spirit and the body. The body obeys the spirit and the soul. The degree to which this intended unity is disrupted is the degree to which we allow our pride to challenge God. For example, if the body is allowed pride of place, then it will drown out the higher faculties of soul and spirit. In that case, we place our higher spiritual nature at the service of our lower animal nature and so our feelings dominate our will (the soul) and ignore the prompting of God (the voice of our spirit). Too many of us justify our sinful actions, using our feelings as the excuse. "I was angry, so I struck him." "I was hurt, so I cannot forgive." "I was sexually aroused, so I committed adultery." People like this have disrupted God's order of authority for our being. Instead of spirit, soul and body, they have decided it should be body, soul and spirit.

Likewise, the soul can assume the ascendency and deliberately initiate and entertain sin by means of thought and a disordered will. Again, the spirit is stifled by the lower faculty of the soul, and the weak body will surely follow.

It is only when true godly harmony exists between our three faculties that we can ever be in true harmony with ourselves and with our God, who made us that way. God is three in one and he designed us to be in his image in that we too are three in one, although unlike God, our threeness is not three *persons* in one but three *faculties* in one. Again we are most unlike god in that he can never be divided against himself, while we can be at war within, which results in disastrous consequences for our personal salvation. Our wholeness, happiness and emotional health depend upon each of our parts adopting its proper place in the Divine design.

Since we are made in the image and likeness of God and since God is love, then we too are called to return love for love and we delight him by means of it. He does not need our love. He is complete without it, but he desires it because he is love. How blessed are we that we can fulfil a desire of our Creator, the almighty God, and this is only possible because we are created in his image and likeness. We are pale reflections of his Divine Splendour, but we are reflections nonetheless.

All of us would do well to remember this awesome reality of human nature when we are tempted to criticize or judge or hurt another human being, whether he or she is a spouse, a relative, a friend or even an enemy. When we attack another person, we are violating a being made in God's image. That is no trivial matter. "What is mortal man that you care for him? Yet you have made him little less than a god. You have crowned him with glory and honour, made him lord of the works of your hands, put all things under his feet" (Ps. 8:4-6).

The individual human person is represented in the diagram by the small brown triangle. The colour brown indicates the dust of the earth, from which Adam was created by God.

In his gratuitous relationship with humanity, God reproduces his image and likeness in three other powerful forms, all of them covenants. A covenant is not simply a contract. A contract usually describes an exchange of goods. A covenant, on the other hand, consists of an *exchange of persons.*

The Church: A Covenant of Salvation

This is the covenant relationship between God and his people. In the Old Testament, it consisted of a solemn agreement between Yahweh, the Levitical priesthood, and the people of Israel. The covenant was solemnised at Mount Sinai, and it supplanted the earlier covenant with Israel whereby all the people enjoyed the privilege of priesthood. After the Israelites had worshipped the golden calf, God stripped the people of their personal priesthood and invested it in the Levites only. Through Moses and the covenant, God promised to hold the chosen people dear to his heart and to watch over them, while Israel promised to be faithful to God's commandments. In the New Testament, God instituted the New Covenant, this time an agreement between himself, the Sacramental priesthood, in the ranks of which Jesus is the High Priest, and the Catholic Church. In this Covenant, God promises always and infallibly to inspire the Church through the Holy Spirit, while the Church, in turn, under the authority of the Vicar of Christ, and through the mediation of Jesus Christ its head, promises to remain faithful and pure. "Then he took a cup, and when he had given thanks, he handed it to them saying, 'Drink from this, all of you, for this is my blood, the blood of the new covenant, poured out for many for the forgiveness of sins'" (Matt. 26:27-28). This new and everlasting covenant was sealed by the blood of Jesus, the Lamb of God, and it consisted of God the Father, Jesus the High Priest, now represented by those ordained to the Sacramental priesthood, and the people of God, who are the Church.

The three-ness of the Church is represented in the diagram by the red triangle. The colour red indicates the blood of Christ, shed for his Church on the cross, and indicates the Church itself as it follows in the blood-stained footsteps of Jesus. It also represents the blood of the martyrs which Tertullian said, "is the seed of Christians."

This is the covenant under whose canopy the remaining two covenants enjoy life and meaning. The first of these is the sacrament of matrimony, and the second is the human family.

The Sacrament of Matrimony: A Covenant of Fidelity

The Catholic church does not regard marriage as a mere contract. It reveals marriage to us as a Sacramental covenant. This covenant is like all other covenants in that it is an exchange of persons. "I will be your husband and you will be my wife." "I will be your wife and you will be my husband."

But it is not merely a solemn exchange of vows between a man and a woman. It is also a covenant between *three* persons, God, man and woman. "I will be your God and you will be my married couple, and you shall become one in flesh with each other and one in spirit with me." The marriage vows, then, include God and place upon us the binding oath to be faithful to God and to one another. There is no room for infidelity in a marriage. Adultery is not only a breaking of the covenant to the spouse, but it also violates the promise we have made to God himself. Adultery is trivialised in today's pagan society but it will never be trivial to God, who is affronted and violated by it.

Most of us know that Jesus solemnised the Sacrament of Marriage at Cana, when he gave his first miracle to the world by changing water into wine. But perhaps we do not realise that marriage was instituted for Adam and Eve by Yahweh himself in the Garden of Eden. "God blessed them, saying to them 'Be fruitful, multiply, fill the earth and subdue it'" (Gen. 1:28). God, then, was the presider over the wedding day of Adam and Eve, just as the priest, standing in for Jesus, is the presider over our Catholic marriages today.

The three-ness of the marriage sacrament is represented in the diagram by the blue triangle. The colour blue indicates the colour of Our Blessed Mother Mary, who was the perfect wife and mother. It was she who prompted Jesus' first miracle at Cana whereby he blessed marriage as a solemn covenant.

The Human Family: A Covenant of Love

The final covenant also has the divine mark of three-ness, since it too comes from God. It consists of the human family, sometimes called the domestic church. Here, the "three-nature" is entirely human, although divinely guided, and it consists of father, mother and child. As with the Divine Trinity, each of these persons is distinct from and equal to each other. The child is, of course, dependent, but nonetheless commands the same dignity as does father and mother. The father derives his paternity from the paternity of God, and his fatherly authority is given to him from the same God the Father. It may surprise some to know that the mother is akin to Jesus in the relationship. Just as Jesus is the one who is known by God the Father, so also the wife is the one who is known by her husband. The love that proceeds from the human father and *equally* from the human mother is the fruit of their union, namely, the child, who may be likened, therefore, to the Holy Spirit. The human family is a creation of God. It is also in the image and likeness of God and so is a reflection of the essence of God. Just as God is a family of three, so the human family possesses three-ness in the form of father, mother and child. This little trinity is designed by God to be the very means by which we come to our salvation. The more the family learns to emulate God's family, the more sanctified it becomes, a privilege that it enjoys through the begetting of God the Father, the redemptive action of Jesus the Son, and the mediation of the Holy Spirit.

The human family is represented on the diagram by the green inverted triangle. The colour green indicates the colour of the life of the earth, and signifies the life-giving and life-receiving nature of the family covenant. The triangle is inverted, with the child at the bottom, because the child is totally dependent upon his parents to provide nourishment for his body and nourishment for his soul. He has yet to become a mature follower of Christ.

It is interesting to note that, together, the two triangles of the marriage covenant and the human family covenant form the Star of David. This is the six-pointed star which has come to represent the Jewish people, the first chosen people of God. Today's Catholic families are also chosen people of God and it seems fitting that the six-pointed star should also represent their special relationship with the Triune God. It was a star over Bethlehem which announced the incarnation of God the Son into a human family, and which continues to announce that Jesus is incarnate, in the Eucharist, to all Catholic families throughout the world.

Inasmuch as God is a Trinity of persons, it follows that:

1. We are trinitarian persons in that we possess a triple nature.
2. Marriage is a trinitarian covenant, solemnised by three persons.
3. We are trinitarian families, whereby two become three in creating new life.
4. We are a trinitarian Church in the triple relationship of God, Jesus (represented by the priest) and the people of God.

The complete trinitarian diagram is placed at the end of this chapter. Note that all of the created likenesses are contained in the Divine Trinity, which is to say, that all things are held in existence within the Divine Mind of God.

The Angel Gabriel told Mary that her Son would be called "Emmanuel," which means "God with us." God is indeed with us, firstly by the creative action of the Father, secondly by the redemptive action of Jesus, thirdly by the sanctifying action of the Holy Spirit, and then by the amazing truth that we have been created in the image and likeness of God.